HEGEL'S CRITIQUE OF LIBERALISM

Hegel's Critique of Liberalism

RIGHTS IN CONTEXT

STEVEN B. SMITH

THE UNIVERSITY OF CHICAGO PRESS
CHICAGO AND LONDON

Steven B. Smith, associate professor of political science at
Yale University, is the author of *Reading Althusser: An Essay
on Structural Marxism* and of numerous articles on political
theory.

The University of Chicago Press, Chicago 60637
The University of Chicago Press, Ltd., London

© 1989 by the University of Chicago
All rights reserved. Published 1989
Printed in the United States of America

98 97 96 95 94 93 92 91 90 89   5 4 3 2 1

Library of Congress Cataloging-in-Publication Data

Smith, Steven B., 1951–
  Hegel's critique of liberalism : rights in context / Steven B.
Smith.

      p.   cm.
  Includes index.
  ISBN 0-226-76349-8
  1. Hegel, Georg Wilhelm Friedrich, 1770–1831—Contributions in
political science.   2. Liberty.   3. Human rights.   I. Title.
JC233.H46S63   1989
323.44'01—dc19   88-14410
                                                      CIP

For my parents

CONTENTS

Preface   ix

A Note on the Texts   xiii

1   Why Hegel Today?   1

2   The Origins of the Hegelian Project   17

   Hegel and the Divided Self   17
   Romanticism and Revolution   31
   Civic Religion, Positivity, and the *Volksgeist*   40
   The Discovery of the Dialectic   49

3   The Critique of the Liberal Theory of Rights   57

   Hegel and the Enlightenment   57
   The Theory of Natural Rights   61
   Critique of Natural Rights, I : Hobbes and Locke   65
   Critique of Natural Rights, IIa : Kant   70
   Critique of Natural Rights, IIb : Fichte   80
   Hegel and the French Revolution: Rousseau   85
   The Politics of Virtue   91

4   Hegel's Theory of Rights   98

   The Concept of Human Rights and Its Critics   98
   The Subject of Rights   103
   The Origin of Rights   115
   The Right of Recognition   122

5   The Hegelian *Rechtsstaat*   132

   Hegel and Practical Philosophy   132
   Civil Society and the Corporation   140
   The Rule of Law   145

The Universal Class   149
The Monarch   152
War and International Relations   156

6   Hegel's Idea of a Critical Theory   165
What Is Dialectic?   165
Immanent Critique and the Foundations of Phenomenology   169
Bildung and Negative Dialectics   175
The Skeptical Moment   180
The Logic of Determinate Negation   187

7   Reason and History   194
Reason and Understanding   194
Contradiction   197
Rational Necessity   204
Absolute Knowledge and the End of History   217

8   Hegel and the Liberal Legacy   232

Index   247

PREFACE

The interpretation of Hegel that emerges in the following pages would have been unthinkable just a few years ago. The rehabilitation of Hegel as a serious political thinker would not have been possible without the revival of interest in Marxism during and after the 1960s. The combination of Marxist and existentialist ideas that formed the spiritual core of the New Left pointed backwards to Hegel. For many of the most thoughtful members of this generation, Hegel was the truly profound source of all of Marx's theories regarding labor, history, dialectics, and alienation. Indeed this synthesis of Marxism and existentialism which proved such a politically and philosophically potent force was prepared earlier by Alexandre Kojève with whose brilliant *Introduction à la lecture de Hegel* (1947) I have found it necessary to contend throughout this study. According to Maurice Merleau-Ponty, who had been introduced to Hegel by way of Kojève's *marxisant* "reading," "All the great philosophical ideas of the past century—the philosophies of Marx, Nietzsche, phenomenology, German existentialism, and psychoanalysis—had their beginnings in Hegel."[1]

The revival of Marxism was at best a necessary but not a sufficient condition for an adequate appreciation of Hegel. For those, like myself, disenchanted with the evident failure of Marxism to realize anything remotely resembling a just or humane society, the publication in 1971 of John Rawls's *A Theory of Justice* appeared to reestablish the intellectual credibility of liberal theory in a way that had previously seemed impossible. Especially important was Rawls's emphasis on human rights as the core of liberalism at a time when talk of rights had become little more than a political slogan or cliché. Rawls's identification of rights with justice and justice with "the first virtue of social institutions" seemed a heady and exciting prospect.

For reasons that I elaborate throughout this study, the recent resurgence of liberal theory has itself left something to be desired. What has inspired many of the post-Rawlsian theorists of "deontological" liberalism is the belief that human practical rationality is capable of providing an objective

1. Maurice Merleau-Ponty, *Sense and Non-Sense,* trans. Hubert L. Dreyfus and Patricia A. Dreyfus (Evanston: Northwestern University Press, 1964), p. 63.

framework for moral and political evaluation. Instead of relying on controversial notions about teleology, these thinkers hoped to generate the conditions for justice out of minimalist assumptions about rational agency and human choice. As a result, not only justice but all the institutions and practices of political life are seen as the outcome of rationally calculated decisions on the part of self-interested agents. Justice and all the other virtues are thus reducible to our calculating desire for peaceful or commodious living. There is, obviously, a close family resemblance between this deontological style of moral and philosophical argument and recent developments in social-choice theory in fields such as economics and political science.

The attempt of liberal theorists to discuss rights and political institutions as if they could be justified on the purely "formal" grounds of rational agency exhibits, to my mind, an impoverished grasp of human psychology and the developmental structure of moral personality. While the revival of liberalism did much to reestablish the primacy of rights and the dignity of the individual, it paid little attention to the cultural and historical context within which rights-claims in fact develop. In particular the attempt of contemporary liberal theorists to ground rights in the social contract methodologies of the seventeenth and eighteenth centuries seems to ignore the quite powerful criticisms of those methodologies, most notably by Hegel. So long as the state is regarded as nothing more than an enforcement mechanism for the maintenance of individual rights, liberalism will be unable to speak persuasively about such properly political matters as citizenship and the public good.

In this study I examine Hegel's critique of the tradition of rights-based liberalism as this presents itself in writers from Hobbes to Kant. This is not to suggest that Hegel is some kind of simple antiliberal. Hegel's method of dialectical or immanent criticism, to be examined at length below, seeks to preserve what he found of value in classic liberalism while reformulating it in ways that are more sensitive to the cultural and historical context of rights. Liberal government, Hegel reasoned, is neither a gift of nature nor the product of purely intellectual reflection, but is the result of a long and arduous historical process which has culminated in the modern constitutional state.

My argument is that Hegel's political philosophy is intended to promote the values and ideals of the *Rechtsstaat,* a term for which there is no precise English equivalent but which, I believe, is best captured in our phrase "the rule of law." The central feature of Hegel's theory of the state is its respect for rights, crucially including the right to recognition (*Annerkenung*). It is the right to have one's "free personality" acknowledged or respected that is a precondition for the enjoyment of all the other social goods that one's situation may afford. For Hegel, the various "categories" that structure social life, chiefly including civil society and the state, are not just conservative restraints on freedom but the necessary context within which our individual powers and capacities can grow and develop. What Hegel calls the institutions of ethical life, or *Sittlichkeit,* are there to preserve and enhance our right to mutual recognition and esteem. Hegel's politics, I conclude, should be of interest not only to political philosophers concerned with the normative problems of liberalism but to more empirically minded political scientists who under the banner of the "new institutionalism" have called for a revival of interest in the state as a central concept orienting political inquiry. A return to the state must *ipso facto* mean at least a partial return to Hegel.

The view of Hegel offered here differs from other interpretations in a number of ways. Unlike the studies of such hostile critics as Rudolph Haym and Karl Popper, my work shows that Hegel is not a reactionary or irrationalist philosopher bent on justifying the status quo however it stands. Likewise, I suggest against the views of Theodor Adorno and the Frankfurt School that Hegel is not a pre-Marxist prophet of emancipation through labor. And finally, I wish to resist the temptation of those who, despairing of the possibilities afforded by liberalism, seek to find in Hegel a source of their own communitarian dreams of a society ruled by what Hegel himself derided as "a genuine communal spirit . . . united by the holy chain of friendship." For reasons that are closely bound up with his metaphysics and philosophy of history, Hegel resisted the appeal of communitarianism as profoundly at odds with the deepest aspirations of modernity. Those interpreters who reject Hegel's general philosophy either as anachronistic (Z. A. Pelczynski) or as "expressive" of some essentially nonrational and untranslatable "vision" (Charles Taylor, Michael Rosen) cannot adequately appreciate Hegel's politics. Accordingly, I argue that Hegel's dialectic of *Geist* is best interpreted pragmatically or nonmetaphysically as specifying some telos of agreement among persons who mutually acknowledge and enhance one another's right to recognition.

It is never easy to say exactly when a book was conceived. My earliest debts must be to Henry Tudor, my supervisor at Durham University, who first helped me work my way through the intricacies of Hegel's political philosophy. Joseph Cropsey, in a memorable lecture course on Hegel's *Philosophy of Right* taught at the University of Chicago, helped me to understand the broader significance of many of the themes treated in this book.

More recently I have been fortunate to have a number of colleagues and students who have all contributed something to the final form of this book. In particular I would like to thank the members of the Yale Political Theory Workshop, who have provided a sometimes good-natured, occasionally spirited, but always stimulating environment for the presentation of many of the ideas contained here. Joseph Hamburger, David Mayhew, David Plotke, Patrick Riley, Ian Shapiro, Stephen Skowronek, and Rogers Smith have all read this manuscript either in whole or in part and I would like to record my thanks.

In addition I want to acknowledge the help of Judith N. Shklar and George A. Kelly, both of whom read this manuscript when it was still in a fairly primitive state and made many useful and encouraging remarks that went far beyond the offices of collegiality. It is with profound regret that I note the passing of George Kelly, perhaps the premier interpreter of the political philosophy of German idealism in our time. His "archaeology" of Hegelian thought served as both inspiration and guide for my own work on the subject.

Finally, I am happy to thank my wife, Susan, for her patience and understanding throughout the time when this work was written.

A NOTE ON THE TEXTS

The following editions and abbreviations have been used in reference to the works of Hegel. Wherever possible, quotations are taken from existing English translations.

Briefe   *Briefe von und an Hegel.* 3 vols. Edited by J. Hoffmeister. Hamburg: F. Meiner, 1952–54.

ETW   *Early Theological Writings.* Edited by R. Kroner. Translated by T. M. Knox. Philadelphia: University of Pennsylvania Press, 1971.

JR   *Jenaer Realphilosophie. Vorlesungsmanuskripte zur Philosophie der Natur und des Geistes von 1805–1806.* Edited by J. Hoffmeister. Hamburg: F. Meiner, 1969.

LHP   *Lectures on the History of Philosophy.* 3 vols. Translated by E. S. Haldane and F. S. Simson. London: Routledge and Kegan Paul, 1955.

LL   *Lesser Logic.* Translated by William Wallace. Oxford: Clarendon Press, 1975.

NL   *Natural Law.* Translated by T. M. Knox. Philadelphia: University of Pennsylvania Press, 1975.

PhM   *Phenomenology of Mind.* Translated by J. B. Baille. London: George Allen and Unwin, 1966.

PH   *Philosophy of History.* Translated by J. Sibree. New York: Dover Publications, 1956.

PM   *Philosophy of Mind.* Translated by A. V. Miller. Oxford: Clarendon Press, 1971.

PR   *Philosophy of Right.* Translated by T. M. Knox. Oxford: Clarendon Press, 1967. References are to the numbered paragraphs and page numbers of this edition. An *R* refers to Hegel's "remarks," while an *A* indicates his "additions" to each paragraph.

PW   *Political Writings.* Translated by T. M. Knox. "Introductory Essay" by Z. A. Pelczynski. Oxford: Clarendon Press, 1964.

SL   *Science of Logic*. Translated by A. V. Miller, London: George Allen and Unwin, 1969.

Werke   *Werke in Zwanzig Bänden*. Edited by E. Moldenhauer and K. M. Michel. Frankfurt: Suhrkamp, 1971. References are to volume and page number of this edition.

1 WHY HEGEL TODAY?

An undeniable feature of the contemporary intellectual landscape has been the revival of interest in Hegel. Only a few years ago such a revival would have been considered unthinkable. First, Hegel seems to belong unalterably to the mystic regions of German speculative thought which, we have been assured by more empirically minded philosophers, has been superseded by the development of increasingly sophisticated logical and factual disciplines. Hegel's formidable "system" seems the very antithesis of the more skeptical spirit driving much of modern philosophy. Second, Hegel's political philosophy in particular is said to be guilty of the organic fallacy, that is, undervaluing the role of individual rights and insisting on the primacy of a politics of the common good. His belief that not just politics but history as a whole embodies a collective rationality operating independently of what individuals think and do is often thought to contradict the open, free, and tolerant spirit that has shaped both the institutions and practices of modern liberalism.

Nevertheless, intellectual currents are notoriously subject to change, and what seemed impossible only a generation ago is now in full swing. Two reasons bear on the rehabilitation of Hegel. First, as a number of recent studies have shown, the differences between Continental and Anglo-American philosophy are not as great as previously believed.[1] Analytically trained philosophers like Charles Taylor, Richard Rorty, and Bernard Williams have recently shown an interest in such thinkers as Hegel, Heidegger, and members of the Frankfurt School. Likewise, European social theorists such as Jürgen Habermas and Karl-Otto Apel have expanded their research to include the insights of Wittgenstein, J. L. Austin, and Oxford linguistic philosophy.

1. For instance, Richard J. Bernstein, *The Restructuring of Social and Political Theory* (Philadelphia: University of Pennsylvania Press, 1976); Fred J. Dallmayr, *The Twilight of Subjectivity: Contributions to a Post-Individualist Theory of Politics* (Amherst: University of Massachusetts Press, 1981); Richard Ro ty, *Consequences of Pragmatism* (Minneapolis: University of Minnesota Press, 1982). I have also dealt with some of these issues in my *Reading Althusser: An Essay on Structural Marxism* (Ithaca: Cornell University Press, 1984).

1

Second, Hegel's political philosophy has provided a useful point of departure for those, like myself, uneasy with the currently dominant strategies for justifying liberalism. Perhaps the most powerful of these approaches is that underlying John Rawls's *A Theory of Justice*. For Rawls and other "deontological" liberals, liberalism is a framework for people to pursue their own self-chosen ends and goals but is neutral with respect to any particular ends or preferred way of life. In the language of contemporary deontological liberalism, the "right" must take precedence over the "good."[2] So conceived, liberalism is said to avoid the problems inherent in utilitarian or collectivist approaches to politics by regarding the state only as a guarantor of basic rights and liberties but not itself committed to any substantive vision of the good as an ultimate object of human aspiration. By asking us to abstract from all the contingently acquired and hence empirical characteristics about ourselves, the aim of these theorists has been to derive a set of legal and political institutions that accord equal "concern and respect" to everyone's interests. Indeed, so successful has this strategy appeared to some that one of its proponents has called it "a new liberal paradigm."[3]

In attempting to articulate this new liberal paradigm, Rawls and others have been led to make extensive use of Kant. Rawls's whole conception of "justice as fairness," he acknowledges, is based upon "a procedural interpretation of Kant's concepts of autonomy and the categorical imperative."[4] And in some of his post–*Theory of Justice* writings, he has gone so far as to describe his project as "Kantian Constructivism in Moral Theory."[5] The idea here and throughout his subsequent works is that political institutions are "fair" if and only if they respect the individual's right to autonomy. The advantage of this procedural interpretation of Kant should be obvious. By specifying the right to autonomy as providing some minimum standard of political decency, Rawls is absolved from having to engage in potentially more controversial systems of evaluating different levels of substantive achievement and distinguishing them by some order of rank.

But here we can already begin to see Rawls's equally significant departures from Kant. In the first place, Kant regarded morality as establishing a realm of freedom. Morality is only worthy of the name when it is chosen for

2. John Rawls, *A Theory of Justice* (Cambridge, Mass.: Harvard University Press, 1971), pp. 30–33, 446–52.

3. James S. Fishkin, "Defending Equality: A View from the Cave," *University of Michigan Law Review* 82 (1984):755.

4. Rawls, *A Theory of Justice,* p. 256.

5. John Rawls, "Kantian Constructivism in Moral Theory: The Dewey Lectures, 1980," *Journal of Philosophy,* 9 (1980):517–71.

its own sake. For Rawls, by contrast, the rules of justice are intended to serve the most felicitous distribution of "primary goods," for example, liberty and opportunity, income and wealth. Morality becomes, then, an instrument by which to distribute essentially nonmoral goods, a prospect that would no doubt have filled Kant with horror. Second, the core Kantian concept is not autonomy but universality. For Kant, an actor is autonomous only if he can universalize the maxim of his action to become a general law. Autonomy is the dependent variable, not the independent one. For Rawls, though, autonomy is more like a natural datum with which we all begin. Whereas Kant had seen it as the highest product of man's moral aspiration, for Rawls it is simply assumed without further argument.[6]

To some extent, I believe Rawls would not necessarily disagree with this characterization of his departures from Kant. His own theory of justice, he admits, "is not, plainly, Kant's view, strictly speaking; it departs from his text at many points."[7] These departures from Kant have characteristically adopted procedures and assumptions from a variety of very non-Kantian sources, especially neoclassical economic theory.[8] These assumptions can be reduced to four. First, rationality is conceived exclusively as a predicate of individual actors and actions; this is the principle of methodological individualism. Second, rationality is concerned with means and not ends. It is a form of calculation that allows the agent to acquire the objects of his desire rather than to prescribe what kinds of objects he ought to desire; this is the principle of value neutrality. Third, the natural goal of each agent is to maximize the number of pleasures and minimize the number of pains; this is the principle of psychological hedonism. And fourth, the problem of politics is conceived as finding ways of limiting the infinity of human desires so that each person can coexist with all under the universal rule of law. This is the principle of the social contract, which in turn is said to generate the conditions for political legitimacy. Out of these purely hypothetical assumptions about human nature, contemporary Kantian political theorists have proceeded to elaborate rules of justice which are claimed to be binding on all rational beings, everywhere and always.

These assumptions have not, however, gone unchallenged. Liberalism of

6. It should go without saying that my use of the terms "Kantian" and "neo-Kantian" in the following pages refer, not to the historical Kant, but to the recent appropriation of his doctrines for a variety of purposes. For a recent attempt to salvage Kant from the various misuses to which he has been put, see Patrick Riley, "The 'Elements' of Kant's Practical Philosophy: The *Groundwork* after 200 Years (1785–1985)," *Political Theory* 14 (1986): 552–83.

7. Rawls, "Kantian Constructivism," p. 517.

8. These assumptions are dealt with in Martin Hollis and Edward J. Nell, *Rational Eco-*

the neo-Kantian type has typically been depicted by its opponents as narrowly legalistic, concerned only with securing formal rights and indifferent to the warmer, more affective bonds of community. According to such Marxist critics as C. B. Macpherson, this kind of deontological liberalism rests upon a false conception of human beings as consumers or "possessive individualists" driven only by such ends as comfort, safety, and security.[9] For political romantics, liberalism appears as unbearably cold, barren, and rationalistic, hostile to the deeper emotional and aesthetic needs of persons.[10] And for conservatives (both neo- and paleo-), the emphasis on equality and rights represents a leveling off of natural differences in talent and ability.[11]

If contemporary liberals have been led to rediscover Kant, liberalism's critics have been forced to reinvent Hegel. Indeed, many of the most trenchant criticisms made of liberalism today—about its abstract, individualist methodology, its excessive concern with private nonpolitical goals, and its insensitivity to public issues of citizenship and civic virtue—were all decisively brought forth near the beginning of the last century by Hegel. In a sense, the whole debate between the defenders of liberalism and its critics has something of the character of a reinvention of the wheel. Today thinkers on both the left and the right seem to agree with Hegel that the solitary, individualistic, or "unencumbered self" of Kantian liberalism is too thin a basis from which to generate a morally or politically satisfying form of community. What is needed, then, is a more historically sensitive and culturally connected form of criticism, if liberalism is to prove defensible.[12]

The claims undergirding this Hegel renaissance are a mirror image of those supporting the neo-Kantian revival. In the first place, the contemporary Hegelians deny the tenet of methodological individualism by arguing that rationality may be predicated not merely of individuals but also of the

nomic Man (Cambridge: Cambridge University Press, 1975), pp. 47–64; see also Brian Barry, *Sociologists, Economists, and Democracy* (Chicago: University of Chicago Press, 1978).

9. C. B. Macpherson, *Democratic Theory: Essays in Retrieval* (Oxford: Clarendon Press, 1973), pp. 87–94.

10. For the variety of romantic reactions to liberalism, see Nancy L. Rosenblum, *Another Liberalism: Romanticism and the Reconstruction of Liberal Thought* (Cambridge, Mass.: Harvard University Press, 1987).

11. See Irving Kristol, "About Equality," *Commentary* (November 1972), pp. 41–47.

12. Some of the more notable of these works include Michael Walzer, *Spheres of Justice: A Defense of Pluralism and Equality* (New York: Basic Books, 1983); Alasdair MacIntyre, *After Virtue* (Notre Dame: University of Notre Dame Press, 1981); Michael Sandel, *Liberalism and the Limits of Justice* (Cambridge: Cambridge University Press, 1982); William A. Galston, *Justice and the Human Good* (Chicago: University of Chicago Press, 1980).

institutions and even the political cultures that make these actions possible. Second, rationality is valued, not simply for its ability to achieve ends, but as an end in itself, something valued for its own sake. Third, the comprehensive good for human beings cannot be regarded as the satisfaction of private pleasures but is intimately bound up with the good of others. We are what we are by virtue of our membership in a community of shared meanings and values. And finally, the political community is not on this account merely an aggregate of individuals peering through a veil of ignorance, but is at least partially constitutive of what it is to be a human being. As one of the proponents of the new communitarianism has put it: "To say that the members of a society are bound by a sense of community is not simply to say that a great many of them profess communitarian sentiments and pursue communitarian aims, but rather that they conceive their identity . . . as defined to some extent by the community of which they are a part."[13]

It seems obvious to me that neither of these positions is completely correct. The neo-Kantians attempt to discover rules for social life that would be binding on all rational agents, but the neo-Kantians' own prescriptions are often so general and abstract as to be void of moral content. Only by abstracting from everything we already know about ourselves, our lives, and our histories will we be in a position to provide a solid and unimpeachable ground for choosing between moral principles. I would argue, however, that this operation of abstraction does not result in a stronger foundation from which the self can choose, but in no foundation at all, since there is literally nothing left to the self.

If the neo-Kantian paradigm suffers from excessive abstractness, the new community or participatory model suffers from the opposite problem, namely, a misplaced concreteness. In its assumption that everything we are we owe to the particular communities of which we are a part, the communitarians often appear dangerously indifferent to the quite-legitimate claims that individuals can make against their communities. All we are told is that particular communities are the outcome of our communal or political nature, which leaves the individual no room to criticize those communities except in their own terms. The result, often the opposite of what is intended, is merely to reendorse existing patterns of social and political life without asking whether those patterns are rational or whether they ought to exist. These "re-endorsement theories," as Ernest Gellner has called them, tend uncritically to accept whatever forms of life or culture happen

---

13. Sandel, *Liberalism and the Limits of Justice,* p. 147.

to exist. "Forms of life and culture," he says, "are precisely what thought does not and need not automatically accept. Cultures must not be judges in their own case."[14]

My purpose here is not so much to pass judgment on this debate as to examine the genesis of the critique of rights-based liberalism in the philosophy of Hegel. One advantage of this approach is that as a critic of liberalism in at least its early modern or classic form, Hegel provides us with an insight into the strengths and weaknesses of the liberal tradition that are simply not available to a more conventional liberal thinker. Hegel's strategy is often to criticize especially the psychological and ethical foundations of classic liberalism, while at the same time praising many of its concrete political and historical accomplishments. This strategy allows him to provide a fuller, richer account of liberalism than one could find in the work of any other member of that tradition, while also expanding and improving upon our understanding of what it means to belong to that tradition. His method of providing a series of comprehensive contrasts between liberalism and its various alternatives allows us to grasp in a particularly illuminating way the specificity of the liberal tradition.

The argument I want to defend in this study is that Hegel provides us with a middle ground between the two alternatives outlined above. Like the modern communitarians, he is critical of the individualistic and ahistorical conceptions of rights underlying the liberal polity, but like many liberals in both his day and ours, he is skeptical of any attempt to return to some form of democratic participatory gemeinschaft based upon immediate face-to-face relations. Put another way, Hegel's goal is to combine the ancient emphasis on the dignity and even architectonic character of political life with the modern concern for freedom, rights, and mutual recognition. To this end, he developed a philosophical theory that sought to prove that the liberal constitutional state instantiated in his own day in the most advanced societies of Northern Europe constituted the legitimate goal of historical aspiration. Instead of rejecting liberalism out of hand, Hegel accepted many of the institutions of the modern "bourgeois Christian" world, especially the rule of law and the separation of civil and political life, as forming the basis of a common culture and a sense of social solidarity. Hegel's political philosophy might be seen as an attempt to reappropriate the terrain of ancient Aristotelian political theory by means prepared by Kant.

To substantiate this claim I will have to show exactly what Hegel thought

14. Ernest Gellner, *The Legitimation of Belief* (Cambridge: Cambridge University Press, 1974), p. 20.

was defective in the tradition of rights-based liberalism as this was transmitted from Hobbes and Locke to Rousseau and Kant. To the best of my knowledge, Hegel referred explicitly to liberalism only once in his writings, in a passage near the end of the *Philosophy of History,* to refer to the individualist and voluntarist traditions of political philosophy set in motion by the French Revolution. "Liberalism," he remarks there, "sets up . . . the atomistic principle, that which insists upon the sway of individual wills; maintaining that all government should emanate from their express power, and have their express sanction."[15] Hegel's critique of this view of government is both methodological and substantive. Methodologically, he opposed, as is well-known, any "atomistic" conception of the individual as an entity stripped of all cultural and historical forms of identification. Whatever modern human beings may say about themselves, we are all "situated" by a variety of traditions and practices that we are not simply free to accept or reject. Substantively, Hegel believed that liberalism was guilty of collapsing the state into civil society. That is, it provides an overly abstract and limited conception of the state which resembles most of all the night-watchman authority proposed by Locke and Hume. As we shall see later, it is just this "state based on need" (*Notstaat*) or "state as the understanding envisages it" (*Verstandesstaat*) that was anathema in Hegel's critique.

Hegel's critique of liberalism, I argue, grew out of the romantic or idealistic belief that while in the Enlightenment man had attained an unprecedented growth in human freedom achieved successively by the Copernican, the French, and the Kantian revolutions, he had done so at a price: the Enlightenment had bequeathed a set of dichotomies between public and private, reason and passion, and the noumenal and phenomenal parts of the self that would have to be resolved if our moral and intellectual lives were to be satisfactory. The experience of what I want to call the "divided self" became for Hegel and others of his generation the chief obstacle to be overcome if the conditions for freedom were to be realized. To be more specific, while the philosophers of liberalism had successfully attacked the abusive practices of the old regime as inconsistent with the essential freedom and dignity of man, they had not sufficiently thought through the moral and psychological basis of human freedom. By continuing the ancient tradition of referring norms of moral and political conduct back to nature, but conceiving nature along modern scientific lines as a vast machine governed by mechanical laws, liberalism saw men as driven by purely animalistic drives and desires.

15. *PH,* p. 452; *Werke* 12:534.

The problem, then, that Enlightenment liberalism had failed to resolve was how freedom could be guaranteed on the basis of a mechanistic physics and psychology. Hume's dictum that reason both is and ought to be slave to the passions was but the most famous expression of this paradox. While liberalism had in one sense liberated modern man from the tyranny of social custom and tradition, it had in another sense left him enslaved to his passions. Thus, whatever its claims, liberalism had not successfully disposed of the ancient problem of mastery and slavery. As much as any scholar of our generation, George A. Kelly has sought to restore an appreciation of the significance of this problem for understanding Hegel. In his masterful "Notes on Hegel's 'Lordship and Bondage,'" Kelley writes:

> Not only for Hegel, but for his great predecessors and his age as a whole, mastery and slavery was a multidimensional problem—and a paradoxical one. The paradox is this. Antiquity, which had sanctioned the institution of slavery, had nevertheless intensely researched the dilemma of man's enslavement of himself. The Enlightenment, by contrast, progressively attacked social bondage as abusive and immoral, while scratching only at the surface of its spiritual dimensions. . . . The revival of antiquity, in substance as well as form, by Rousseau on the one hand and the German idealists on the other—even when the battle of ancients and moderns had been seemingly won by the latter—is in part a response to this perplexity. The Enlightenment had furnished a sense of progress; it had not restored the conviction of harmony.[16]

The task, then, that Hegel and his contemporaries set for themselves was to combine the liberal or enlightened belief in life, liberty, and the pursuit of happiness with the ancient Aristotelian conception of politics as a collective pursuit aimed at some idea of a public good. Such a task may seem akin to squaring the circle. As we shall see in greater analytical and historical detail later, Hegel's answer to this apparent conundrum was his purified and revivified doctrine of *Sittlichkeit,* or ethical life. Ethical life is more than a set of formal procedures for arriving at moral decisions. It is rooted in the customs, traditions, and practices of a community. It forms definite structures and ways of life and thus prescribes specific rights and duties. At the same time, however, Hegel insists that these structures and ways of life not be simply imposed on us, as they are in premodern or traditional societies. The institutions and practices of ethical life must be reflectively accepted; they must be an adequate expression of the will or they would lack legiti-

---

16. George A. Kelly, "Notes on Hegel's 'Lordship and Bondage,'" *Hegel's Retreat from Eleusis: Studies in Political Thought* (Princeton: Princeton University Press, 1978), p. 45.

macy. Thus, these institutions—family, civil society, and the state—provide an ethical context within which modern freedom is possible.[17]

Before going on to consider the substance of Hegel's critique of liberalism, let me allude to one initial difficulty. Clearly, much of Hegel's assessment of liberalism depends on how we interpret the broader purposes of his philosophy. This is no easy task. Readers with only the most superficial acquaintance with Hegel's writings will know his famous dictum in the Preface to the *Philosophy of Right,* that philosophy is "its own time apprehended in thoughts" and that every philosopher is therefore a child of his age. But if, as Hegel tells us, philosophy always comes on the scene too late to give advice, it would seem that any criticism it can offer is already beside the point. The very idea of a Hegelian critique would seem oxymoronic. A cynic might suggest that Hegel is doing no more than congratulating rulers and states on what they have done by themselves without explicit philosophical guidance and calling for more of the same. The argument against the possibility of a genuine Hegelian critique was first made by Marx and the generation of the 1840s, who were more concerned with changing reality than interpreting it.[18]

Nevertheless, it would be rash to make everything hinge on a prefatory remark to a single work. Despite Hegel's claim that it was not the philosopher's business to offer advice, he himself theorized in a way that is difficult to square with that claim. To be sure, Hegel was not a radical or alienated critic of society. His criticisms of liberalism will no doubt appear far too modest for those on both the left and the right who see liberalism more as a problem to be overcome than an occasion to be explored. Hegel's strictures against prescriptivism notwithstanding, he offered a conception of philosophy at once rational and reconstructive. Philosophy for Hegel not only describes; it also tries to bring out the rationality or necessity of events by showing the inner (and inter) connections between them. His famed dialectical procedure consists of discerning the movement of spirit and criticizing those aspects of reality that do not accord with its highest possibilities. Contemporary positivistic distinctions between description and prescription, fact and value, fail to grasp Hegel's richer dialectical procedure of bringing out the implicit rationality from within the apparently arbitrary and contingent features of social life.

17. For a recent interpretation along these lines, see David Kolb, *The Critique of Pure Modernity: Hegel, Heidegger, and After* (Chicago: University of Chicago Press, 1987).

18. The best recent study of this theme is John E. Toews, *Hegelianism: The Path Toward Dialectical Humanism, 1805–1841* (Cambridge: Cambridge University Press, 1980).

The general assumptions underlying Hegelian philosophy will be treated at length in chapters 6 and 7 of this study. For now it is enough to say that Hegel will emerge in the following pages as the great champion of a form of philosophical practice that I want to call immanent critique. By an immanent critique I mean a form of theorizing that seeks standards of rationality within existing systems of thought and forms of life. Rather than seeking in the manner of, say, Descartes or Fichte some apodictic first principle or foundation for knowledge, Hegel's aim is to enter into and critically engage the various systems of thought and life on their own terms. Thus, he does not proceed by deduction from a set of necessary and sufficient conditions that could be specified in advance, but rather from the world of conventional opinions and understandings. The famous statement cited above, that philosophy is "its own time apprehended in thoughts," is intended to point to a more historically and hermeneutically sensitive form of cultural criticism—one which, we shall see later, is at least partially constitutive of the reality which it takes as its object. Philosophy no longer occupies the status of a disinterested observer looking down on life from some Archimedean point, but is far more intimately related to the world of ordinary experience. A central tenet of Hegelian philosophy, I believe, is that thinking is not simply about the world—it is something that takes place in the world. Any appreciation of Hegel's critique of liberalism must begin from this premise.

The approach to Hegel I adopt in this study, while by no means unprecedented, should still be distinguished from two competing perspectives.[19] One of these, which I call the political interpretation, has been championed by scholars like Joachim Ritter, Manfred Riedel, Shlomo Avineri, and Z. A. Pelczynski. Their interpretations have done much to blunt the still widespread belief that Hegel was a partisan of a conservative, if not reactionary, politics. As will become clear below, I am in general agreement with the political thrust of these interpretations. Where I part company with them is in thinking that, while they make Hegel a more attractive political thinker than he has often been assumed to be, they have done so at the cost of blunting some of his more arresting and even visionary ideas. While I have probably not gone as far in rehabilitating Hegel's metaphysics as some readers might like, I argue that Hegel's critique of liberalism makes sense only within the broader context of the arguments concerning immanent criticism and historical progress that they presuppose.

19. For a good review of some of the literature, see Anthony Quinton, "Spreading Hegel's Wings," *New York Review of Books,* 25 May 1975, pp. 34–37; and 12 June 1975, pp. 39–42; see also James S. Schmidt, "Recent Hegel Literature," *Telos* 46 (1980–81): 113–47.

The other approach, which might be called the metaphysical interpretation, is in fact a much older view which has recently been revived. According to this line of interpretation, Hegel was a "panlogicist," that is, a thinker who ruthlessly and consistently subordinated the facts of experience to the categories of logical analysis. Hegel is seen here as part of the great metaphysical and speculative tradition of thought going back to Plato. One of the most articulate defenders of this interpretation, Stanley Rosen, has argued in his book *G. W. F. Hegel: An Introduction to the Science of Wisdom* that "Hegel is first and foremost a logician and not a philosopher of history, a political thinker, a theologian, or a *Lebensphilosoph*." Accordingly, "none of [Hegel's] writings or lectures can be read in a proper manner without a grasp of the main tenets of his logic." According to Rosen, Hegel's "greatest innovation" was his development of "a new doctrine of contradiction and negativity . . . which attempts to resolve the *aporia* of classical rationalism at a higher, more comprehensive, and so genuinely rational level."[20]

My disagreement with this interpretation was already implied in what I said above. By viewing Hegel as "first and foremost" a logician and speculative metaphysician, this approach tends to isolate Hegel's philosophy proper from the rudimentary human and political concerns that were never far from its center. This is not to say that I regard Hegel's systematic philosophy as a mere appendage to his ethical and political writings—an ironical *jeu d'esprit* designed to divert the reader. Indeed, more than most philosophers, Hegel took pains to emphasize the extraordinary degree of unity and systematicity that he believed he had attained. And yet to see Hegel's logic as a first philosophy from which the content of politics and history can be deduced takes insufficient account of his warnings against any such foundationalism in philosophy. I cannot hope to dispose here of a problem that has occupied generations of Hegel interpreters. I can only wonder whether Hegel is better understood, not as doing some kind of fundamental ontology, but as practicing a form of cultural hermeneutics.

Before embarking directly on these matters, I need to say a few words about the organization of this study. In chapter 2 I develop the theme alluded to briefly above. Hegel's philosophy, I argue, grew out of an attempt to overcome the phenomenon of the divided self. This is a term I use to describe a species of the moral life, deeply rooted in the Western philosophic tradition, according to which man is a being divided between such warring compounds as body and soul, reason and sensibility, and material and spiritual elements. In a reaction to this split personality which they

20. Stanley Rosen, *G. W. F. Hegel: An Introduction to the Science of Wisdom* (New Haven: Yale University Press, 1974), pp. xiii, xvii–xviii.

believed dominated the Western tradition, Hegel and others of his generation, especially Hölderlin and Schelling, turned back to the Greeks as a
paradigm of both rational autonomy and moral coherence. But whereas
Hölderlin and Schelling saw the overcoming of dissonance and disharmony
as possible only through the experience of art, Hegel turned to politics and
the revolutionary efforts in France to recapture something of ancient republicanism. Brought up on the republican theorizing of Montesquieu and
Rousseau, the young Hegel saw in the Revolution an attempt to recreate
conditions of polis democracy. It was only after the Revolution's failure to
revive past political forms in historically very different circumstances had
become apparent to all that Hegel was led to a more sober appreciation of
the opportunities afforded by modernity.

In chapter 3 I advance the themes of chapter 2 by turning to Hegel's
critique of the liberal theory of rights. I begin by showing how the liberal
theory is related to the broader philosophical project of the Enlightenment,
with its goal of the liberation of men from the sway of prejudice and tradition. After examining a number of features central to the liberal theory of
rights, I turn to Hegel's objections to two dominant views of his time,
namely, the empirical naturalism of Hobbes and Locke and the moral formalism of Kant and Fichte. After sketching Hegel's methodological objections to the doctrines of these philosophers, I turn to what he regarded as
their undesirable political consequences. It was Rousseau's moral and political formalism that conceived the self as prior to all natural or empirical
ends that gave rise to Robespierre's terrorist conception of politics. Indeed,
Hegel traces the failure of revolutionary politics to recreate anything remotely resembling polis democracy to its inability to grasp the essential
situatedness or enrootedness of persons.

In chapter 4 I elucidate the structure of Hegel's theory of rights (Recht).
The concept of right is here defended against various modern detractors,
especially Marxists, utilitarians, and cultural relativists. Rights, I argue, are
not simply a natural property of the human will but are rather the product
of historical struggle. The dialectic of master and slave is presented as the
paradigmatic account of this struggle culminating in the demand for mutual recognition. I argue that for Hegel, the right of recognition—the right
to be treated with civility, decency, and respect—is the core human right.
Furthermore, the right to recognition is not just an empty demand but
must be instantiated in a particular way of life—a form of Sittlichkeit—
which contains a definite set of roles and social structures which gives objective content to our life choices.

In chapter 5 I examine the institutional context within which human rights can be secured. I argue that the Hegelian *Rechtsstaat,* characterized by such features as the rule of law, an impersonal civil service, the private corporation, and the monarchy, is a sufficient, although not a necessary, feature for the defense of rights. I also attempt to locate the *Philosophy of Right* within the context of the tradition of practical philosophy as this derives from Aristotle. The work, I try to show, is not a piece of deductive theory but is based on the classical humanist's desire to write something useful for citizens, especially university students, preparing to begin the practical conduct of life.

In chapters 6 and 7 I provide a reconstruction of the overall philosophical framework and assumptions underlying Hegel's critique of liberalism. Central to Hegel's critical theory is his concept of immanent critique. The locus classicus of this conception is in the Introduction to the *Phenomenology of Mind,* where Hegel rejects the attempts of both Locke and Kant to provide a set of permanent or apodictic foundations for knowledge. Hegel, we shall see, rejects the modern Enlightenment conception of knowledge as something that develops between a subject and an object, and also the correspondence theory of truth that this implies. Knowledge instead grows out of conversation or dialogue, not between a self and an other, but between selves. His theory is dialectical in the original sense of the term, seeing knowledge less as correspondence than as agreement or consensus. This conversational mode is in turn said to generate a process of "determinate negation," whereby higher and more rational manners of thought and life grow out of the contradictions, incoherences, and anomalies of the ones they replace. Contrary to a number of modern criticisms, Hegel believes that this process creates a logic or necessity of its own capable of ensuring standards of moral and epistemic validity. A key task for anyone broadly sympathetic to Hegel's approach is to determine what kind of necessity or logic he claims to be operating with. After considering a number of possible candidates, I conclude that Hegel is operating with a teleological conception of necessity. This conception of teleological necessity leads, finally, to a consideration of Hegel's controversial views on the end of history. I interpret Hegel's end of history thesis to entail a community of language users whose goal is consensus achieved through dialogue and discussion.

In chapter 8 I try to put Hegel's arguments in a present-day context. I suggest that the primacy he accorded to the state has special significance for the so-called new institutionalism in political science, with its call to "bring the state back in." Likewise, the importance he attributed to the ethical context of moral argument provides a much-needed corrective to the ahistorical individualism of liberal theory. Whatever their defects, I suggest that Hegel's views provide a more useful point of departure for thinking through some of the problems of liberalism than any of the dominant alternatives.

As in all studies in the history of political thought, a word about methodology is inescapable. In carrying out this study I have tried to remain true to Hegel, while at the same time addressing questions that will be of interest to the general political theorist. This decision stems from my sense of what political theory is and where it is going. It is now generally agreed that ideas have a historical component, although exactly what that means remains a subject of considerable debate. While any interpretation of a text must seek to discover what the author meant in writing it, it is impossible to keep from raising questions about the significance of the author's ideas for later political and philosophic controversy. The question of the significance of a work cannot be neatly distinguished from an author's intention in writing it, especially if part of the intention was to influence the future. For this reason, it is never enough to interpret a text by placing it only within its author's own time and place. Authors not only address their immediate contemporaries but their predecessors and posterity as well. Language, we are frequently told today, has a performative function, and part of the interpreter's business must be to discover exactly what an author was attempting to do with words. Nowhere is this more necessary than in the case of Hegel, whose works were written, I intend to show, with a clear practical purpose in mind. No one today who seriously seeks to understand the shape of the modern world can avoid coming to terms with Hegel.

In general I am in agreement with the claim advanced by hermeneuticists and linguistically sensitive analytic philosophers, that ideas must be studied in context, and that it is always inappropriate to judge their meaning by prevailing standards of rationality and coherence. If Hegel taught us anything, it is that reason has a history and that ideas which from the current standpoint might seem simply false or absurd may turn out to have been functional for the people who held them. At the same time, I believe we cannot avoid recognizing that ideas enter into the stream of history and thus help to shape later contexts, including our own. Past and present may be situated in different historical times, but they are still part of one continuous history. The idea that we can stand over and above history in order to view it objectively has always, in my opinion, been untenable. The interpreter of a text, just like the text itself, is always situated *in* history.

The kind of historicist hermeneutic I have just described has often been used to show that ideas have no abiding significance and that attempts to enlist the past to explain the present must always court anachronism. According to Quentin Skinner, a leading proponent of this view: "To demand from the history of thought a solution to our immediate problems is thus to commit not merely a methodological fallacy, but something like a moral error."[21] But I believe a different moral is in order here. Political thinking need not be tied down exclusively to local contexts with their own particularist and empirical problems. To conclude, as the above passage does, that political thought is always concerned with "immediate problems" is to disallow dogmatically the possibility that at least some thinkers might have had larger ambitions—to speak across the centuries or even for all time. What I would like to suggest is that to study the thought of the past is never just to study something detached from ourselves, related to us in a purely external, contingent manner. All history, Hegel taught, is the history of mind, of what mind has done and what it has become. There is in every historical investigation a kind of identity of subject and object, between the thinker and the object of his inquiry. Every investigation of thought is at least in part a form of self-inquiry.

Finally, like many people who work in the area known as "the history of political thought," I believe the study of ideas can never be simply an antiquarian activity. The study of the political thought of the past is itself a political act, or at least has something political about it. Great works of the tradition force us to consider anew the substantive themes of political philosophy—themes like freedom, rights, warfare, and justice. I find myself in a large measure of agreement with those critics who have argued that the distinction between first-order and second-order works, between the grand tradition of political philosophy and the history of commentary on that tradition, is not as great as is sometimes believed.[22] As children of a historical age, we tend to believe that substantive theorizing about politics is best when it grows out of a critical engagement with great works of the tradition. I realize, of course, that emphasizing the political side of commentary may lead to all manner of abuse. If, in the history of political thought, commentary is itself a political act, what is to distinguish works of genuine scholarship from ideological special pleading? Or if scholarly works are ac-

21. Quentin Skinner, "Meaning and Understanding in the History of Ideas," *History and Theory* 8 (1969):53.
22. See Deborah Baumgold, "Political Commentary on the History of Political Thought," *American Political Science Review* 75 (1981):928–40.

tive engagements with the world, what might not be considered political? There are no a priori ways of putting these objections to rest. For this reason, I have not sought to avoid a certain degree of partisanship. I only hope that the image of Hegel that appears in the following pages is not false to the original.

2 THE ORIGINS OF THE HEGELIAN PROJECT

HEGEL AND THE DIVIDED SELF

Iris Murdoch once remarked, "It is always a significant question to ask of any philosopher: what is he afraid of?"[1] In the case of Hegel the answer would have to be division, diremption, and contradiction. Indeed, the experience of diremption (*Entzweiung*), he wrote in his first published work, is the source of need for philosophy. "The need for philosophy arises when the power of unification disappears from the life of man."[2] It is only when this "power of unification" dissolves that men turn away from the world of politics and community life to seek consolation in philosophy. Philosophy is both the symptom of and the cure for a culture that has become problematic. Hegel's own critical reflections grew out of, and in a sense were a response to, the bifurcation of modern political culture into such rigid antinomies as public and private, legal and moral, practical and theoretical.

It is, then, the desire to overcome the experience of division, diremption, and discord that provides the thread of coherence running through Hegel's doctrine from his earliest manuscripts from when he was a student in the politically charged atmosphere of southern Germany in the 1790s to his works of maturity from when he was a professor of philosophy in the peace and tranquillity of restoration Berlin. If diremption is the source of the need for philosophy, then "to overcome such solidified contradictions is the single interest of reason."[3] Rationality is not simply an analytic faculty used for drawing distinctions, but is a synthetic capacity for reunifying and making whole what has been torn apart. Since "reason is but one,"[4] its aim is to bring together all the diverse aspects of experience into a complete, harmonious whole.

Hegel's desire to overcome the contradictions and restore the unity of life was no mere idiosyncratic concern but was an intense longing he shared with some of the most powerful minds of his age: Goethe, Schiller, Hölder-

1. Iris Murdoch, *The Sovereignty of Good* (Boston: Ark, 1985), p. 72.
2. *Werke* 2:22.
3. *Werke* 2:21.
4. *Werke* 2:172.

lin, and Schelling. To varying degrees, all of these thinkers were moved initially, not by strictly philosophical concerns with the nature and limits of knowledge, but by an essentially practical problem posed by the modern age. The problem is that in the modern or postclassical world, we are in a sense forced to live a dual existence, torn between the philosophic demands for rights, equality, and rationality, on the one hand, and an existing order that is everywhere seen to violate those demands, on the other. It was this experience of what I want to call the divided self that Hegel felt was the problem to be overcome if our activity was to prove morally and intellectually satisfying.

I have used the term the "divided self" to indicate a species of moral life which emphasizes the ideas of conflict and struggle, as well as their eventual resolution. On this account of morality, which has dominated much of Western thought and culture at least since the Greeks, human nature is depicted as deeply at odds with itself, torn between conflicting sets of moral demands. Furthermore, it is important for this conception of morality that the cause of the diremption is not something outside of us, over which we have no control, but is the result of two basic elements of human nature, each vying for supremacy. In one of the most memorable depictions of this standpoint, the soul is likened to a charioteer who drives two horses, one noble but docile, the other wanton, lecherous, and aggressive.[5] The moral life consists of the constant struggle of the charioteer and the first horse away from the life of hedonic, sensual gratification represented by the second horse. Underlying this view, then, is clearly a kind of depreciation of the goods of the body and a striving toward an ideal world of truth, beauty, and perfection. Morality consists of adopting an essentially negative posture toward the realm of the senses and an aspiration, so far as is possible, toward eternity.

This conception of the moral life involves, then, an overcoming of the divided and self-contradictory aspects of human nature. In the Greek tradition, this duality could be overcome only in thought. Both Plato and Aristotle, whatever their differences may have been, saw in reason a transcendent activity capable of soaring high above the contingencies of human experience and grasping the infinite. Indeed, Plato's image of the divided line in book 6 of the *Republic* remains one of the most powerful expressions of the soul's longing to liberate itself from the harsh exigencies of the human world and become one with the eternal. But this liberation is not available to everyone. Only through a unique act of noetic insight, Plato believed,

5. Plato *Phaedrus* 246a–d.

could the mind move beyond the visible world of flux and instability to the world of ideas or forms—the unchanging, imperishable principles that account for the whole. These principles stand outside the knower, in the sense that they are independent of his activity, and as such become objects worthy of contemplation.

Corresponding to the classical conception of a transcendent reason was a fairly neat division between theory and practice. *Theoria,* as Aristotle described it in book 10 of the *Nicomachean Ethics,* is a quasi-divine activity guided by nothing but an interest in truth for its own sake.[6] Aristotle also thought that the life of the mind was the surest way to happiness, or *eudaimonia,* but for now this argument need not bother us. *Theoria* was chiefly taken to be distinguished from the practical and productive arts, respectively. The practical arts, ethics and politics, have activity (praxis) as their end.[7] Their goal is not some fabricated object but the activity itself performed well. Thus, the goal of ethics is the regulation and direction of the passions, while politics aims at participation in decision making and deliberation. Only the productive arts, or *technai,* such as economic activity, aim at the creation of those goods required for the sustenance and preservation of life.

Each of these activities was ranked by Aristotle in accordance with its proper degree of self-sufficiency. The productive arts were clearly least self-sufficient, ministering exclusively to the needs of the body. Praxis and *theoria* were closer to being ends in themselves, since they were concerned, not just with the preservation of mere life, but with the good life, or what makes life worth living.[8] But here contemplation was held to surpass politics in dignity to the same degree that politics surpassed all other activities. While the political way of life was ultimately dependent upon signs of honor and esteem from fellow citizens, only the philosopher was capable of realizing that part of the divine nous that linked him to the cosmos. As Aristotle put it in one of his biological writings, man is the only animal who shares not only in life but in a good life, because he alone of all the animals has a share in something divine.[9]

Classical political philosophy sought an answer to the problem of man's divided self by subordinating praxis and *techne* to *theoria.* The contemplative life was identified with freedom from necessity, including the necessity

6. Aristotle, *Nicomachean Ethics* 10.7; for a good treatment see Trond Berg Eriksen, *Bios Theoretikos: Notes on Aristotle's "Ethica Nicomachea"* 10.6–8 (Oslo: Universitetsforlaget, 1976).
7. Aristotle *Nicomachean Ethics* 1.1095a.5.
8. Aristotle *Politics*, 1.1252b.28–30; 1253a.30–39; 3.1280b.5–15; 1281a.1–5.
9. Aristotle *De partibus animalium* 2.10.656a.

to engage in politics. Whatever differences existed between the Platonists and the Aristotelians and the Stoics and the Skeptics, they all subscribed to the superiority of the contemplative life as the chief means of overcoming the contingencies of worldly existence. Contemplation has essentially three advantages over the other ways of life. First, it is an activity chosen for its own sake and thus admits no mixed motives or admixture of pain. Second, the philosopher is concerned with truth, a higher value on the scale of forms than the goals of other activities. And third, there is a stability about contemplation that arises from the fact that it is the only good whose goodness is not diminished by being shared.[10]

This celebration of the *bios theoretikos* was later exploded by the advent of the Judeo-Christian God, which presented itself, not as a rational principle knowable through our share in divine nous, but as the Creator of all that is and whose ways cannot be known but only accepted. Reason was no longer something that participated in the divine, but was reduced to a faculty cut off from any cosmic purpose. Above all, the Judeo-Christian God introduced a much sharper sense of the sheer contingency of being. By contingency is not meant here the fact that all things come into being and pass away. The ancients had developed a highly sophisticated conceptual vocabulary for relating the mutability of the individual to the imperishability of the species. Christianity introduced a much deeper sense of the dependence of the species and nature as a whole upon the will of God. "In the beginning God created the heavens and the earth," the book of Genesis begins. Such a statement, implying the creation of the universe ex nihilo, would have been unintelligible to Aristotle—as unintelligible as God's revelation to Moses: "I am that I am." Natural human reason, from this perspective, is incapable of grasping the one thing all men most deeply desire to know: the reason for creation, or why God does what he does. It thus becomes only through a life of faith (*pistis*) that we can be said to have any share in God's plan. Reason can do no more than lead men toward, and prepare them for, the truths of revelation.

The implications of this view were understood only imperfectly and developed gradually over a long period of time, reaching a culmination in the nominalism of William of Ockham. Unlike the Aristotelians, with their belief in a humanly relevant and dependable cosmos, the nominalists asserted God's creation of the world ex nihilo. This doctrine, which was already contained in Saint Augustine's first book, *De libero arbitrio,* was given sys-

10. See Martha C. Nussbaum, *The Fragility of Goodness: Luck and Ethics in Greek Tragedy and Philosophy* (Cambridge: Cambridge University Press, 1986), pp. 147–48.

tematic expression in Ockham's teaching regarding "divine omnipotence" and the inscrutability of God's will. By emphasizing the absolute omnipotence of God, Ockham underscored the radically contingent nature of all finite beings. The result of this bifurcation between the finite and the infinite—what Hegel would later refer to as the experience of the "unhappy consciousness"—was the disappearance of any sense of order from the universe, where God, the source of that order, was conceived as so thoroughly unfathomable by human reason as to leave him all but irrelevant for practical purposes. Out of this impasse emerged what Hans Blumenberg has called a new form of human "self-assertion," that is, a new edginess or anxiety "from which springs the incomparable energy of the rise of the modern age." [11] "The destruction of trust in the world," Blumenberg writes in one of his characteristically Nietzschean moments, "made [man] for the first time a creatively active being, freed him from a disastrous lulling of his activity." [12]

One strategy adopted in the early phases of modernity for coping with the *aporiai* of medieval Christianity was proposed by René Descartes. The very titles of his two major works, *Discourse on Method* and *Rules for the Direction of the Mind,* already tell us a great deal about the direction of his thought. The key terms, "method" and "rules," indicate the following of an intellectual regimen which, if followed scrupulously, holds out the possibility of great intellectual and scientific advances. [13] While Descartes is generally regarded as the founder of modern philosophy, with all of its attendant metaphysical and epistemological problems, it is, on my reading, plausible to see the Cartesian project more as a response to the sense of anxiety and unrest produced by the understanding of ourselves as contingent, finite creatures, wholly dependent upon an all-powerful deity for every moment of our existence. The famous method advocated by Descartes can thus be seen as a kind of surrogate theology which might liberate those who follow it from the uncertainty and doubt brought on by problems of a fundamentally religious nature. The "Cartesian Anxiety," as it has been called, has more the character of an existential, than a strictly metaphysical, problem. [14]

The escape from uncertainty was thought to be achieved by a unique act of the cogito—the thinking subject—which must be taught "to accept

11. Hans Blumenberg, *The Legitimacy of the Modern Age,* trans. Robert M. Wallace (Cambridge, Mass.: MIT Press, 1983), p. 148.

12. Blumenberg, *Legitimacy of the Modern Age,* p. 139.

13. For some of the implications of Descartes's methodological turn, see Sheldon Wolin, "Political Theory as a Vocation," *American Political Science Review* 63 (1969): 1062–82.

14. Richard J. Bernstein, *Beyond Objectivism and Relativism: Science, Hermeneutics, and Praxis* (Philadelphia: University of Pennsylvania Press, 1983), pp. 16–20.

nothing as true which I did not clearly recognize to be so: that is to say, carefully to avoid precipitation and prejudice in judgments and to accept in them nothing more than what was presented to my mind so clearly and distinctly that I could have no occasion to doubt it."[15] Only when we can discover a class of truths which is sufficient to command the assent of all reasonable onlookers will it be possible both to safeguard knowledge from the corrosive blasts of skepticism and to establish a "firm and permanent" foundation for the sciences.[16] The first absolute certainty that emerges from the experience of radical uncertainty is the fact of doubt itself. There is something that not even an "evil genius" (*malin génie*) can make us doubt, namely, the act of doubt itself. Skepticism is dispelled, then, by reference to the *I,* the cogito, which becomes the new locus of certainty in a world impregnated by insecurities.

It is arguable that Descartes's method has purchased certainty at the price of vacuity. As Hegel would argue later on, beginning with the "self-certainty" of the ego, Descartes is never able to escape from its subjective limitations. Descartes's answer to the charge of subjectivism is that from the "fact" of doubt, other, more substantive, facts can be inferred. Among this class of facts is the existence of a beneficent deity who sustains us at every moment of our existence and guarantees that our knowledge and the external world will in fact correspond. While Descartes's theology is a disputed topic, it is essential to his argument that he be able to argue from the certainty of the cogito to the existence of God. Crudely stated, Descartes's argument is that we are finite, fallible creatures who can nevertheless recognize our imperfections by measuring them against some standard of perfection that is presupposed. Since this standard cannot be derived from ourselves alone, the idea of God, the ultimate standard, must be implanted innately in our minds, or else we would be unable to conceive it. While Descartes denied that knowledge of God as the locus of limitless perfection could provide us with insight into our rights and duties, he did believe that we could derive from it the "laws of nature," as well as those "passions of the soul" which are part of the natural order.

What plausibility Descartes's injunctions contain depend upon the introduction of God as a sort of deus ex machina designed to ensure the possibility of objective knowledge. But while Descartes thought it legitimate to cast doubt upon the opinions and beliefs of his predecessors, especially the beliefs contained in "the Greek and Latin books," he nonetheless sought to

15. René Descartes, *Oeuvres philosophique,* ed. Felix Alquie (Paris: Garnier, 1963), 1:586.
16. Descartes, *Oeuvres* 1:404.

avoid direct confrontation with the political authorities. Thus, in the *Discourse on Method*, he elaborated a code of "provisional morality," the first principle of which was "to obey the laws and customs of my country, adhering constantly to the religion in which by God's grace I had been instructed since my childhood." And to this he added the corollary that "amongst many opinions all equally received, I chose only the most moderate, both because these are always most suited for putting into practice and probably the best for all excess has a tendency to be bad."[17] Descartes's maxim to adhere to the established religion and obey the laws and customs appears to be the basis for the outward conformism and conservatism of which he has often been accused. Indeed, his decision to abstain from political activity and to harmonize his conduct "with the ideas of those with whom [he] had to live" would seem to confirm the suspicion that Cartesian doubt is merely subjective, leaving the world no different after it than it was before.

Yet the accusation of conservatism is perhaps too hasty. Descartes's *morale provisoire* is exactly what he claims it is: provisional. The provisional morality is not his definitive morality. Whatever the status of this morality may be within Descartes's "legislation" as a whole, it is clear that the obligation to obey the law is not intended to command absolutely. A policy of outward conformity masks an attitude of ironical distance that Descartes put between himself and the world. Thus, in the *Discourse* he says that because of "the corrupt state of our manners there are few people who desire to say all that they believe," and elsewhere he states that his morality was written under the force of social pressure and does not necessarily represent his true convictions.[18]

However, the alleged conservatism of Descartes seems to be further substantiated by the third maxim of his provisional morality, according to which one must "try always to conquer [oneself] rather than fortune, and to alter [one's] desires rather than change the order of the world."[19] Like the Stoics to whom he has often been compared, Descartes emphasizes self-control and restraint as the core of moral virtue. Virtue is the knowledge of what is and what is not within our powers to control. And since "there is nothing entirely within our power but our own thoughts," he seems to be cautioning against a Machiavellian or Baconian project of conquering na-

17. Descartes, *Oeuvres* 1:592, 594.

18. René Descartes, *L'entretien avec Burman*, trans. Jean-Marie Beyssade (Paris: Presses Universitaires de France, 1981), p. 144.

19. Descartes, *Oeuvres* 1:595.

ture or "fortuna." But here again, the appearance is misleading. In *The Prince,* Machiavelli counsels a policy of ruthlessness as a means of conquering fortune; in the *Discourse,* Descartes offers a policy of firmness and resoluteness as a means of overcoming the "disorders of passions," which are prone to afflict us. Once we adopt the correct method, we will be able to master not only the passions but external nature as well. The self-control of reason and its withholding of assent from all things that do not pass the test of "clarity and distinctness" are the foundation of a mathematical physics that can ultimately render us "masters and possessors of nature."[20] It is not, then, extreme Stoic piety or submission to nature, but in the final analysis, our self-emancipation from nature that made Descartes not only a profound student of Machiavelli but a particular favorite of Nietzsche, as well.[21]

Exactly what Descartes means by making us the masters and possessors of nature is tied to his morality of *générosité.* Descartes means by generosity that "passion of the soul" which "causes a man to esteem himself as highly as he legitimately can."[22] The true cause of these feelings of self-approbation or esteem is the "firm and constant resolution" of the will, but a secondary cause comes from a desire to benefit "the general good of all mankind."[23] Cartesian generosity is not, then, simply an inward-looking passion; it is a political passion or virtue whose aim is to find new and more useful ways of benefiting "the public." Cartesian generosity is the bearer of a particular technique which "is not merely to be desired with a view to the invention of an infinity of arts and crafts which enable us to enjoy without any trouble the fruits of the earth and all the good things which are to be found there, but also principally because it brings about the preservation of health, which is without doubt the chief blessing and the foundation of all other blessings in this life."[24]

The posture that Descartes chooses to adopt for himself is clearly that of the embattled philosophe fighting against the entrenched forces of darkness and superstition. The *générosité* of which he is the bearer is not necessarily that of political or moral justice but of a promised kingdom of heaven on earth, what Joseph Cropsey has called a "Mechanical Jerusalem," made possible by the power of both mathematical physics and the science of medi-

20. Descartes, *Oeuvres* 1:634.

21. The best treatments of Descartes's "Machiavellianism" are Pierre Mesnard, *Essai sur la morale de Descartes* (Paris: Boivin, 1936), pp. 190–212; Raymond Polin, "Descartes et la philosophie politique," *Mélanges Alexandre Koyré* (Paris: Hermann, 1964), 2:381–99.

22. Descartes, *Oeuvres* 3:1067.

23. Descartes, *Oeuvres* 1:634.

24. Descartes, *Oeuvres* 1:634.

cine.[25] The *Discourse* concludes with an eschatological vision in which Descartes holds open the possibility that through the beneficence of his science, one day (perhaps soon) we may even transcend the infirmities of old age. While the aims of science will not be achievable in the life of one man, or even one generation, Descartes speaks of sharing his insights with the public: "by joining together the lives and labors of many we should collectively proceed much further than any one in particular could succeed in doing."[26] In the same way as Bacon, Descartes sees that it is only through the principle of the division of labor that his own discoveries will bear fruit and, perhaps more importantly, that his own good name will survive his body.

Finally, Descartes realized that the new science of which he was a founder was more likely to bear fruit, not in monarchic France, but in commercial Holland, where "the armies which are maintained seem only to be of use in allowing the inhabitants to enjoy the fruits of peace."[27] Only in a commercial society where people are "more concerned with its own affairs than curious about those of others" will one be able to engage in the kind of scientific and scholarly pursuits that will both enhance the lives of the "unlearned" public and call attention to the generosity of their benefactor. It was only by refraining from, and even explicitly disavowing, any effort to reform public law that Descartes was able to bring men such nonpolitical or private goods as health, comfort, and long life.

What Descartes in his *Discourse* called his "provisional morality" was given its definitive shape by the Enlightenment of the seventeenth and eighteenth centuries. The famous doctrine of natural law, to be examined in more detail in chapter 3, was the Enlightenment's great attempt to unite reason and nature by making moral judgments natural. Typically the founders of the Enlightenment appealed to some prepolitical state of nature as the source of man's rights and obligations. Only by appealing to a putative condition antedating civil society could they discover some universal fact of nature which, if obeyed, could instruct us about our duties. While different thinkers disagreed about the precise content of the natural law, they were in general accord that underlying the superficial diversity in manners, customs, and habits there was a single and simple moral order available to everyone not blinded by prejudice or *parti pris*. Furthermore, this moral order could be discovered, not by trying to intuit the will of

25. Joseph Cropsey, "On Descartes's Discourse on Method," *Political Philosophy and the Issues of Politics* (Chicago: University of Chicago Press, 1977), p. 289.

26. Descartes, *Oeuvres* 1:635.

27. Descartes, *Oeuvres* 1:601.

God, but by consulting the undeniable facts of human nature and man's needs, interests, and relationships. Such laws, when properly understood, governed the manner in which men operated, not the purposes for which men were created.

The Enlightenment essentially envisaged a research program which attempted to read off moral characteristics from certain alleged uniformities of nature. Hobbes, perhaps the prototypical Enlightenment naturalist, regarded natural law as the factual experience of man's powers, needs, and will that lead him to seek peace when all others agree to do so as well. Similarly, for Pierre Bayle, author of the *Dictionnaire historique et critique,* natural law is revealed through a "natural light" which is foreign to all forms of revelation but which speaks directly to all those who but consult their reason. His was an entirely naturalistic or empirical theory of morality. "It is necessary," Bayle wrote, "to submit all moral laws to the idea of natural equity which . . . illuminates every man coming into the world." There are sentiments of honesty inscribed in the souls of men, sentiments that can only be likened to "natural and eternal law which proves to all men the idea of honesty that holds for pagans, Christians, and atheists alike." [28] Finally, David Hume, for all of his famed skepticism, sought "to introduce the experimental method of reasoning into moral subjects." This method attempted to establish what can only be described as a moral and political physics with the same rigor and exactitude as mathematics. In his *Enquiry Concerning Human Understanding,* we read: "Would you know the sentiments, inclinations, and course of life of the Greeks and Romans? Study well the temper and actions of the French and English. . . . Mankind are so much the same, in all times and places, that history informs us of nothing new or strange in this particular. Its chief use is only to discover the constant and universal principles of human nature." [29]

The pleasing harmony between reason and nature that natural law theorists hoped to discover could not be sustained in the face of increasingly skeptical assaults. In the first place, the sanctions for transgressing these laws were usually vague and remote, thus rendering natural law of questionable utility for civic purposes. Second, there was a certain equivocation in the term "natural" in the phrase "natural law." For some, the term still carried residues of the discredited Aristotelian teleology, while for others it implied some kind of spontaneous biological drive or impulse. Third, for

28. Pierre Bayle, *Oeuvres diverses* (La Haye, 1737), 2:368, 369.
29. David Hume, *Enquiry Concerning Human Understanding,* ed. L. A. Selby Bigge (Oxford: Clarendon Press, 1902), pp. 83–84.

thinkers with a more historical cast of mind, like Montesquieu and Herder, the whole issue of the state of nature and a primordial natural law was questionable at best. While these thinkers did not deny the existence of certain human uniformities persisting across space and time, they believed that it was the particular culture of a people, their unique esprit, that contributed most to their humanity.

Perhaps the most important assault upon the naturalistic empiricism of the Enlightenment came from Rousseau. For Rousseau, the precedence given to nature and natural law seemed to carry over an essential reductionism into the comprehension of moral duty. Morality cannot simply be read off certain natural propensities, like the desire for life or property. Thus, Rousseau's critique of the natural law school in his *Discourse on the Origins and Foundations of Inequality* speaks more with the idealism and romanticism of the nineteenth century than with the generalizing and positivistic science of the Enlightenment. In the *Second Discourse*, Rousseau denied the Enlightenment premise of the essential homogeneity of nature and hence of a unified natural and social science. The natural law, for Rousseau, is not a moral law. The law of nature is simply the law of the strong, from which no moral obligations can be drawn. "Nature treats them [natural men] precisely as the law of Sparta treated the children of citizens," Rousseau observed; "it renders strong and robust those who are well constituted and makes all the others perish."[30] The moral law requires us not to conform to nature but to transcend it. And the way we transcend nature is by acting in accordance with reason, where reason is understood, above all, by form. The form of reason, its universal applicability, becomes more important than its content. From this line of thought the modern idea of an "autonomy" of reason and of the rational human essence emerged.[31]

Rousseau offered the following reasons for rejecting Enlightenment naturalism. Depicting the naturalistic monism of Hobbes and Spinoza as "dangerous dreams," Rousseau looked at human beings under two aspects: the "physical" and the "metaphysical and moral." Conceived as physical objects—as a part of nature—we are nothing more than "ingenious machines" constituted by certain appetites and desires which can be studied and known through the laws of mathematical physics. Seen from the moral and metaphysical angle, however, human beings are decisively or qualita-

30. Jean-Jacques Rousseau, *Discourses on the Origins and Foundations of Inequality, First and Second Discourses,* trans. Roger D. Masters and Judith R. Masters (New York: Saint Martin's, 1964), p. 106.

31. Deiter Henrich and David S. Pacini, "The Contexts of Autonomy: Some Presuppositions of the Comprehensibility of Human Rights," *Daedalus* (Fall 1983) 255–77.

tively different. We are primarily free agents whose capacity for willing and choosing makes possible progress or "perfectibility."[32]

Rousseau explains this dualism in the following passage: "Nature commands every animal and the beast obeys. Man feels the same impetus, but he is free to acquiesce or resist; and it is above all in the consciousness of this freedom that the spirituality of his soul is shown."[33] It is this capacity to resist or deny the sway of instinct and to choose for ourselves that most importantly marks the distinction between man and beast and makes it possible for us to behave morally. A being ruled by necessity alone, whose every action is determined by the rule of instinct, is scarcely to be held responsible for its acts and is therefore incapable of morality. Only beings who have some capacity for free and spontaneous action, who can decide to do or not to do, can escape the determined order of nature.

The implications of Rousseau's attack upon the Enlightenment were fully realized only by Kant. Kant is the thinker properly called the founder of that line of modern thought known as "idealism" or "critical idealism." He invented the critical philosophy in conscious opposition to the empirical realism of his early modern predecessors. Indeed, Kant's critical philosophy is sometimes regarded as but a deepening and radicalization of Rousseau's. John Rawls, for one, has suggested that "among other things, Kant is giving a deeper reading to Rousseau's remark that 'to be governed by appetite alone is slavery, while obedience to a law one prescribes to oneself is freedom.'"[34] For Kant, Rousseau was the first thinker to express the "honor" and "dignity" due to mankind by virtue of its humanity alone. Kant saw in Rousseau's formula of the general will—that the criterion of law resides in its form alone—a kind of anticipation of his own Categorical Imperative.[35]

Where Kant and Rousseau part company is with Kant's attempt to give a universal, or "cosmopolitan," significance to the general will that Rousseau would never have allowed. While Rousseau saw the general will as purely local and political, operative only in small polislike communities, the entire thrust of Kant's critical idealism was toward universally binding moral norms that would obligate persons as such. But Kant's cosmopolitanism came at a price, namely, severing the will from all natural or observable

32. Rousseau, *Origins of Inequality,* pp. 113–15.

33. Rousseau, *Origins of Inequality,* p. 114.

34. John Rawls, *A Theory of Justice* (Cambridge, Mass.: Harvard University Press, 1971), p. 264.

35. Kant, cited in Ernst Cassirer, *Rousseau, Kant, Goethe* (New York: Harper & Row, 1963), p. 1.

facts of human experience. In the *Groundwork of the Metaphysic of Morals,* his first major contribution to ethical theory, Kant described the good will as the one thing "good without qualification," which would still "shine like a jewel" even if it were to prove practically impotent.[36] The Kantian idea of a "kingdom of ends" was to be an ideal community of persons cooperating in the colegislation of moral laws. Thus, while Rousseau conceived the general will as a purely procedural formula for testing the legitimacy of civil laws, the Kantian good will was intended to apply "to the personal maxims of sincere and conscientious individuals in everyday life."[37]

Despite Kant's frequent disclaimers, he did not regard the free will of the moral agent as irrelevant to political life. There is clearly a connection between Kant's kingdom of ends in the *Groundwork* and his preference for republican politics in his political writings. His definition of the kingdom of ends as "a systematic union of different rational beings under laws" points the way to a republican form of government based on the "rights of man." "A true system of politics," he says in his article "Perpetual Peace," "cannot take a single step without first paying tribute to morality."[38] While Kant never went so far as to deny the distinction between the moral and the political realms and even admitted that civil society would be possible among a nation of "devils," so long as they were rational,[39] the consistent tendency of his thought was to blur the distinction between the politically possible and the morally permissible.[40]

Nonetheless, Kantian critical philosophy begins with the attempt to provide a more articulate defense of Rousseau's dualism between nature and morality. This attempt is expressed in the famous opposition between the realm of nature (phenomena) and the realm of freedom (noumena). The realm of nature is the realm of things or objects (including human beings) in their appearance or manifestation. We might call this the empirical world, because it is the world as it comes to be known through the senses and can be formulated and analyzed according to the laws of natural science. The realm of freedom, or noumena, on the other hand, is the world

36. Immanuel Kant, *Groundwork of the Metaphysic of Morals,* trans. H. J. Patton (New York: Harper & Row, 1964), pp. 61, 62.

37. John Rawls, "Kantian Constructivism in Moral Theory: The Dewey Lectures 1980," *Journal of Philosophy* 9 (1980):552.

38. Immanuel Kant, "Perpetual Peace," *Political Writings,* trans. H. B. Nisbet (Cambridge: Cambridge University Press, 1970), p. 125.

39. Kant, "Perpetual Peace," p. 112.

40. For a recent treatment of this problem, see Patrick Riley, *Kant's Political Philosophy* (Totowa, N.J.: Rowman & Littlefield, 1982).

opened to morality. Accordingly, this morality cannot be based upon any natural or empirical facts about human beings as we perceive them. To attempt to find a basis for morality in nature would be for Kant tantamount to collapsing human beings back into the determined order of natural necessity. If Kant is, then, to avoid confusing human beings as they appear or as they behave empirically from how they are as moral creatures, he must be able to deduce or infer a purely a priori morality or, to paraphrase the title of one of his later works, a morality within the limits of reason alone.

For our purposes, the most important feature of Kant's dualism is his belief in the autonomy of morality, that is, his belief that moral duty can be derived from no source outside itself. Even God, Kant says, is to be revered, not because he is the source of, but because he embodies, the moral law. In particular, Kant wants to avoid the kind of ethical naturalism expressed by writers like Spinoza, Bayle, Hume, and the utilitarians, for whom morality is bound up with the increase of human happiness or with certain feelings of pleasure and pain. For Kant, all such feelings are "pathological" in the sense that they can be reduced to and explained by natural processes and the "laws of mechanism." Like many later antinaturalists, Kant denies that any mere matter of fact, including the facts of human psychology, is sufficient to derive a genuinely moral "ought," but says that the two inhabit mutually distinct realms with mutually distinct logics. This is the basis for Kant's famous assertion that no *ought* can be derived from an *is*.

It was this putative diremption between *is* and *ought,* given its most uncompromising expression in Kantian philosophy, to which Hegel and others of his generation felt obliged to respond. The division of man between two orders of being, between the phenomenal natural world subject to universal causality and the noumenal world of moral freedom and independence of mind, was the specifically Kantian form of the morality of the divided self that Hegel tried to overcome. For Kant, morality presents itself as a constant struggle between our phenomenal and our noumenal selves, between our physical and psychological urges and inclinations and the command of duty. While our inclinations and desires will be invariably self-seeking, by duty is meant obedience to a rational principle or law that is universally binding on all rational beings. For the Kantian moralist, then, duty requires a constant effort to transcend the empirically given side of our nature, which can only serve as a temptation to immorality.

The Kantian depiction of human nature provides a textbook case of the morality of the divided self described above. A standard criticism of this morality turns on its alleged overreliance on an abstractly conceived set of moral principles or rules. For an action to be moral, according to Kant, it had to be explicable in terms of certain principles that could be universalized. Only in acting for the sake of (out of "respect" for) principle could a person escape from being causally determined by the desire for pleasure and other nonmoral motives. Typically, Schiller and other early critics of this viewpoint took the reliance on moral rules as an attempt to deny humanity by submitting it to the cold order of law. Consider, for instance, the following speech by Karl Moor from Schiller's play *The Robbers:*

> Am I to squeeze my body in stays, and straightlace my will in the trammels of law? What might have given rise to an eagle's flight has been reduced to a snail's pace by law. Never yet has law formed a great man: 'tis liberty that breeds giants and heroes.[41]

What are at issue here are clearly two different conceptions of freedom. For Kant, freedom is only possible within a framework guaranteed by law, while for Schiller, law only serves to frustrate the legitimate human desire for freedom. Kant's conception of morality is singularly democratic, setting down a uniform standard of conduct for all; Schiller, by contrast, is concerned with the cultivation of moral "giants and heroes" whose special abilities should be regarded as virtues precisely because they cannot be subsumed under common moral rules. For our purposes it is not necessary to inquire whether this represents an entirely accurate picture of Kantian morality. What the romantics were rebelling against was a view of morality as obedience to a purportedly fixed code of behavior or a set of rules designed to impose order and restraint on the unruly passions. Since only what can be subsumed under law can count as morality, any personal oddity, eccentricity, or quirk must be repressed as an affront to the rules of right conduct. Such rules, made for ordinary men under ordinary circumstances, can only harden into dogma that confronts the individual as alien or other to his own personality.

ROMANTICISM AND REVOLUTION

Hegel's hope to resolve the persistent tensions within this view of the moral life provides the basis for his critical efforts. In his early writings, Hegel, like many of his generation, harked back to ancient Greece and the classical ideal of the polis as providing the paradigm of cultural wholeness and integrity.[42] Indeed, Schiller's *Letters on the Aesthetic Education of Mankind,*

41. Friedrich Schiller, *The Robbers*, 1:2.

42. The classic account of this problem is still E. M. Butler, *The Tyranny of Greece over Germany* (Cambridge: Cambridge University Press, 1935); for other studies see J. Glenn Gray, *Hegel's Hellenic Ideal* (New York: King's Crown Press, 1941); Henry Hatfield, *Aesthetic Paganism*

which Hegel immediately hailed a "masterpiece," provided him with an early insight into the beauty of Greek life.⁴³ What Hegel and others of his generation saw in this work was a call for liberation from the dominant ethos of the *Aufklärung,* namely, materialism and utility.⁴⁴ Writing under the direct impact of the reign of terror, Schiller connected his hopes for spiritual and aesthetic liberation with the political aspirations of the French Revolution. "Man," he says, "has roused himself from his long indolence and self deception and . . . is demanding restitution of his inalienable rights."⁴⁵ And later in the *Letters* he remarks that for the aesthetic culture to at last replace utilitarianism "a complete revolution in [man's] whole way of feeling is required."⁴⁶

In the *Letters,* Schiller set out to contrast the harmony and cohesion of the ancient world to the fragmentation and division of modern society. How did this transformation come about? Schiller presents this transition as a falling away from a primordial natural harmony which was destroyed by the growth of the speculative intellect. What nature made whole, mankind has torn asunder. "Why was the individual Greek qualified to be the representative of his time, and why can no single Modern venture as much?" Schiller asks. "Because it was all-uniting Nature that bestowed upon the former, and all-dividing intellect that bestowed upon the latter, their respective forms."⁴⁷ Schiller's account of the rise of modern intellectual culture goes beyond the romantic opposition of nature and intellect. His insights incorporate elements of the expanding disciplines of sociology and political economy. Drawing on his reading of Adam Ferguson's *Essay on the History of Civil Society,* Schiller lays particular emphasis on the intensification of the division of labor as the source of this fragmentation.⁴⁸

in *German Literature* (Cambridge, Mass.: Harvard University Press, 1964); Jacques Taminiaux, *La Nostalgie de la Grece à l'aube de l'idéalisme allemand* (The Hague: Martinus Nijhoff, 1967); Judith Shklar, "Hegel's Phenomenology: An Elegy for Hellas," *Hegel's Political Philosophy,* ed. Z. A. Pelczynski (Cambridge: Cambridge University Press, 1971), pp. 73–89.

43. Friedrich Schiller, *On the Aesthetic Education of Man,* trans. Elizabeth Wilkinson and L. A. Willoughby (Oxford: Clarendon Press, 1967); for Schiller's influence on Hegel during these early years, see George A. Kelly, "Social Understanding and Social Therapy," *Hegel's Retreat from Eleusis* (Princeton: Princeton University Press, 1978), pp. 55–89.

44. Schiller, *Aesthetic Education,* p. 7.

45. Schiller, *Aesthetic Education,* p. 25.

46. Schiller, *Aesthetic Education,* p. 205.

47. Schiller, *Aesthetic Education,* p. 33.

48. For Ferguson's influence on Schiller and German romanticism, see M. A. Abrams, *Natural Supernaturalism: Tradition and Revolution in Romantic Literature* (New York: W. W. Norton, 1971), pp. 210–11; Raymond Plant, *Hegel* (London: George Allen & Unwin, 1973), pp. 21–24.

Through the specialization of functions, man's faculties have become ener-
vated and narrow until he is now only a partial, abstract, caricature of what
he once was. In modern society, individuals are but "fragments" of the
whole, so that "one might almost be tempted to assert, the various faculties
appear as separate in practice as they are distinguished by the psychologist
in theory." The division of labor, which may be useful for increasing efficiency, has led to a "more rigorous separation of ranks and occupations,"
where in place of an "organic" system we have "an ingenious clockwork in
which out of the piecing together of innumerable but lifeless parts, a mechanical kind of collective life ensued."[49]

Schiller's work is a classic statement of what later sociological theorists
like Tönnies and Durkheim would call the transition from gemeinschaft to
gesellschaft, or from organic to mechanical solidarity.[50] What is distinctive
to Schiller's vision, however, is the belief that the self-division and fragmentation that human powers have undergone in the present are in the service
of the reunification of human nature to come. "It must be open to us,"
Schiller writes in the famous sixth letter, "to restore by means of a higher
art the totality of our nature which the arts themselves have destroyed."[51]
The "higher art" (*höhere Kunst*) to which Schiller here alludes is nothing
short of the principle of a new civilization where the previous antagonism
between sensuousness and reason, *Stofftrieb* and *Formtrieb,* will be overcome. In passages that sound reminiscent of the young Marx, Schiller argues that only a culture that produces, not according to need or utility, but
by "the laws of beauty" will restore a higher, nondivided humanity. While a
return to the earlier prereflective harmony of the Greeks is declared to be
impossible, Schiller holds open the possibility of a higher unity based on
exposure to art. The idea is that the artist can create the conditions for
harmony which the Greeks had merely taken for granted. In fact this new
harmony would even be superior to the earlier one for being created in full
self-awareness of the multiple alternatives open to us.

The final goal is, then, what Schiller calls an "aesthetic state." Schiller
presents this as a "third realm" (*drittes Reich*) transcending the subordinate
spheres of legality and morality. The principle of this state is nothing less
than taste. "Taste alone," he writes, "brings harmony into society, because it
fosters harmony in the individual. All other forms of perception divide

49. Schiller, *Aesthetic Education,* p. 35.

50. See Ferdinand Tönnies, *Community and Association,* trans. C. Loomis (London: Routledge & Kegan Paul, 1955); Emile Durkheim, *The Division of Labor,* trans. G. Simpson (New
York: Macmillan, 1933).

51. Schiller, *Aesthetic Education,* p. 43.

man, because they are founded exclusively either upon the sensuous or upon the spiritual part of his being; only the aesthetic mode of perception makes of him a whole."[52] Beauty is not for Schiller simply an ornament for a new *Gelehrtenrepublik*. It is to be the unifying principle for collective life where reason, community, and freedom are at last joined in a new and higher harmony. From the liberation of the play impulse, he expects "the fetters of serfdom [to] fall from the lifeless and living alike. In the Aesthetic State everything—even the tool which serves—is a free citizen having equal rights with the noblest. . . . Here therefore in the realm of Aesthetic Semblance, we find the ideal of equality."[53]

The basic theme to emerge from Schiller's *Letters,* then, and from the writings of other early romantic critics of existing society is that the highest human aspiration is the drive for unity. However, this is a unity of a special kind. It is a unity that presupposes and even welcomes diversity and conflict. Thus, Schiller and, following him, Hölderlin and Hegel, came to regard life as a movement from an original paradisaic condition into one of extreme conflict and tension, to be followed by a final stage of reunion with our alienated past. This movement actually constitutes a development where the integration of life's opposing tendencies is placed even above the restoration of the original unity. This integration of life into a whole is then understood as beauty in the truest sense of the term. But what remains crucial here is the path or the way toward this end. In his prose poem *Hyperion,* Hölderlin referred to this development as a path without a center, an "eccentric circle" (*exzentrische Bahn*):

> We all pass through an eccentric path, and there is no other way possible from childhood to consummation. The blessed unity, Being (in the only sense of that word) is lost to us, and we had to lose it if we were to gain it again by striving and struggle. We tear ourselves loose from the peaceful *en kai pan* of the world, in order to restore it through ourselves. We have fallen out with nature, and what was once one, as we can believe, is now in conflict with itself, and each side alternates between mastery and servitude. . . . Hyperion too was divided between these two extremes.[54]

In his early years, Hegel shared with his contemporaries, Schelling and Hölderlin, an enthusiasm for an aesthetic utopia conceived along Schillerian lines. Together they celebrated the French Revolution for its promise to re-

---

52. Schiller, *Aesthetic Education,* p. 215.
53. Schiller, *Aesthetic Education,* p. 219.
54. Friedrich Hölderlin, "Erste Hyperion-Vorrede," *Sämtliche Werke. Historisch-Kritische Ausgabe* (Berlin: Propylaen, 1923), 2:545.

create the cult of ancient virtue, which they interpreted somewhat inconsistently to be compatible with the Kantian demands for moral autonomy and self-determination. They saw in the Revolution not only an internal spiritual liberation from the political and religious dogmas of the ancien régime but (in the words of John Towes) "the historical possibility of a radical transformation of 'the whole previous constitution of the world.'"[55] As early as 1795, Hegel equated the political acquisitions of the French Revolution with Kant's "Copernican Revolution" in morals. In a programmatic letter to Schelling from this period, he notes: "From the Kantian system and its ultimate conclusion, I expect a revolution in Germany—a revolution which will take its point of departure from already existing principles and which only needs to be generally applied to all previously existing knowledge."[56]

Needless to say, Hegel did not expect that this revolution would be confined to the sphere of mind only. Richard Kroner, for one, has noted "the breathtaking speed" and "explosive character" of post-Kantian idealism.[57] The concept of revolution, which made its way into modern European vocabularies originally through the language of literary criticism to describe the changes of fortune of a character from one state to another, later came to imply a process of historical development or acceleration towards new and theretofore unpredictable states of affairs.[58] Revolution in this new sense came to imply a capacity for novelty and an openness to change that were often seen as the root of the two great upheavals of the eighteenth century. In the decades before and after 1789, the term was expanded by enlightened thinkers to apply to areas as diverse as law, morality, religion, economics, and politics. Thus, by 1772, Louis Sebastian Mercier could observe that "[t]out est revolution dans ce monde."[59] And Robespierre could announce at the height of the French Revolution that "[t]out a changé dans l'ordre physique; et tout doit changer dans l'ordre moral et politique."[60] Robespierre saw himself as the executor of a moral justice to be secured by force, a belief reiterated by Tom Paine, who interpreted the American and French Revolutions as involving an absolute turn of events. From the eighteenth century onward, the term "revolution" acquired overtones of an

55. John Toewes, *Hegelianism: The Path Toward Dialectical Humanism, 1805–1841* (Cambridge: Cambridge University Press, 1980), p. 31.

56. Letter to Schelling, 16 April 1795, *Briefe* 1:23.

57. Cited in Abrams, *Natural Supernaturalism,* p. 348.

58. R. G. Collingwood, *The New Leviathan* (Oxford: Clarendon Press, 1942), pp. 199–200.

59. Cited in Reinhart Koselleck, "Historical Criteria of the Modern Concept of Revolution," *Futures Past: On the Semantics of Historical Time,* trans. Keith Tribe (Cambridge, Mass.: MIT Press, 1985), p. 45.

60. Cited in Hannah Arendt, *On Revolution* (New York: Viking Press, 1965), p. 39.

almost irresistible movement that would inaugurate a new era of human happiness in which autocracy would be exploded, superstition banished, and republican government established as the only political regime rational in theory and tolerable in practice.

Kant's position on the French Revolution can here serve as a kind of barometer for the new moral attitude. In his essay "The Contest of the Faculties" (1798), he could claim to find evidence of a moral tendency toward progress evinced in "an occurrence of our times." This event, the French Revolution, proved to Kant that moral factors did play a part in history, however small, but that these factors were to be found not in the political actors themselves but in the "disinterested spectators" who observed their actions. This moral tendency is to be discovered in the enthusiasm for revolution regardless of what the consequences of that enthusiasm might be. Thus, Kant could write near the end of his life:

> The revolution which we have seen taking place in our own times in a nation of gifted people may succeed, or it may fail. It may be so filled with misery and atrocities that no right-thinking man would ever decide to make the same experiment again at such a price, even if he could hope to carry it out successfully at the second attempt. But I maintain that this revolution has aroused in the hearts and desires of all spectators who are not themselves caught up in it a *sympathy* which borders almost on enthusiasm, although the very utterance of this sympathy was fraught with danger. It cannot therefore have been caused by anything other than a moral disposition within the human race.[61]

That Kant could decry the execution of Louis XVI as a sin worse than murder, but still admire the principle of revolution by which that action was carried out, is stark testimony to the Janus-like character the concept had acquired. From Kant onwards, it acquired an almost transcendental significance, which later thinkers would transmute into the idea of historical necessity. Starting from Kant and proceeding in an unbroken line from Hegel and Marx to Lenin and Trotsky, revolution became a kind of moral duty undertaken by selfless men claiming to act in accordance with the highest liberal principles.[62]

The various changes I have been describing here have as their background the emergence of the idea of history as a collective force giving shape to the modern world. In its earliest meaning, revolution implied a return to first principles, indicated by the prefix *re* in the Latin word *revo-*

---

61. Kant, "Contest of the Faculties," *Political Writings*, p. 182.
62. William A. Galston, *Kant and the Problem of History* (Chicago: University of Chicago Press, 1975), pp. 23–38.

lutio.[63] When applied to political affairs, it signified the eternal recurrence of a few fixed forms of government, the essential character of which had long been known. For the Greeks and Romans, history was understood as a cyclical pattern of birth, growth, decay, and regeneration conceived along naturalistic lines. This meant that human affairs followed a pattern in which a few forms recurred with the same irresistible force that made the stars follow their paths in the heavens. This pattern constituted a revolution in the original lexical sense of circulation. Thus, Plato's cycle of regime transformation in books 8 and 9 of the *Republic* was followed closely by Aristotle's typology of regimes in the *Politics*. The same cyclical pattern occurred in the *Histories* of Polybius, who used the concept *anakuklosis politeion,* or cycle of constitutions, to indicate the sempiternal recurrences into which human affairs are driven, as if by nature. The cycle was a *physis,* a natural process, through which regimes were bound to pass unless by a stroke of good fortune they were able to escape this fate.[64]

The original meaning of the term "revolution," then, implied a return to some previously occupied position and not an overturning of all that had gone before. It is more than a semantic peculiarity, then, that the term meant something almost directly opposite what it has come to mean today. Even Locke, in the famous nineteenth chapter of the protorevolutionary *Second Treatise of Government,* could describe "the dissolution of government" as a return of the legislative power to its original hands. For Locke, as for Burke later on, revolution properly signified a restoration of the original constitution, a retrieving of ancient liberties. Thus, Locke could call King William the "Great Restorer" and describe the "Glorious Revolution" of 1688 as glorious precisely because it lacked what in the modern sense we call revolutionary.

The concept of revolution acquired its distinctively modern meaning only with the advent of the philosophy of history, which at least since the French Revolution has become the paradigm for understanding political change. This philosophy of history was possible only once the ancient conception of regime transformation as a *physis* was exploded by later Christian millennialist notions. While early Christian thinkers like Saint Augustine used the term *procursus* to describe the distance between the earthly and heavenly cities, it was left to the founders of modernity to describe history as a *progressus* owing nothing to God, nature, or any external

63. See Koselleck, "Historical Criteria of the Modern Concept of Revolution," p. 42; Arendt, *On Revolution,* pp. 35–36.

64. Polybius, *Histories,* 5.7–12; for a useful discussion, see Robert D. Cumming, *Human Nature and History* (Chicago: University of Chicago Press, 1969), 1:95–97, 149–51.

agency. History, understood as the totality of human deeds, came to be seen as having an immanent logic or development that the founders of the modern age called the idea of progress. In spite of its theological origins, the new conceptual formation offered historically immanent patterns of explanation not dependent upon divine intervention. Progress thus came to signify a process of improvement that does not have a precise telos, or goal, but does have a general direction. It is measured by our ever-expanding power over external nature based on the steady accumulation of scientific knowledge. Henceforth, the human good would not be teleologically limited in advance but would be projected into a glorious but indefinite future where man would become a power the equal of, if not superior to, nature itself. Indeed, it is perhaps not too much to say that for the idea of progress, the good simply *is* the future.[65]

Hegel ties himself to this new conception of revolution in the early letter to Schelling quoted above. In particular, he associates the French Revolution with the vindication of "the rights of man," which have become a sort of revolutionary force in their own right. Thus, he goes on to say:

> I believe that there is no better sign of the times than the fact that humanity is being represented as worthy of dignity and esteem in itself. . . . The philosophers demonstrate this dignity, the people will learn to feel it; and they will no longer be content to demand their rights which have been reduced to dust, but will seize them, appropriate them. . . . Thanks to the propagation of ideas which demonstrate how things ought to be, the indolence of those who confer eternity on everything that exists is disappearing. The vitalizing power of ideas—even if they do always carry a limitation such as country, constitution, etc.—will elevate the spirits and they will learn to devour these ideas.[66]

The political radicalism expressed in this letter was no doubt partly influenced by Hegel's association with Schelling, who before Hegel had sought to discover a metaphysical foundation for freedom. In the preface to his first published work, *On the Ego as the Principle of Philosophy,* Schelling remarks that his aim "is no mere reform of a discipline but a complete reversal of its principles, that is, a revolution." The nature of this revolution will be "to liberate mankind to remove it from the terrors of the objective world," and to do this it will only be necessary to demonstrate that "the essence of man consists of freedom and only of freedom, that man is not a thing, not a chattel, and in his very nature no object at all."[67] What

---

65. For a recent discussion, see Robert Nisbet, *A History of the Idea of Progress* (New York: Basic Books, 1980).

66. Letter to Schelling, 16 April 1795, *Briefe* 1:24.

67. Friedrich W. J. Schelling, *The Unconditioned in Human Knowledge: Four Early Essays (1794–1796),* trans. Fritz Marti (Lewisburg: Bucknell University Press, 1980), pp. 67–68.

Schelling means by freedom here is not yet civil or political freedom but the freedom of the ego to abstract itself from all objects met with in experience. It is a metaphysical freedom produced by an act which Schelling calls "intellectual intuition," in which we are able to soar above all the limitations and restrictions of the "objective world."

While Hegel refrained from criticizing his friend in print, there is already discernible a difference in their understandings of freedom, which would only be exacerbated later. The problem with Schelling's view is that freedom is never actualized or made immanent in the world of practical activity. Stuck on the Kantian dualism between noumenal freedom and phenomenal causality, for Schelling the attempt to structure the world in accordance with freedom was always frustrated by stubborn and recalcitrant causal laws. The material world, the nonego, can never be made to correspond fully to the freedom inherent in the subject. The only answer is, then, a mystical withdrawal from the world into a vaccum of pure contemplation.

Skeptical about deducing moral and political consequences from a philosophy of the ego, Hegel sought to secure the conditions of human autonomy through the acts of a free citizen of a republic. His differences with Schelling are already apparent *in nuce* in the "Earliest System-Programme of German Idealism," where we read:

> From nature I come to the work of man. The idea of mankind being premised, I shall prove that it gives us no idea of the state, since the state is a mechanical thing, any more than it gives us the idea of a machine. Only something that is an objective of freedom is an idea. So we must go even beyond the state!—for every state treats free men as cogs in a machine; and this it ought not to do; so it must stop.[68]

From here it goes on to say that it is necessary to outline the principles for a history of mankind in which "the whole wretched human work" of state, government, constitution, and the legal system will be laid bare. From this will follow the rooting out of ignorance and superstition, as well as the extirpation of the clergy. Only then will the achievement of absolute freedom be possible. Such a philosophy, the author concludes, is as much poetic as it is intellectual. "The philosopher, as much as the poet, requires the possession of aesthetic power. The men without aesthetic sensibility are textbook philosophers [*Buchstabenphilosophen*]. The philosophy of spirit is an aesthetic philosophy. One cannot be intellectually rich in anything, not even historical reasoning—without aesthetic sensibility."[69]

68. *Werke* 1:234–35.
69. *Werke* 1:235.

It is generally accepted that the "System-Programme" is a work of Schelling's which was later copied down in full by Hegel, indicating, it would seem, that it at least represented a project of which he approved.[70] It was during their early years as radical critics of existing society that Schelling and Hegel found themselves allied. But it is not difficult to detect within this sketch a latent, as yet unstated, difference between them which would later become open. What Schelling really wants, as we have seen, is a transcendental freedom beyond the state which entails the complete annihilation of the finite, temporal world. What Hegel wants, however, is merely the destruction of one particular kind of state, the state which treats men as "cogs in a machine," or which treats them as means and not ends. For Hegel, then, the state is not a limitation on, but a condition for, human freedom. While Schelling desires a liberation from the state and all external restraint, Hegel, at least in his early writings, desires a regeneration of politics along quasi-classical lines.

CIVIC RELIGION, POSITIVITY, AND THE *VOLKSGEIST*

Hegel's enthusiasm for Greece and the classical republican model was given initial expression in his "early theological writings" (*theologische Jugendschriften*), so-named by their first editor, Hermann Nohl. These writings, composed at various times in Tübingen (1788–93), Bern (1793–96), and Frankfurt (1797–1800), gave first expression to that longing for community that both Hegel and the early romantics prescribed as the cure for the problem of alienation and diremption that they imagined they saw around them. Still, the title is perhaps unfortunate, because there is nothing theological about these writings, at least in the conventional sense of the term. Rather, they attempt to examine the dynamic interaction between politics and religion within the contexts of three distinct cultures: ancient Greece, Judaea, and modern Christianity. This does not, of course, vindicate the judgment of Georg Lukács, for whom the attribution of an "early theological period" to Hegel can be dismissed as a "reactionary legend."[71] I suspect rather that Raymond Plant is nearer the mark when he writes that because "Hegel is not concerned with the problem of truth tests in theology but

70. That the "System-Programme" was an original work by Hegel has been suggested by H. S. Harris in *Hegel's Development: Toward the Sunlight, 1770–1801* (Oxford: Clarendon Press, 1972), pp. 249–57; Otto Pöggeler, "Hegel der Verfasser des ältesten Systemprogramms des deutschen Idealismus," *Hegel-Studien* 4 (1969): 17–32; Herbert Marcuse (*Reason and Revolution: Hegel and the Rise of Social Theory* [Boston: Beacon Press, 1954], pp. 11–12) also believes that this fragment was an original work by Hegel, although no evidence is adduced for this.

71. Georg Lukács, *The Young Hegel: Studies in the Relations between Dialectics and Economics*, trans. Rodney Livingstone (London: Merlin Press, 1975), p. 16.

with the cultural effects of religious belief," this does not prevent him from "belong[ing] to a recognizable theological genre, namely civil or social theology."[72]

The most important concept to emerge in these writings is that of the *Volksgeist,* of which three features may be noted. The first is methodological. Hegel uses the term to bring out the essential relatedness of all aspects of a culture. As opposed to the methodological individualism of the Enlightenment, with its penchant for analytical abstractions, Hegel's point is to show that the whole is essentially prior to its parts. The term is used to encompass the whole of a people's conditions of existence. "The spirit of a people," he writes, "its history, the level of political freedom, cannot be treated separately either with respect to their mutual influence, or in characterizing them in isolation. They are woven together in a single bond."[73] In this respect, the Hegelian *Volksgeist* bears a family resemblance to what Montesquieu had called the *esprit général* of a nation.[74] Hegel even applauds Montesquieu for his efforts to view the spirit of a people within its particular historical setting and for not abstracting it from its spatiotemporal limitations. Where they differ is perhaps in that Montesquieu tended to see the spirit as a secondary phenomenon produced by a nation's distinct economic, cultural, and even linguistic history, while Hegel's *Volksgeist* has a more idealistic, even mythological, character about it. "The spirit of a people is drawn down to earth and held fast by a light bond which resists through a magical spell all attempts to break it, for it is completely intertwined in its essence."[75] It is less the product of the empirical arrangements of a society than the creative force behind those arrangements.

The second feature is normative. The idea of the *Volksgeist* is not simply a descriptive label but is intended to convey an ideal of social solidarity informing all the aspects of a people's collective life. Thus, Hegel commends the Greek civic religions which, unlike Christianity, with its essentially private character, were bound up with the life of the polis. Indeed, the harmonious political culture of the ancient city, in which there was an immediate identity between the individual and the common good, was best expressed through the religion of its people. "Civic religion," he writes,

72. Plant, *Hegel,* p. 32n.

73. *Werke* 1:42.

74. See Guy Planty-Bonjour, "L'Esprit général d'une nation selon Montesquieu et le *Volksgeist* hégélienne," *Hegel et le siècle des lumières,* ed. Jacques d'Hondt (Paris: Presses Universitaires de France, 1974), pp. 7–24; for a further comparison, see Michael Mosher, "The Particulars of a Universal Politics: Hegel's Adaptation of Montesquieu's Typology," *American Political Science Review* 79 (1984): 179–88.

75. *Werke* 1:42–43.

"which generates and nourishes noble dispositions goes hand in hand with freedom."[76] The religion of a people is, ideally, inseparable from their political constitution and thereby fosters good citizens.

Hegel's preference for the civic religion of the ancients plainly owes a great deal to Machiavelli, who, in the *Discourses on Livy*, castigated Christianity for leading to the decline of republics by teaching men to be more concerned with their souls than with their countries.[77] Similarly, he draws inspiration from Rousseau, who in the *Social Contract* had said, "Christian law is fundamentally more harmful than useful to the strong constitution of a State." Since it is preoccupied with other-worldly matters, its spirit is ultimately more favorable to tyranny. "True Christians are made to be slaves," he put it in one of his typically Machiavellian asides.[78] For Rousseau, Christianity is the root of the modern problem of the divided self for its attempt to sever the individual from the particular community of which he is a part and to bind him instead to the entire species. "Our religion," Hegel writes, "aims to educate men to be citizens of Heaven whose gaze is ever directed thither so that human feelings become alien to them."[79] For Hegel and the whole civic humanist tradition, the cosmopolitanism and lack of patriotism of Christian doctrine are in the final analysis at odds with the *Volksgeist*, or the established national character of a people.

As for the third feature, the Hegelian idea of the *Volksgeist* has a historical dimension that is not to be found in the works of either Montesquieu or Rousseau. The *Volksgeist* is not a static entity, but is tied to the idea of *Bildung*, a quasi-biological metaphor implying processes of growth, change, and development. It was to Herder more than to any other of his contemporaries that Hegel owed this idea. *Bildung*, for Herder, was primarily a process of "humanization"—the process whereby humanity rises from early stages of isolation and independence and sees itself as a single interrelated whole. This process of collective self-education is no doubt marked by conflict, struggle, and war, although its aim—its immanent teleology—is the full expression of human powers, which can only be developed within a nation (*Volk*).[80]

76. *Werke* 1:41.
77. Niccolò Machiavelli, *Discourses on Livy,* trans. Leslie J. Walker (Harmondsworth: Penguin, 1970), 1:11–12 (pp. 139–46); 2:2 (pp. 274–81).
78. Jean-Jacques Rousseau, *On the Social Contract,* trans. Judith R. Masters (New York: Saint Martin's, 1978), 4.8 (pp. 127, 130).
79. *Werke* 1:42.
80. F. M. Barnard, *Herder's Social and Political Thought* (Oxford: Clarendon Press, 1965), chap. 5.

For Hegel, the dominant image that appears here is that of a "road" or "journey" (*Weg*) where the mind is shaped, from its earliest stage of "natural consciousness," to the "understanding" marked by self-division and conflict, to mature "self-consciousness," characterized by an awareness of the human situation as one of irreducible plurality. The *Bildungsideal* is marked, then, by a mature acceptance of increasing complexity as necessary for the unfolding of the widest variety of human possibilities. The peculiar characteristic of this modern *Bildungsideal* is set out later in the preface to the *Phenomenology of Mind,* as a contrast between two quite different forms of moral education, what the Greeks called *paideia:*

> The manner of study in ancient times is distinct from that of the modern world, in that the former consisted in the cultivation and perfecting of the natural mind. Testing life carefully at all points, philosophizing about everything it came across, the former created an experience permeated through and through by universals. In modern times, however, the individual finds the abstract form ready made.[81]

The difference to which Hegel is alluding here is between the modern world and the Greek world, which attained a natural harmony based on an immediate faith or trust in the goodness of its institutions and way of life. "Natural" is here understood as effortless; it is to be contrasted, not with conventional or customary, but with reflection or conceptual thought (*Verstand*). On Hegel's highly idealized account, the Greeks, unlike ourselves, did not draw a sharp distinction between themselves as individuals and the appointed social functions and roles that they shared as members of particular communities. They had not yet come to regard their roles and institutions as alienating and oppressive. What characterized "the beautiful happy freedom of the Greeks" was precisely the absence of discord between the public and the private or, in Rousseau's language, between the regimes of the bourgeois and the citizen.[82]

All three meanings of the term *Volksgeist*—the methodological, the normative, and the historical—can be found in Hegel's first major essay, a lengthy critique of Christianity, entitled "On the Positivity of the Christian Religion." Here he contrasts the private, apolitical character of Christianity with the public civic religion of the Greeks. By a positive religion, Hegel

81. *PhM,* p. 94; *Werke* 3:36–37.
82. Jean-Jacques Rousseau, *Emile or on Education,* trans. Allan Bloom (New York: Basic Books, 1979), p. 40: "Public instruction no longer exists and can no longer exist, because there is no longer fatherland, there can no longer be citizens. These two words, *fatherland* and *citizen,* should be effaced from modern languages."

means something very much like the morality of the divided self discussed above. It is a system of religious propositions which must be held as truths independently of the opinions of the believer. These truths are laid down in the form of positive laws or commands which the individual is simply constrained to obey. By contrast to Christian positive religion, Hegel juxtaposes something like a natural religion based on the supremacy of man's moral autonomy. Only a religion which stems from our moral rationality alone and not from any external transcendent source can provide for the kind of civic virtue typified by the actions of a citizen of a republic. In fact, this nonpositive natural religion of practical reason can be seen as an attempt to reinterpret the Greek civic religion—in which the gods were perceived as embodied in the democratic collectivity of the polis—in the light of Kant's *Religion Within the Limits of Reason Alone.*[83]

By positivity, then, Hegel means a renunciation of man's "inalienable right" to moral self-determination.[84] For the positive Christian religion, the moral law is not something derived from the autonomy of the subject but is rather external to him, something given. Hegel's critique of Christianity here is aimed at freeing man from ecclesiastical domination and returning to him the right to think and act for himself. Only through the critique of religion could men begin to recover the freedom lost under the hegemony of positive Christianity. This freedom, which Hegel believed to be immanent in his own time, could not be actualized through contemplative withdrawal from the world but only through the political activity of a citizen of a republic. Hegel's answer, then, to the persistent problem of positivity in modern culture is the creation of a republican community supported by a civic religion of practical reason, which alone could induce a sense of political virtue.

The longest and, for our purposes, most interesting section of this essay is entitled "On the Difference between the Imaginative Religion of the Greeks and Christian Positive Religion." Hegel here takes up the familiar problem of how Christianity, which emerged as a nonpolitical sect among a subject people, could have conquered the pagan civil religion which for centuries had been intimately bound up with the political constitution. He rejects as too facile the explanation that Christianity triumphed over paganism because of its rational superiority. In words taken almost literally out of Schiller's sixth letter, he remarks that the pagans, too, had intellects, and "in everything great, beautiful, noble, and free they are so far our superiors that

83. *Werke* 1:190–96.
84. *ETW*, p. 145; *Werke* 1:190.

we can hardly make them our examples but must look up to them as a different species at whose achievements we can only marvel."[85]

If the rise of Christianity cannot be explained in purely intellectual terms, it can only be accounted for by a change in "the spirit of the age." Using for the first time the concept of *Geist* for purposes of historical explanation, Hegel says: "Great revolutions which strike the eye at a glance must have been preceded by a still and secret revolution in the spirit of the age, a revolution not visible to every eye, especially imperceptible to contemporaries, and as hard to discern as to describe in words."[86] This "secret revolution" consists in the historical transition from the ancient republic, based upon civic virtue, to the modern bourgeois Christian world, in which the individual is cut loose from the ties of the community and freed to pursue his own private interests.

Hegel depicts this revolution in terms of a decline of the ancient city and the public civic religion that sustained it. In the eyes of the classical citizen, the republic was the highest form of reality before which his own individuality seemed paltry and insignificant. Like the long line of "civic humanists" and republicans on whom he draws, Hegel here regards the life of the citizen as the only life worth living.

> As free men the Greeks and Romans obeyed laws laid down by themselves, obeyed men whom they had themselves appointed to office, waged wars on which they had themselves decided, gave their property, exhausted their passions, and sacrificed their lives by thousands for an end which was their own. They neither learned nor taught [a moral system] but evinced by their actions the moral maxims which they could call their very own. In public as in private and domestic life, every individual was a free man, one who lived by his own laws. The idea of his country or of his state was the invisible and higher reality for which he strove, which impelled him to effort; it was the final end of *his* world or in his eyes the final end of *the* world, an end which he found manifested in the realities of his daily life or which he himself co-operated in manifesting and maintaining. Confronted by this idea, his own individuality vanished; it was only this idea's maintenance, life, and persistence that he asked for, and these were things which he himself could make realities. It could never or hardly ever have struck him to ask or beg for persistence or eternal life for his own individuality. Only in moments of inactivity or lethargy could he feel the growing strength of a purely self-regarding wish. Cato turned to Plato's *Phaedo* only when his world, his republic, hitherto the highest order of things in his eyes, had been destroyed; at that point only did he take flight to a higher order still.[87]

85. *ETW*, p. 153; *Werke* 1:204.
86. *ETW*, p. 152; *Werke* 1:203.
87. *ETW*, pp. 154–55; *Werke* 1:204–5.

The crucial factor in the demise of the ancient religion occurred with the transition from a small self-sufficient republic to a large commercial empire. Despite the initial moral austerity and strictures against inequality, successful campaigns abroad brought about an increase in wealth and luxury, as well as the rise of an indolent aristocratic class. The free republic, formerly based upon a stern martial asceticism, could not sustain these changes, and the spirit of virtue slowly lost its vigor. When cynical young aristocrats established a dictatorship maintained through force of arms, there followed the extinction of all political freedoms, and this led to the rise of a religion tailored for men who had given up hope of every finding happiness in this world. In a passage which shows the marked influence of Tacitus, as well as the modern "pragmatic" historians, Montesquieu and Gibbon, Hegel writes:

> The picture of the state as a product of his own energies disappeared from the citizen's soul. The care and oversight of the whole rested on the soul of one man or a few. Each individual had his own allotted place, a place more or less restricted and different from his neighbor's. The administration of the state machine was intrusted to a small number of citizens, and these served only as single cogs deriving their worth solely from their connection with others. Each man's allotted part in the congeries which formed the whole was so inconsiderable in relation to the whole that the individual did not need to realize this relation or to keep it in view. Usefulness to the state was the great end which the state set before its subjects, and the end they set before themselves in their political life was gain, self-maintenance, and perhaps vanity. All activity and every purpose now had a bearing on something individual; activity was no longer for the sake of a whole or an ideal. Either everyone worked for himself or else he was compelled to work for some other individual. Freedom to obey self-given laws, to follow self-chosen leaders in peacetime and self-chosen generals in war, to carry out plans in whose formulation one had had one's share—all this vanished. All political freedom vanished also; the citizen's right gave him only a right to the security of that property which now filled his entire world. Death, the phenomenon which demolished the whole structure of his purposes and the activity of his entire life, must have become something terrifying, since nothing survived him. But the republican's whole soul was in the republic; the republic survived him, and there hovered before his mind the thought of its immortality.[88]

This passage testifies to Hegel's appreciation of the split between the public and private realms that he believed emerged only with the decline of classical antiquity. Like his French counterpart, Benjamin Constant, Hegel was especially mindful of the contrast between ancient and modern lib-

88. *ETW,* pp. 156–57; *Werke* 1:206.

erty that had been drawn by his predecessors.[89] Thus, in *De l'esprit des lois,* Montesquieu contrasted the "principle" of the ancient democracies to that of the modern commercial states. The principle of the democratic regime was virtue, not Christian moral virtue, but political virtue: love of country, love of equality, in short a wholehearted devotion to the good of the commonwealth. Far from being inimical to freedom, Montesquieu regards this kind of austere, self-sacrificing patriotism as a component of it.[90] The ancients, on his interpretation, understood freedom as collective self-determination, or participatory freedom, which requires virtue, equality, and frugality as its supports. Only when citizens can be induced to place public needs above private interests can this kind of freedom prevail.

Modern freedom, like that found in eighteenth-century England, is based less on the ability to participate in the collective fate of one's country than in "that tranquility of mind which arises from an individual's opinion of his security."[91] Security here means not only life in the present but also the assurance of life in the future. Such life is possible only with the protection of private property. While the ancients had believed freedom required restraint and frugality, Montesquieu presented modern liberty as based on the liberation of man's competitive and acquisitive propensities and especially the desire to acquire and accumulate property.[92] Thus, while ancient freedom tended to concern politics, modern liberty tends to concern economics. This insight led Rousseau to remark, "Ancient politicians incessantly talked about morals and virtue, those of our time talk only of business and money."[93]

At this point, however, Hegel joined ranks, not with the sensible Montesquieu, but with the radical Rousseau in his search for a political community, "un corps moral et collectif," in which each individual will desire only what is generally willed.[94] The Hegelian *Volksgeist* is intended to recapture the moral harmony and coherence of the early Greeks and Romans that Rousseau's *volonté générale* promised to keep alive. But unlike Rousseau in

89. See Benjamin Constant, "De la liberté des anciens comparée à celle des modernes," *De la liberté chez Modernes,* ed. J. Gauchet (Paris: Pluriel, 1980), pp. 491–517.

90. Montesquieu, *De l'esprit de lois,* ed. R. Derathé (Paris: Garnier, 1973), 4:6; 5:5, 7, 8; 6:3, 9; 8:16.

91. Montesquieu, *De l'esprit des lois* 11:6 (p. 169).

92. Montesquieu, *De l'esprit des lois* 5:6; 20:1; see also Albert O. Hirschman, *The Passions and the Interests: Political Arguments for Capitalism before its Triumph* (Princeton: Princeton University Press, 1977), pp. 60, 70–81.

93. Rousseau, *Discourse on the Arts and Sciences,* p. 51.

94. Rousseau, *Social Contract,* 1.6.

this respect, Hegel regarded Christianity not so much a cause as a symptom of political decay. It was only after the prior liberation of the individual from the bonds of communal life that Christianity came to make any impact. Under these changed circumstances, the older civic religion no longer made sense. But even while Roman despotism had transformed the classical citizen into a mere bourgeois, it could not destroy his need for an absolute which transcends the insignificance of his own individuality. It was the introduction of Roman law, which reduced everyone to a legal person, that severed the relationship between the citizen and the commonwealth which had formerly been the mark of freedom. Roman law reduced each individual to his own solitary atomistic self, unrelated to his fellows except as a property owner. And when this law was formalized and codified, it bore little resemblance to the old law, which was based upon custom and habit and which, while nowhere written in words, was known to everyone by heart.

Like other civic humanist writers, Hegel concluded his work with a plea for the regeneration of civic virtue. His hope was for the appearance of a semimythical "legislator" or "prince" who, like Solon for the Athenians, or Lycurgus for the Spartans, or Moses for the Jews, could provide a new nonpositive civic religion for contemporary Germany.[95] Indeed, his call was for a modern-day Theseus who could use religion as the basis for political revival. He went on to blame Christianity for putting an end of the old indigenous national imagery and popular culture upon which such a revival could be based:

> Christianity has emptied Valhalla, felled the sacred groves, extirpated that national imagery as a shameful superstition, as a devilish poison and given us instead the imagery of a nation whose climate, laws, culture, and interests are strange to us and whose history has no connection whatever with our own. A David or a Solomon lives in our popular imagination, but our country's own heroes slumber in learned history books, and, for the scholars who write them, Alexander or Caesar is as interesting as the story of Charlemagne or Frederick Barbarossa. Except perhaps for Luther in the eyes of the Protestants, what heroes could we have had, we who were never a nation? Who could be our Theseus, who founded a state and was its legislator? Where are our Harmodious and Aristogiton to whom we could sing scolia as the liberators of our land?[96]

At the time when he completed "On the Positivity of the Christian Religion," Hegel's call for a German Theseus to arise and turn Germany into a

95. Machiavelli, *Il Principe,* chap. 26; Rousseau, *Social Contract,* 2.7.
96. *ETW,* p. 146; *Werke* 1:197–98.

state could not but appear as a species of wishful thinking. When he re-
turned to this image some years later, first in *The German Constitution* and
then in his Jena lectures on the *Philosophy of Mind,* it is clear that he had
come to regard Napoleon as just such a "tyrant" capable of a political
founding.[97] Nevertheless, until that time, his hopes were still with the
French Revolution and its claim to have established a "virtue religion" as the
foundation of the state. As we shall see in the next section, Hegel's Kantianism as a pendent to his republicanism did not survive the crisis in his
own thought.

THE DISCOVERY OF THE DIALECTIC

This rather abrupt change in Hegel's thought, alluded to above, was first
registered in the longest and most nearly complete of his so-called early
theological writings entitled "The Spirit of Christianity and its Fate." Indeed, T. M. Knox, Hegel's translator, has said that between the Kantianism
of the essay on positivity and this new work, "there is a gulf so wide, that
the later essay, written as it is with such assurance, such passion, and such
independence of mind, may seem at first as if could scarcely have come
from the same pen."[98] Were this change in outlook simply of a psychological nature, it would scarcely be of interest here. I believe, however, that this
crisis was at least in part occasioned by Hegel's changing perception of the
role of politics in the modern world and in particular of the inability of the
French Revolution to achieve anything remotely resembling classical polis
democracy. It was this disillusionment with the experiment in radical republicanism, I would suggest, that led Hegel ultimately to disown his
earlier Kantianism and to adopt a far more conciliatory attitude toward
Christianity and the type of society it affords. What we see in this essay is
a turning away from republicanism and the cult of civic virtue towards a
position which is far more recognizably "Hegelian."

The central concept to emerge in this essay is the idea of *Geist,* a notoriously elusive word which can be rendered as either "mind" or "spirit." We
have already been introduced to the possibility that the spirit of a people, or
Volksgeist, is the product of antecedent developments in a nation's history,

97. See *PW,* pp. 219, 241; *Werke* 1:553, 580; see also *JR,* p. 246; Shlomo Avineri, *Hegel's
Theory of the Modern State* (Cambridge: Cambridge University Press, 1972), pp. 60–61 has
some useful remarks on this point.
98. T. M. Knox, "Hegel's Attitude to Kant's Ethics," *Kant-Studien* 49 (1957–58):72; for
further evidence of a break in Hegel's thought see the letter to Nanette Endel, 2 July 1797,
Briefe 1:53; also the letter to Windischmann, 27 May 1810, *Briefe* 1:102. For a careful analysis
of this "crisis" see Lukács, *The Young Hegel,* pp. 101–5; Harris, *Hegel's Development,* pp. 258–70.

its customs, habits, and laws. Since the spirit of one nation appears related to the spirit of others, what we are now asked to consider is whether there is some controlling power, or "world spirit," in terms of which the development of each of the lesser national minds must be understood. The idea that there is some "Infinite Mind" or demiurge directing the course of events opens up the horizon of a universal philosophy of history. Rather than regarding history, as did Montesquieu and Herder, as the disharmonious development of individual national spirits, each with its own unique culture, tone, and taste, Hegel is now inclined to regard history as a whole as a process whereby humanity would be revealed as one.

But this is not all. *Geist* becomes manifest in what Hegel calls the "fate" (*Schicksal*) or history of a people. Fate is, for Hegel, an "iron necessity" immanent within history, before which the individual is powerless and to which he must submit. This conception of history as an immanent fate marks a significant departure from Hegel's earlier speculations. While in his "Kantian" writings, his emphasis had been on man's power of practical reason and self-determination, giving laws to himself, the emphasis is now on an overall historical fate which he must learn to face with patience and equanimity. It is because this fate is necessary that man must learn to reconcile himself to reality and the type of society it offers. This desire to be reconciled with the world becomes evident in the far more conciliatory attitude Hegel adopts toward Christianity in particular and the modern world in general. Thus, while he had earlier said to Schelling that philosophy must take its point of departure from "what ought to be," Hegel is now far more concerned with finding a way back to what "is."

The means by which Hegel hopes to effect this reconciliation with the world is through religion and, in particular, Christianity, which he now sees as a religion of love (*Liebe*). In another manuscript from this period, to which Hegel's editor gave the title "Liebe," he treats love as the striving for unity that Schiller and Hölderlin had earlier attributed to beauty. Love is said to overcome the formal Kantian insistence on self-sufficiency and autonomy. It establishes not only a more satisfying metaphysical relationship between man and God but a more satisfying moral relationship between human beings:

> True union, or love proper, exists only between living beings who are alike in power and thus in one another's eyes living beings from every point of view; in no respect is either dead for the other. This genuine love excludes all oppositions. It is not the understanding, whose relations always leave the manifold of related terms as a manifold and whose unity is always a unity of opposites. It is not reason either, because reason sharply opposes its determining power to what is determined. Love neither restricts nor is restricted; it is not finite at all. It is a

feeling, yet not a single feeling. A single feeling is only a part and not the whole of life; the life present in a single feeling dissolves its barriers and drives on till it disperses itself in the manifold of feelings with a view to finding itself in the entirety of this manifold. This whole life is not contained in love in the same way as it is in this sum of many particular and isolated feelings; in love, life is present as a duplicate of itself and as a single and unified self. Here life has run through the circle of development from an immature to a completely mature unity: when the unity was immature, there still stood over against it the world and the possibility of a cleavage between itself and the world; as development proceeded, reflection produced more and more oppositions (unified by satisfied impulses) until it set the whole of man's life in opposition; finally, love completely destroys objectivity and thereby annuls and transcends reflection, deprives man's opposite of all foreign character, and discovers life itself without any further defect. In love the separate does still remain, but as something united and no longer as something separate; life senses life.[99]

What Hegel here attributes to the power of love will later be replaced by reason, a term which, we shall see, is broader than mere ratiocination but incorporates the essentially erotic character of love.

Far from castigating the "positivity" and dead "objectivity" of Christianity, he now commends it for setting forth "the subjective in general."[100] This conception of love emerges most forcefully in the Christian teaching of the relationship between God and man. As opposed to the Judaic conception that this relationship is one of unquestioning obedience to authority, Jesus, whom Hegel describes as "setting himself against the entire Jewish fate," taught that this is a relationship based upon love.[101] The idea of a loving disposition between man and God did not occur to the Jews, apparently because of their intellectualist standpoint. The intellect (*Verstand*) is described as the power of discursive reasoning, which is here set in direct opposition to the power of love. Because the Jews were dominated by logic, they elevated the intellect as "absolute division, destruction of life," to "the pinnacle of spirit." While the intellect bifurcates and reifies experience into rigid and irreconcilable antinomies, love designates a way of thinking and feeling whose different parts and states are integrated into a complete unity. Thus, for the first time we see Hegel attempting to work out through an analysis of love a distinctively dialectical method attuned to the logic of history and human events. One example will suffice to demonstrate this method.

Hegel's remarks on love in "The Spirit of Christianity and Its Fate" are

99. *ETW*, pp. 304–5.
100. *ETW*, p. 209; *Werke* 1:321.
101. *ETW*, p. 205; *Werke* 1:317.

intended clearly as a rebuttal not only of what he perceived to be the authoritarianism of established Jewish practice but of the Kantian ethic which he himself had earlier adopted. Oddly enough, his argument is that the Kantian postulate of practical reason is but the counterpart of Mosaic legalism. In the Mosaic code, Hegel maintains, law is an arbitrary command handed down as though from a master to a slave, the Jews being like slaves to their far-off transcendent deity. Kantian morality, by contrast, appears to free itself of this relation, since the moral law emanates from the will alone. The only reason we have for obeying the law is that its determining ground is in us. But this is not what Hegel wants to argue. For when one examines it closely, one can see that the whole Kantian framework, far from abolishing the coercive power of law, merely succeeds in internalizing it. By setting up a distinction between inclination and reason, the phenomenal and the noumenal self within us, Kant transfers the master-slave relationship from the social to the psychological dimension.[102] As Hegel sees it, then, there is no qualitative difference between a slave who must obey the externally imposed commands of his master and the Kantian moralist who obeys his own self-imposed commands of duty:

> By this line of argument, however, positivity is only partially removed; and between the Shaman of the Tungus, the European prelate who rules church and state, the Voguls, and the Puritans, on the one hand, and the man who listens to his own commands of duty, on the other, the difference is not that the former make themselves slaves, while the latter is free, but that the former have their lord outside themselves, while the latter carries his lord in himself, yet at the same time is his own slave.[103]

Hegel believes it possible to overcome this diremption within our moral experience only in an ethic of love, which he sees as embodied in Christ's Sermon on the Mount. Here he presents Jesus's message as "an attempt, elaborated in numerous examples, to strip the laws of legality, of their legal form."[104] In the Sermon on the Mount Jesus taught a loving disposition which both fulfills the law and at the same time annuls it. When motivated by love, men carry out their duties, not because they have been commanded, but because of a "liking to perform all duties."[105] When we act in the spirit of love, we are not acting out of a motive that is "pathological," but in such circumstances we find reason and inclination acting in har-

---

102. See Kelly, "Hegel's Lordship and Bondage," *Hegel's Retreat from Eleusis,* pp. 29–54.
103. *ETW,* p. 211; *Werke* 1:323.
104. *ETW,* p. 212; *Werke* 1:324.
105. *ETW,* p. 213; *Werke* 1:325.

mony. The result is a new kind of morality, which at one place Hegel describes as an "elevation above the sphere of rights, justice, equity."[106] The result is, then, that when we allow love to act as the determining ground of our behavior, we find law to be dialectically *aufgehoben* in the precise sense of that term: negated, preserved, and superseded. And those aspects of life that traditional morality had torn asunder we find united in a new type of humanity "raised above morality."[107]

What Hegel has proposed here is two ideal moral orders—one based on rules, the other based on love. The legal order which appeared first in Judaism and later in Kantianism is equated with the reign of private property and the penal code. Hegel here appears to anticipate Marx's later critique of the purely formal character of law which abstracts from the more substantive needs of individuals. The core of the juridical order is punishment. "Retribution," Hegel writes, "and its equivalence with crime is the sacred principle of all justice, the principle on which any political order must rest."[108] The early Christian community showed how a society could be united, not by obedience to law, but through participation in a common way of life. Love becomes here the new principle of community:

> The supper shared by Jesus and his disciples is in itself an act of friendship; but a still closer link is the solemn eating of the same bread, drinking from the same cup. This too is not a mere symbol of friendship, but an act, a feeling of friendship itself, of the spirit of love. But the sequel, the declaration of Jesus that "this is my body, this is my blood" approximates the action to a religious one but does not make it one; this declaration and the accompanying distribution of food and drink, makes the feeling to some extent objective. Their association with Jesus, their friendship with one another, and their unification in their center, their teacher, are not merely sensed. . . . A spectator ignorant of their friendship and with no understanding of the words of Jesus would have seen nothing save the distribution of some bread and wine and the enjoyment of these. Similarly, when friends part and break a ring and each keeps one piece, a spectator sees nothing but the breaking of a useful thing and its division into useless and valueless pieces; the mystical aspect of the pieces he has failed to grasp. Objectively considered, then, the bread is just bread, the wine just wine; yet both are something more.[109]

This "something more" is no mere natural property "in which the different things, the things compared, are set forth as severed, as separate, and all

106. *ETW*, p. 222; *Werke* 1:335.
107. *ETW*, p. 212; *Werke* 1:324.
108. *ETW*, p. 218; *Werke* 1:331.
109. *ETW*, pp. 248–49; *Werke* 1:365–66.

that is asked is a comparison, the thought of the likenesses and dissimilars" but is rather "*this* link between bread and persons [where] difference disappears, and with it the possibility of comparison." And in a phrase that will turn out to be of much greater significance, he concludes: "Things heterogeneous are here most intimately connected."[110]

At the same time that he was extolling the redemptive power of love, Hegel could not but recognize the failure of Jesus to promote his teachings as a civil religion appropriate to men in the postclassical age. He accounted for this failure in terms of the historical context in which Jesus lived. On the one hand, he could have attempted to reform Jewish society from within, but run the risk of compromising his message of love. On the other hand, he could have divorced himself entirely from this society, retaining the purity of his message intact but foregoing the possibility of realizing it. Of these two alternatives, Jesus chose the latter. Rather than corrupt the original beauty of his teaching, he preferred to flee from any association with his people and concentrate his efforts upon the edification of immediate friends and disciples. His attempt to reconcile man and God and thereby establish the foundation of a true community proved to be too radical to make any impact upon the culture of his age. Being at odds with the general spirit of the times, his message could not but fall upon deaf ears.

Hegel describes Jesus as a "beautiful soul" who refuses to take any interest in earthly existence. Jesus exhorted his followers not to succumb to the violence of life. By withdrawing into himself, he fled from life and remained no longer vulnerable to its injuries. Any misfortune which occurred to him was merely tolerated as part of the human condition. Thus, while he had come to reconcile man and God, Christ was forced to the conclusion that the Kingdom of God is not of this world. The life of Jesus became a separation from the political world and a flight into heaven, where human relations can proceed only from the most disinterested love. This dualism between the earthly and heavenly cities was to be the fate of the Christian religion and through it the fate of modernity. "In all the forms of the Christian religion," Hegel writes, "which have been developed in the advancing fate of the ages, there lies this fundamental characteristic of opposition. . . . And it is the fate that church and state, worship and life, piety and virtue, spiritual and worldly action, can never dissolve into one."[111]

By the end of "The Spirit of Christianity and Its Fate," it could be said that Hegel had developed the outline of a full-blown philosophy of history.

110. *ETW,* p. 249; *Werke* 1:366.
111. *ETW,* p. 301; *Werke* 1:418.

This philosophy is based upon the concept of *Geist,* or world spirit, as embodied in the fate of various lesser nations and cultures. But the movement of *Geist* through history is not characterized by movement towards greater harmonization and unity. Rather it is marked by deep division, diremption, and opposition. This spiral or progressive vision of history, which sees us as moving away from an early simplicity and concreteness in the direction of greater differentiation and abstractness, is expressed by Hegel in terms of a movement from an "unmediated" to a "mediated" condition. The former had been attained by the Greeks, who had achieved their synthesis through unreflective feeling and intuition. And according to Hegel, Christianity had tried to recapture the early simplicity in its ethic of love. But this original harmony had to die as the precondition for the development of *Geist,* and with it the growth of the reflective intellect, as well as the demands of moral autonomy. This is not only what has made a return to the Greek synthesis of political life and religion an impossibility. It is also what has made the present opposition between them a necessity. The growth of reason and morality, on the one side, had to be at odds with the claims of sensibility and feeling, on the other. Thus, rather than seeking a solution to the problem of history by a nostalgic longing for the past, we must try to solve the problem through the fullest development of the possibilities of the present.

Hegel's philosophy is, then, marked by an intense realism. This realism can best be explained on the basis of a combination of personal and political factors. At the political level, I have already indicated (and will document it more fully below) that Hegel came to reject the aims of the French Revolution and therewith the radical idealism of his youth. This idealism, deriving ultimately from the Kantian philosophy of the *ought* and its ahistorical demands for the realization of the rights of man, seemed to do nothing more than legitimate the deeds of Robespierre and the Terror. This *ought,* which Hegel would later castigate as the "bad infinity," is characterized by an endless striving for freedom which rejects any attempt to limit the will or man's power of creative activity. The culmination of this demand for radical freedom is, then, a repudiation of everything "positive," everything that would act as a constraint on the will or as a barrier to complete human emancipation. Hegel's return to history should be seen as an attempt to discover some relatively stable ground upon which political institutions and normative structures could be based. Hegel regarded history as the last barrier to that kind of revolutionary nihilism, what he called the "fury of destruction," that accompanied the modern liberation of the will from nature.

What I have called Hegel's discovery of the dialectic, then, resulted from an attempt to accord a type of recognition or legitimacy to the rationality inherent within historically concrete institutions and practices. Henceforth, freedom must not be sought in the extreme demand for autonomy and self-determination which implies a rejection of everything that we have not ourselves created. Rather, true freedom consists in an acceptance of what the *Geist* working in and through history has made necessary for us. Of course what is meant by "necessity" here is a vexed question. For now, however, it is enough to say that only through the philosophical interpretation of history could the world be made more rational and the iron necessity of fate be made more tolerable for thoughtful men. Not by attempting to change the world but by understanding it can the rational be made real. In a letter written to Schelling just on the eve of his departure for Jena and for the more public part of his philosophic career, Hegel expressed himself as follows:

> In my own development which began with the most elementary needs of man, I was necessarily pushed towards science and the ideals of my youth necessarily became a form of reflection, transformed into a system. I ask myself now, while still engaged in this, how to find a way back to the lives of men.[112]

It is, then, in terms of this desire to return to "the lives of men" that any assessment of Hegel's mature reflections must be understood.

112. Letter to Schelling, 11 November 1800, *Briefe* 1:59.

3 THE CRITIQUE OF THE LIBERAL THEORY OF RIGHTS

HEGEL AND THE ENLIGHTENMENT

It has been argued, with considerable justification, that Hegel's philosophy is best understood as a response to the Enlightenment.[1] The Enlightenment, as the name implies, grew out of an unprecedented attempt by modern philosophers to submit existing laws, practices, and institutions to the test of their own critical rationality. Enlightened thought is here conceived by contrast to the claims of tradition. Living by tradition means living in a manner time-honored by custom, convention, and received opinion. Tradition is based on the primeval identification of the good with the ancestral, and on living in the way of one's fathers and ancestors simply because they are "one's own." Tradition, so understood, is the polar opposite of enlightened rationality, which is the professed slayer of traditionalism. Rationality and scientific knowledge are typically presented as excluding belief in anything that cannot be demonstrated by methodical observation and logic, whereas traditional beliefs have never been so tested.

Enlightenment and tradition therefore represent two radically opposed ways of legitimating society: one by means of critical deliberation and reflection, the other by long experience and awestruck reverence for the past. Of course in practice, reason and tradition are never as hostile to one another as they are in theory. No society, however traditional it may appear, can dispense entirely with rationality and innovation if it is to adapt to changing circumstances. And likewise, patterns of reasoning and scientific method are not discovered de novo by each generation but are handed down at least in part by tradition. As ironic as it sounds, we can speak of a "scientific tradition," a "rationalist tradition," and even the "modern tradition," without falling into absolute incoherence. In short, it is probably fairer to say that traditions entail rationality and rationality involves tradition.[2]

1. The best studies are Charles Taylor, *Hegel and Modern Society* (Cambridge: Cambridge University Press, 1979); Lewis Hinchman, *Hegel's Critique of the Enlightenment* (Gainesville, Fl.: University of Florida Press, 1984).
2. For a useful treatment, see Edward Shils, *Tradition* (Chicago: University of Chicago Press, 1981).

From its inception, however, the Enlightenment was considered a special case of Western rationalism. The "century of philosophy" and the "age of critique" were just two expressions used by the eighteenth-century philosophers to describe man's self-movement from tradition to reason, from darkness to light, from ignorance and superstition to liberation and truth. While modern scholars debate among themselves about whether the Enlightenment is to be understood as one or many, a period of skepticism or of dogmatism, the birth of secular humanism or the last gasp of an age of faith, it seems reasonable to me to identify it with the comprehensive unmasking of prejudice. This new form of critical rationalism was concerned especially with unmasking various forms of illusion and error which stood in the way of a correct apprehension of the truth. Underlying this conception of the critical process, then, was the metaphor of knowledge as perception. The prototypical activity of the eighteenth-century Enlightenment philosophe became one of getting the agent to see things with his own eyes, to submit judgment unconditionally to his own standards of observation and reflection. If the conditions for perception are right, the truth will be transparent, as the numerous works dealing with sight and its opposite, blindness—such as Diderot's *Lettres sur les aveugles* and Berkeley's *Essay Toward a New Theory of Vision*—were to testify.

For the founders of the Enlightenment, then, reason or truth was taken as standing at the opposite pole from error or, more specifically, prejudice.[3] Prejudice, for these thinkers, became a kind of all-purpose term to symbolize the Enlightenment's struggle against inertia or the merely "given." Strictly speaking, a prejudice means a pre-judgment, a meaning captured better in the French *préjugé* or the German *Vorurteil* than in the English. A prejudice is, then, an unfounded judgment or a judgment given before all the facts necessary to determine a case have been given. What distinguishes a prejudice from mere error is not an insufficiency of knowledge but a perverted or distorted direction of thought. Prejudice is not a matter of mistaken belief but of systematically distorted thought, a form of delusion or superstition, what today we might call an "ideology." In its assumption that the typical situation in which human beings find themselves is one of distortion or prejudice, the Enlightenment did no more than follow the rule of modern science, given its canonical manifesto in Descartes's *Discourse on Method,* where he advised his readers to doubt everything that does not appear absolutely indubitable.

Prejudices in turn have two sources. The first, as we have seen, is merely

---

3. See Hans-Georg Gadamer, *Truth and Method* (New York: Seabury, 1975), pp. 238–53.

a subjective error of judgment which results from overhastiness or carelessness. Such errors are corrigible by the diligent application of the correct method. But the second, and more dangerous, source of error, is less easily correctable, since it stems from human authority. Power and authority can serve as independent sources of error and delusion. Power is invariably bound up with the abuse of power, so that the aim of reason becomes the systematic opposition to all established authority and tradition. It was the general aim of the Enlightenment not to accept any authority but to decide everything before the judgment seat of reason alone. Reason, not tradition, constitutes the ultimate source of authority. Since traditions are simply repositories of prejudice and popular credulity, there is a strong antiauthoritarian, if not anarchistic, streak running through the eighteenth-century Enlightenment. This is captured beautifully in the opening paragraph of Kant's famous essay, "What is Enlightenment?" where he formulates the principle of his age as having the courage to use one's own understanding.[4]

To be sure, the whole history of political philosophy, from the Platonic critique of *doxa* onwards, has exercised a critical function by seeking to liberate men from error, deception, and opinion. What distinguishes the Enlightenment from earlier philosophical movements, though, was its proponents' conception of it as a "project" for translating their ideas directly into reality. The theoretical core of this project was the new science of nature associated with such names as Galileo, Bacon, Descartes, and Hobbes, to name but a few. The goal of this new science was no longer the disinterested pursuit of knowledge for its own sake, but the mastery and conquest of nature. From the beginning, modern science was aimed chiefly at the practical goal of the improvement of man's condition by giving him power over a hostile environment. And furthermore, the new science promised to deliver its goods, not through a long and arduous process of education, but through the methodical application of a few simple rules and principles already worked out in advance.

This new activist conception of science necessarily had political implications. Because scientific knowledge is potentially universal in scope, it can only progress by overcoming the limitations and parochialism of existing societies, each with their own national traditions and cultures. Because science requires the unimpeded flow of ideas across national boundaries and across generations, there is a tendency to favor open, liberal, and tolerant

---

4. Immanuel Kant, "What is Enlightenment?" *Political Writings,* trans. H. B. Nisbet (Cambridge: Cambridge University Press, 1970), p. 54.

societies as the best way to secure progress. The Enlightenment thus requires that societies forego their claims to exclusivity and open their doors to the potentially beneficial effects of science. Thus, in its battle against throne and altar and the religious superstitions that sustained them, the Enlightenment took on a distinctively moral and political dimension. It culminated in a preference for republican states that would guarantee civil liberties at home and a federation of such states that would establish perpetual peace in the international order.

From the eighteenth century onwards, then, the cause of the Enlightenment was linked to that of republicanism. Here, as in most things, Kant can serve as a kind of ideological litmus test. While in ancient political thought the republic was the one generic form of constitution from which all others were derived, the Enlightenment tended to interpret it narrowly as the only regime compatible with the requirements of human freedom. Thus, in his *Metaphysical Elements of Justice,* Kant remarks that the republic is "the only enduring political constitution in which the law is autonomous and is not annexed by any particular person."[5] A republican form of government meant for Kant one in which each individual had some share in forming the laws. It is a form of government which requires the maximum degree of participation in the shaping of public decisions.

The new meaning of republicanism and its link to the idea of progress has been elegantly captured by Reinhart Koselleck, who remarks:

> Republicanism was therefore a concept of movement which did for political action what "progress" promised to do for the whole of history. The old concept of "republic," which had previously indicated a condition, became a telos, and was at the same time rendered into a concept of movement by means of the suffix "ism." It served the purpose of theoretically anticipating future historical movement and practically influencing it. The temporal difference between all previously experienced forms of rule and the constitution that was to be expected and toward which one should strive was in this way embodied in a concept which had a direct influence on political life.[6]

The idea of progress is, then, crucially bound up with the Enlightenment's self-understanding. Progress is concerned with the growth and transmission of scientific knowledge, and the essence of this science is

5. Immanuel Kant, *The Metaphysical Elements of Justice,* trans. John Ladd (Indianapolis: Bobbs-Merrill, 1965), p. 112.

6. Reinhart Koselleck, "'Space of Experience' and 'Horizon of Expectation': Two Historical Categories," in *Futures Past: On the Semantics of Historical Time,* trans. Keith Tribe (Cambridge, Mass.: MIT Press, 1985), p. 287.

technology. Modern science is less concerned with contemplating the limits of nature than with furthering the dynamic or Faustian ends of human self-assertion and the desire for power. Thoughtful critics of modernity have themselves begun to wonder whether or for how long this process can continue unchecked. While scientific and technological advances hold out the promise of material comfort and well-being on a previously undreamt of scale, along with this has come increasing anxiety about the costs at which this well-being has been purchased. Genetic engineering and the amassing of nuclear weaponry are just two of the most worrying consequences of the Enlightenment project. Indeed, it is just these negative destructive aspects of modernity that contemporary critical theorists have taken to calling the "dialectic of Enlightenment." In addition, one may begin to wonder whether progress has become just another name for a steamroller or a juggernaut that is now driving out of control. Heinrich Heine was only one of the first to question whether the relief of suffering and the humane goals that are the Enlightenment's positive accomplishments have not concealed a built-in tendency to devalue the present as a mere means to some glorious but indefinite future.[7]

THE THEORY OF NATURAL RIGHTS

At the core of the Enlightenment, I have suggested, was a new teaching about nature in general and human nature in particular. In contrast to the ancient teachings, for the first time human beings were regarded as the possessors of certain natural or inalienable rights. According to the authors who first promulgated this doctrine, rights are justifiable claims that belong to individuals as such. Individuals are not indebted to government or political society for their rights; rather government has its origins in the rational desires of individuals to protect and defend their preexisting rights as human beings. This conception of rights already signaled an important shift in the way people thought about the legitimacy or justice of government. Prior to the seventeenth century, government made no reference to rights as their standard of legitimacy. To the extent that rights existed at all, they were considered derivative from a person's membership in a particular family, estate, or political community. The idea of universal human rights which belonged to individuals as such and against which established authority was to be judged was a conception which would have been unintelligible.

7. Heinrich Heine, *Verschiedenartige Geschichtsauffassung, Sämtliche Schriften,* ed. Klaus Briegleb (Munich: Hanser, 1968–71), 3:22.

In the remainder of this chapter I want to present Hegel's critique of the doctrine of natural rights as the doctrine was presented in the writings of Hobbes, Locke, Rousseau, and Kant. To be sure, these thinkers differed from one another in a number of important respects, but in attempting any comparative survey a few key features are worth bearing in mind.

Egalitarianism   Thomas Hobbes was perhaps the first to assert the categorical equality of the human species as a foundation for political society. In the thirteenth chapter of *Leviathan,* he depicts the natural condition of men as one of roughly equal physical and mental capacity. While Hobbes was not so foolish as to deny real differences between human beings, nevertheless, "the difference between man and man is not so considerable as that one man can thereupon claim to himself any benefit to which another may not pretend as well as he." Hobbes deduces the physical equality of men from the fact that "the weakest has strength to kill the strongest, either by secret machination or by confederacy with others." Furthermore, while men may differ in their abilities to acquire "science," or "the arts grounded upon words," when it comes to "prudence," or the knowledge necessary for success, he remarks that we find "a greater equality amongst men than that of strength" for "prudence is but experience which equal time equally bestows on all men."[8]

Finally, underlying both physical and mental equality, Hobbes presupposes an original equality of desire. This is not to say that all men desire the same things. Quite the opposite. Contrary to Aristotle, Aquinas, and what is spoken of "in the books of the old moral philosophers," Hobbes denies that there is some single substantive goal, the attainment of which renders life happy and complete. But whatever the qualitative differences there may be in the various objects we desire, we all require a quantitative degree of power to secure them. Thus, Hobbes writes that he "put for a general inclination of all mankind, a perpetual and restless desire of power after power, that ceaseth only in death."[9]

Individualism   Whereas classical political philosophy had adopted the premise that man is by nature, a "political animal," modern natural rights theories assume that we are radically asocial. In fact, our asociality derives from our equality, since political order assumes distinctive capacities on the part of rulers and ruled which nature does nothing to provide. Lacking any

8. Thomas Hobbes, *Leviathan,* ed. M. Oakeshott (London: Macmillan, 1962), chap. 13, p. 98.

9. Hobbes, *Leviathan,* chap. 11, p. 80.

basis for natural order, natural rights theorists see men as lonely, isolated, and fearful. The natural condition is one of maximum fear, where, in Hobbes's famous expression, life is "solitary, poor, nasty, brutish, and short." Beginning from the premise that there are no natural ties or obligations between us, the problem is to explain the legitimacy of the obligations that we do incur. The answer, we shall see, is that all authority, especially sovereign authority, is by convention or agreement. Since nature provides no measure for politics, all rule must be artificial or by the consent of the governed.

Voluntarism   Since our natural condition provides no basis for authority, the standard of political legitimacy is volition, or an agreement among consenting adults. This doctrine of the will is at the core of the famous social contract which is taken to be the origin of all legitimate government. As Hobbes says, "[t]he right of all sovereigns is derived originally from the consent of everyone of those that are to be governed," and human wills "make the essence of all covenants."[10] While Hobbes is notorious for using voluntarist arguments to support an absolutist theory of government, it is arguable that his voluntarism not only served to undermine the older Biblical justification for kingly authority but prepared the way for later liberal theories of limited government and the right of rebellion.

This is not to say that premodern political theories were ignorant of the will and of voluntary action with allied notions of moral responsibility. In the *Nichomachean Ethics,* Aristotle depicts morality as the sphere of voluntary actions where judgments of praise and blame apply. "A voluntary action," he writes, "would seem to be one in which the initiative lies with the agent who knows the particular circumstances in which the action is performed."[11] Voluntary actions are those which are preceded by forethought (*proairesis*) and deliberation rather than by either internal or external compulsion. If an act is not the product of free deliberation, it is removed from the moral sphere altogether.

What distinguishes Aristotle from Hobbes is that for the latter a voluntary act is one that proceeds from the will, but the will itself is formally defined as "the last appetite in deliberating."[12] A voluntary action, then, is not one that is chosen or deliberated upon but one that is demanded by the passions. Hobbes seems to have abolished the Aristotelian distinction be-

10. Hobbes, *Leviathan,* chap. 42, p. 416.
11. Aristotle, *Nicomachean Ethics,* 3.1111a.20–23.
12. Hobbes, *Leviathan,* chap. 6, p. 54.

tween the voluntary and the involuntary and in the process obscured the distinction between covenants freely incurred and those produced by fear. The irony is that Hobbes, the founder of modern natural right, understood the sovereign by consent or agreement as similar to the sovereign by acquisition or conquest, since men through fear of one another consent to subject themselves to be ruled.

Reductionism   Following the methods of mathematical physics, Hobbes and his followers saw all genuine knowledge as analytical and reductivist. Just as the physicist can obtain knowledge of the physical world by reducing it to a few simple or lawlike regularities, so knowledge of the social world can be obtained by resolving it into parts, namely, individuals and their most rudimentary passions and desires. Human behavior can be understood in terms of a mechanistic psychology of the passions or those forces that either attract or repel us. The crowning desire of all human life is, of course, the desire for self-preservation, a passion that we share with the lower species. Since it was the most rudimentary passion, Hobbes equated the desire for self-preservation with right: the right of all things to preserve themselves in any way they feel necessary. Only after asserting the primacy of our right to do "all things" did Hobbes go on to deduce the natural law or our duties toward others. Duty here is derivative of and secondary to right. Indeed, Hobbes even shows that this right remains operative within civil society, where no man can, for instance, be made to testify against himself. Furthermore, in those matters where the law is silent, we retain our natural freedom to do, or forebear from doing, as we please.

Universalism   While there was a strong universalist component in Stoic and Christian doctrines, among the ancients the tendency toward universalism and cosmopolitanism was moderated by the quality of prudence. The best regime was not applicable everywhere and always but only under favorable, usually exceptional, circumstances. Politics was thus more a matter of prudent adjustment of general principles to less than perfect conditions. Modern natural right, however, is concerned less with the maximum possibility than with the minimum requirement for a good, decent, or just society. Following Machiavelli's strictures that the ancients had constructed their principalities in the air, modern theorists used their doctrines as a guide to action in the here and now, irrespective of time, place, and circumstance. Hobbes's theory of sovereignty, just like Locke's views on limited government and Rousseau's general will, is presented as a revolu-

tionary doctrine seeking to establish once and for all the conditions for political legitimacy. In the hands of first the English and later the American
and French revolutions, natural rights became a powerful ideological weapon with which to attack the perceived injustices and irrationalities of the
old regime.

CRITIQUE OF NATURAL RIGHTS, I: HOBBES AND LOCKE

Hegel's critique of the natural rights tradition is developed most cogently in
a book-length essay published almost twenty years before the *Philosophy of
Right* and called *On the Scientific Ways of Treating Natural Law* (1802). His
attempted reconstruction of this tradition begins with an analysis of the two
most important methodological approaches to the study of rights. The first
he identifies with the empirical approach, by which he means the early
modern theories of Hobbes and Locke. Unlike a number of prominent
present-day scholars who see Locke especially as a mixture of modern and
late-scholastic elements coming out of the neo-Thomist revival of the sixteenth century, Hegel adopts a more traditional reading of both Hobbes
and Locke, according to which they broke decisively with the older classical and medieval traditions. While the traditional Thomistic conception of
natural right was treated within the context of theology, early modern theorists like Hobbes and Locke tended to treat it "naturalistically" as derivable
from man's passions and inclinations. Consequently natural right came to
be perceived less as a moral and more as a legal doctrine specifying the
necessary and sufficient conditions for political legitimacy.

In describing Hobbesian-Lockean theories of rights as empirical, Hegel
means that they attempted to derive human rights from certain purportedly
natural needs or desires that all human beings have in the prepolitical state
of nature. The first and most basic need that we have is self-preservation,
which Hobbes turns into the most fundamental natural right. Hobbes, for
instance, defines a right of nature as "the liberty each man has to use his
own power as he will himself to the preservation of his own nature—that is
to say, of his own life."[13] Right is defined here in purely naturalistic terms as
the power each person has to get what he wants. For Hobbes, then, it is the
root human need for life itself that is the foundation for all subsequent
rights. It is, of course, arguable, as many modern philosophers have claimed,
that an empirical or naturalistic theory like Hobbes's is not a moral theory at
all. The attempt to derive a statement about rights from a statement about
certain biological or physiological drives is to commit the "naturalistic fal-

13. Hobbes, *Leviathan,* chap. 14, p. 103.

lacy" of deriving an *ought* from an *is*. For Hobbes, however, the factual claim that all men have a desire for self-preservation cannot be separated from the moral claim that no one should be blamed for following this desire. And this entails the additional premise that we should acknowledge the rights of others to self-preservation as well. The right to self-preservation, then, dictates a duty to seek out peace and security whenever our lives are not threatened.

Hobbes's naturalistic schema is complicated by Locke, who introduced rationalistic as well as theological arguments in support of human rights.[14] At times he writes as if he were a semi-Hobbesian basing rights upon a universally implanted desire for self-preservation. The idea is that the desire to preserve life is simply so overwhelmingly powerful that it must be the basis for all society whatever. Since the brute desire for life is the mainspring for all human action, we must concede to men the right to that which they are powerless not to obey. Yet at other times Locke appeals to reason and divinity to support his views on rights. In the *Essay Concerning Human Understanding,* Locke speaks, not of natural law, but of "divine law," which he calls the law "God has set to the actions of men" and which is known through either "the light of nature or the voice of revelation."[15] While animals, Locke appears to say, are motivated directly by instinct, the human species requires reason ("the light of nature") or the teachings of scripture. Man, Locke implies, has a greater flexibility in his actions precisely because he can contravene nature by following other sources. As an example of what this means Locke tells us elsewhere that the "general rule which Nature teaches all things," that of self-preservation, can be overcome when circumstances dictate. Thus, when it comes to protecting our young, "Individuals act so strongly to this end, that they sometimes neglect their own private good for it."[16]

The same identification of reason, nature, and revelation is made again in the *First Treatise,* where Locke asserts that the desire for preservation has been planted in us by God, and reason, which is but the voice of God, teaches us to pursue that desire.[17] He explains that the "Foundation" of all

14. For a clear statement of Locke's position, see Ian Shapiro, *The Evolution of Rights in Liberal Theory* (Cambridge: Cambridge University Press, 1986), pp. 84–89.

15. John Locke, *Essay Concerning Human Understanding,* ed. A. C. Fraser (New York: Dover, 1959), 1:475.

16. John Locke, *Two Treatises of Government, First Treatise,* ed. Peter Laslett (Cambridge: Cambridge University Press, 1960), sec. 56.

17. Locke, *First Treatise,* sec. 86; see also sec. 101, where speaking of paternal power, Locke refers to ". . . the Law of Nature which is the Law of Reason. . . ."

right is the "first and strongest desire God planted in Men," namely, the desire for self-preservation. And in the same passage, he asserts that in addition to the desire to preserve themselves, "God planted in men a strong desire also of propagating their kind, and continuing themselves in their Posterity."[18] A similar style of reasoning is found again in the *Second Treatise,* where Locke goes so far as to identify the natural law with reason, stating that the state of nature has "a law of nature to govern it," and reason, "which is that law," teaches man not to harm others either in their "Life, Health, Liberty, or Possessions." The law of nature, then, "willeth the Peace and Preservation of all Mankind" so long as it "comes not in competition" with ourselves.[19] Locke argues that because all men are born equally rational, they all have the capacity to apprehend the natural law unless their reason has been corrupted by social circumstances and upbringing.

Hegel's objection to empirical theories of natural right turns not so much on their conclusions as on the method by which they purport to arrive at them. Empirical theorists like Hobbes and Locke claim to discover the most universal features of human beings by means of a kind of thought experiment, hypothetically stripping or peeling away everything man has acquired through the influences of history, custom, and tradition, in order to discover the state of nature and the natural man behind them. "If we think away," Hegel writes, "everything that someone's obscure inkling may reckon amongst the particular and the transitory as belonging to particular manners, to history, to civilization, and even to the state, then what remains is man in the image of the bare state of nature, or the abstraction of man with his essential potentialities; and we have only to look in order to find what is necessary."[20]

The problem is that insofar as it aspires to be a theory of rights at all, empiricism cannot establish what it wants to prove. For if empiricism wants to be more than just a description of what rights we happen to enjoy, it must have some way of showing these rights to be necessary and universal. It must, in other words, have some way of showing that these rights are rooted in certain permanent features of human nature. But, according to Hegel, this is just what empiricism is incapable of showing. For categories like "necessity" and "universality" are not given in experience or discoverable through observation but must be gleaned through other means. In Hegel's own language, empiricism is incapable of distinguishing between

18. Locke, *First Treatise,* sec. 88.
19. Locke, *Second Treatise,* secs. 6, 7.
20. *NL,* pp. 63–64; *Werke,* 2:445.

the necessary and the contingent. "Empiricism lacks . . . all criteria for drawing the boundary between the accidental and the necessary; i.e., for determining what in the chaos of the state of nature or in the abstraction of man must remain and what must be discarded."[21]

The strength of the empirical method lies in its recognition of the simple truth that all knowledge must come from experience. "The main lesson of empiricism," Hegel writes in the *Lesser Logic,* "is that man must see for himself and feel that he is present in every facet of knowledge which he has to accept."[22] The weakness with this approach is not that it is too critical, but that it is not critical enough. The method of abstraction or attempting to discover what is natural behind what has been acquired through history is naive and unsophisticated. While it is perfectly compatible with "the common understanding" (*der gemeinen Verstand*) to seek ways of distinguishing the necessary from the contingent, empiricism tends merely to reinforce existing prejudices. Thus, when dealing with actual social institutions like the family, property, or criminal law, the empiricist will simply select out some particular feature of that institution, for example, procreation or the reform of the criminal, and read this back into its cause. While the moral reform of the criminal may be the current raison d'être of penal law, it would be a mistake to assume that this was also its original cause. The Lockean argument that society exists for the sake of the protection of property tells us more about the structure of Locke's own society than the actual origins of society. Thus Hegel seems to anticipate Nietzsche's later barb that not all men desire pleasure, but only Englishmen.[23]

Hegel's point is that there is an irreducible circularity at the core of empiricism which does no more than put back into nature what it took out in the first place.

> After the fiction of the state of nature has served its purpose, that state is abandoned because of its ill consequences; this simply means that the desired outcome is presupposed, the outcome namely of an harmonization of what, as chaos, is in conflict with the good or whatever goal must be reached. Alternatively, a ground of transition is introduced directly into the idea of original qualities as potentialities, such as gregarious instinct.[24]

21. *NL,* p. 64; *Werke,* 2:446.
22. *LL,* par. 38, p. 61; *Werke,* 8:108.
23. Friedrich Nietzsche, *Twilight of the Idols,* trans. R. J. Hollingdale (Harmondsworth: Penguin, 1968), p. 23.
24. *NL,* p. 65; *Werke* 2:447.

Hegel's objection to empiricism is, then, that it is caught in self-contradiction. What is true or useful in empiricism is the demand that "philosophy should take its bearings from experience" and its "obstinate opposition" to any "artificial framework of principles."[25] Furthermore, empiricism "rightly prefers" the "inconsistency" and "confusion" of what actually exists to the artificial and "absolute distinctions" imposed by abstract speculation. Following up upon his earlier romantic critique of the intellect, Hegel denounces philosophy for "the dismemberment [of the phenomena] and this elevation of unsubstantial abstractions and details to absoluteness."[26]

The contradiction enters when empiricism is no longer willing simply to leave itself as an antiphilosophy but aspires to become a philosophy. An empirical philosophy is an oxymoron. For if it remains true to itself, "an empirical attitude would have every right to assert itself against such theorizing and philosophizing, and to treat the mass of principles, ends, laws, duties, and rights as not absolute but as distinctions important to the culture through which its own vision becomes clearer to it."[27] But if empiricism expects to generate findings that have more than limited validity, it will have to import principles that cannot be discovered in experience alone. Thus, despite the empiricists' claims to have built their theories of natural rights on the simplest and most elementary needs, their methods of determining these needs are already "theory loaded." Their descriptions of these needs are not simply neutral but invariably commit them to adopting a particular view of society and the future. There is, as Rousseau would later complain, an implicit teleology smuggled in through the back door.

The empirical theory of rights falls far short, then, of the necessity and universality attributed to it by Hobbes and Locke. It is rather "entangled in such concepts as have become fixed in the culture of the day as 'healthy common sense' and so seem to have been drawn directly from experience."[28] The Hobbesian-Lockean deduction of natural rights is caught in a halfway house: their theories of rights are either too empirical or not empirical enough. Hobbes and Locke are insufficiently empirical insofar as they attempt to return to nature as the standard for moral and political conduct; they are too empirical insofar as their views of nature seem to be

25. *NL*, p. 69; *Werke* 2:451.
26. *NL*, p. 69; *Werke* 2:452.
27. *NL*, p. 69; *Werke* 2:452.
28. *NL*, p. 70; *Werke* 2:453.

taken from what is simply at hand or from "such hardened and ad hoc conventionally fixed abstractions."[29]

CRITIQUE OF NATURAL RIGHTS, IIA: KANT

The second method for studying rights discussed by Hegel in *Natural Law* is the formal or transcendental approach ascribed to the philosophies of Kant and Fichte. In describing Kant's and Fichte's theories of rights as formal, Hegel intends to underscore two things. First, the theories are formal in the sense that Kant and Fichte hold them to be strictly universal. And second, the theories are formal because Kant and Fichte sought a ground for right not by means of an empirical extrapolation from all properties we can know about human beings through ordinary empirical means. If human rights are to have the kind of universality and necessity that we attribute to the laws of nature, then they must be grounded in something that transcends our empirically limited desires. This something is the will, which is for Kant and Fichte not the sort of thing that can be discovered through inductive argument, but is a presupposition that must hold if our talk about rights is to be morally intelligible. This is what is sometimes referred to as a transcendental argument. It begins with some empirical or factual premise and moves backwards to deduce its conditions of possibility. With this transcendental turn in the argument, Kant and Fichte take the discussion of rights to a significantly higher and more abstract level than that of Hobbes and Locke. Rather than beginning with such typically mundane concerns as the desire for life, liberty, and property, Kant and Fichte sought to endow rights with a greater moral dignity and absoluteness.

Hegel's objections to moral theories of the Kantian-Fichtean type vary widely in character and scope. Some relate to the logical structure of the theories, while others concern the specific details of the systems. Sometimes he treats the theories of Kant and Fichte as if they were the same, while elsewhere he distinguishes carefully between them. And while he often appears to reject Kant's and Fichte's doctrines out of hand, he also pays them the most lavish tribute and ends by incorporating a great many of their teachings into his own. My main task here, however, will not be to assess Hegel's reliability as a critic of his predecessors but to single out those features of the Kantian-Fichtean theories of rights which bear on the construction of Hegel's own doctrine.

29. *NL*, p. 70; *Werke* 2:453.

Antihistoricism   At the most general level, Hegel is famous for his critique of what he regarded as the "abstract" or antihistorical character of Kantian morality. Kantian *Moralität* is typically and correctly identified by Hegel as claiming to inhabit a realm of its own outside of other dimensions of human thought and action. Indeed, the autonomy and independence of morality from all contingent empirical circumstances was regarded by Kant as crucial for the sustenance of the "moral point of view." For according to Kant, if we came to believe that morality is a feature of social life just like any other, its commands would cease to appear as binding categorically. Morality would become just a set of prudential maxims followed for reasons of self-interest or utility. If the basic structure of morality were open to essential alteration, the result would be an invitation to immorality and evil.

Hegel's response to the abstract character of Kantian morality is to stress that moral duty has a history and that to conceive it as something apart from social and political circumstances is to misconceive it. Such antihistorical theories are false because they simply fail to grasp the nature of human diversity in all of its detail. This point is made forcefully by Alasdair MacIntyre in his book *A Short History of Ethics*. Here MacIntyre rejects the view associated with "some philosophers" who "have even written as if moral concepts were a timeless, limited, unchanging, determinate species of concept, necessarily having the same features throughout their history." Claiming that this view is "obviously false," he goes on to argue that "moral concepts are embodied in and are partially constitutive of forms of social life." Thus, "to understand a [moral] concept, to grasp the meaning of the words which express it, is always at least to learn what the rules are which govern the use of such words and so to grasp the role of the concept in language and social life."[30] Furthermore, theories of the Kantian type purport to address some timeless, universal subject, the moral agent, who is supposedly prior to and independent of any of the ends or purposes he pursues. This modern "absoluteness of the subject," as Hegel calls it, appears "on a lower plane" in Enlightenment doctrines of eudaimonism, but achieves a higher conceptual form in the philosophies of Kant and Fichte, which Hegel does not hesitate to call "anti-socialistic."[31]

Morality, as Hegel tries to show, is not the product of autonomous individual reflection on how to live as this is portrayed in the rationalistic phi-

---

30. Alasdair MacIntyre, *A Short History of Ethics* (New York: Macmillan, 1976), pp. 1, 2.
31. *NL,* p. 70; *Werke* 2:454.

losophies of his predecessors but is rooted in the prereflective customs and habits (*Sitten*) of a people. Hegel confirms this point by a linguistic allusion to the Greek word for ethics, *ethos,* which he contrasts to "the newer systems of ethics [which] in making independence and individuality into a principle, cannot fail to expose the relation of these words. This inner allusion proves so powerful that these systems, to define their subject-matter, could not misuse these words and so adopted the word 'morality.'"[32] Duties, then, are far less a product of deliberative reflection than of social and cultural development. In the words of Michael Oakeshott, the ethics of a people are "not a habit of reflective thought but a habit of affection and conduct."[33]

What Hegel says here is not intended as a description of a merely primitive form of moral life. In identifying moral conduct as part of the broader ethical life of a people, he is in a sense returning to an older quasi-Aristotelian conception of a community as a structure of relations within which our moral powers can develop. Rather than regarding the community as a necessary evil or an uneasy compromise with our "heteronomous" natures, Hegel sees it as the appropriate context for the development and realization of certain moral qualities that we cannot choose not to have or to be without. The idea here is that moral life is "situated" within the objective structure of communal norms, so that "what is good and bad or right and wrong are supplied by the laws and customs of each state, and there is not great difficulty in recognizing them."[34]

The important methodological point that Hegel is making here is that morality is connected to other spheres of social life by a network of internal relations. No part can be abstracted out and made the cause of the others, as the empiricist believes, but the whole must rather be seen as an "expressive totality," or, as he puts it in *Natural Law:* "the absolute ethical totality is nothing other than a people."[35] The modern theorist who came closest to grasping this principle was Montesquieu, for whom "all parts of the constitution and the laws, all specific details of ethical relationships are entirely determined by the whole and form a structure in which no joint and no

32. *NL,* p. 112; *Werke* 2:504.

33. Michael Oakeshott, *Rationalism in Politics and Other Essays* (London: Methuen, 1962), p. 61.

34. G. W. F. Hegel, *Lectures on the Philosophy of World History: Introduction,* trans. H. B. Nisbet (Cambridge: Cambridge University Press, 1975), p. 80.

35. *NL,* p. 92; *Werke* 2:481: ". . . *die absolute sittliche Totalität nichts anderes als ein Volk ist . . .*"

ornament has been independently present a priori."³⁶ Thus, in *De l'esprit des lois* Montesquieu sought to comprehend "both the higher relationships of constitutional law and the lower specifications of civil relationships down to wills, marriage laws, etc. entirely from the character of the whole and its individuality."³⁷

Empty Formalism A second, equally important charge is that Kantian ethics amounts to an "empty formalism" incapable of generating an "immanent doctrine of duties."³⁸ Kant's supreme principle of morality, the Categorical Imperative—"Act only on that maxim through which you can at the same time will that it should become a universal law"—is criticized for providing no content or direction for human action. Kant's almost exclusive concern with the purity of motives can thus be reduced to a "preaching" of "duty for duty's sake."³⁹

Hegel's charge of empty formalism has until recently been more or less accepted by generations of interpreters. Specifically, it is alleged, by concentrating on the form of moral judgment, that is, with how something is willed, Kant left himself open to the charge of indifference to what is willed. What action or actions does the moral law prescribe? To this question Kant gives only the sketchiest of answers, suggesting in the *Groundwork* only that whatever is done must be in accordance with duty. According to Hegel, Kant's reticence to supply an answer to this question follows from the very formalism of Kant's principle, because the moment he attempts to specify some content for morality he would immediately violate the canon of universality. Hegel reasons as follows:

> For practical reason is the complete abstraction from all content of the will; to introduce a content is to establish a heteronomy of choice. But what is precisely of interest is to know *what* right and duty are. We ask for the content of the moral law, and this content alone concerns us. But the essence of pure will and pure practical reason is to be abstracted from all content. Thus it is a self-contradiction to seek in this absolute practical reason a moral legislation which would have to have a content, since the essence of this reason is to have none.⁴⁰

It is claimed, probably correctly, that Hegel's view of Kant derives from an undue attention to the first formulation of the Categorical Imperative

36. *NL,* p. 128; *Werke* 2:524.
37. *NL,* p. 128; *Werke* 2:524–25.
38. *PR,* par. 135R, p. 90; *Werke* 7:252.
39. *PR,* par. 135R, p. 90; *Werke* 7:252.
40. *NL,* p. 76; *Werke* 2:461.

which emphasizes the universality of its form, and not enough from the second, which commands respect for persons or treating others as "ends in themselves." Had he done so, he might well have found in Kant a set of objective ends that he criticizes him for not having. Kant's moral imperative may well be formal, but it need not be empty. As Patrick Riley has noted, the command to treat humanity as an end and never as a means is to put some "nonheteronomous teleological flesh" upon "the bare bones of universality."[41] Also, it can be shown that in Kant's other writings, notably the *Metaphysics of Morals* and the *Anthropology from a Pragmatic Point of View,* he brings out many of the contextual and empirical features necessary for morality which he elsewhere neglects.

But even if it is correct that Hegel's description of Kantian ethics as an "empty formalism" is only a half-truth, it still remains half true. To illustrate his point, Hegel refers explicitly to an example that Kant himself used on a number of occasions to illustrate the moral law.[42] The example is that of an agent who has been entrusted with a sum of money, the owner of which has since died and has left no evidence of its whereabouts. In one of his more extreme formulations of this example, Kant asks us to imagine that through no fault of his own, the trustee has suffered complete financial collapse, while the heirs of the deceased are "rich, uncharitable, thoroughly extravagant, and luxurious, so that it would make little difference if the aforesaid addition to their property were thrown into the sea."[43] Even under these conditions, Kant claims, the trustee would be wrong to keep the deposit, for reasons that would be plain to "a child of around eight or nine years old," namely, that to universalize the maxim of that action, that it is right to embezzle deposits whenever it is in my interests to do so, or whenever I know that I will not be caught, could not be generalized without contradiction. To universalize this maxim would be to destroy the conditions of trust and confidence that make not only deposits but all safety and security possible. It would be to destroy the very condition of the social contract itself.

Hegel's answer to this application of the moral law is well-known but still deserves to be cited in full:

> But where is the contradiction if there were no deposits? The non-existence of deposits would contradict other specific things, just as the possibility of deposits

41. Patrick Riley, *Kant's Political Philosophy* (Totowa, N.J.: Rowman & Littlefield, 1982), p. 49.

42. *NL,* p. 77; *Werke* 2:462.

43. See Kant, "Theory and Practice," *Political Writings,* pp. 70–71.

fits together with other necessary specific things and thereby will itself be necessary. But other ends and material grounds are not to be invoked; it is the immediate form of the concept which is to settle the rightness of adopting either one specific matter or the other. For the form, however, one of the opposed specifics is just as valid as the other; each can be conceived as a quality, and this conception can be expressed as a law.[44]

Hegel's point here is that Kant is unable to derive any substantive social and political prescriptions from the purely formal standard of universality. In the above example, Kant uses the principle of universality to deny the legitimacy of theft. Yet Hegel's point is that universalization can only ensure the consistency of our actions. To say that the embezzlement of deposits is wrong assumes that if such a practice were generalized it would result in a world where the continued existence of deposits, and hence property, would be thrown into question. Yet even on Kant's own account, it is not possible to say that a world without deposits would be morally inferior to the one in which we now live. It would only be a different world. Kant's example, then, would only be efficacious against those who already accept the institutions of private property but not against those, for example, the committed anarchist, who do not.[45]

One cannot help but notice, then, that behind Kant's purely formal deduction of natural right there is presupposed the legitimacy of certain social and political institutions and practices. To be sure, there is, as his political writings bear out, a certain homology between the anonymity and impersonality of the moral law and the impersonal network of market and exchange relations governing modern civil society. This helps further to explain Kant's preference for liberal, cosmopolitan societies living in a condition of "perpetual peace." Thus, at the end of *Natural Law* Hegel condemns "the shapelessness of [Kant's] cosmopolitanism" and "the void of the Rights of Man . . . or a world republic" in which one finds only "abstractions and formalisms filled with exactly the opposite of ethical vitality."[46] Hegel's argument here is both the empirical one that by abolishing war the Kantian commercial republic in effect destroys "the ethical health of peoples" and the logical one that through a conceptual "sleight of hand" the legitimacy of modern bourgeois liberalism is simply assumed.[47]

44. *NL*, p. 77; *Werke* 2:462.

45. W. H. Walsh, *Hegelian Ethics* (London: Macmillan, 1969), p. 23.

46. *NL*, pp. 132–33; *Werke* 2:529–30.

47. See Georg Lukács, *The Young Hegel: Studies in the Relations between Dialectics and Economics,* trans. Rodney Livingstone (London: Merlin Press, 1975), p. 160.

The Beautiful Soul   Hegel is, as I have indicated, concerned not only with the logical structure of the Categorical Imperative but also with the kind of moral character produced by Kantian morality. Unlike contemporary Kantians (e.g., Rawls), for whom the core of ethics is "the study of the conception and outcome of a suitably defined rational decision," Kant was crucially concerned with the type of human being that his doctrine would promote.[48] For Kant, the essence of moral character was the good will, or an ability to purge one's attitudes of all motives other than respect for the moral law. This is not to say that no other motives or habits of mind may be present to the agent, but that only when such respect represents the determining ground of one's will can one's actions be deemed moral. It is this austere conception of respect or acting for the sake of duty alone that for Hegel "constituted the merit of Kant's moral philosophy and its loftiness of outlook."[49]

It is often believed that Kant proposed a moral philosophy that was indifferent to issues of human character. Contemporary anti-Kantians have pointed out that the Kantian moral agent is curiously bereft of moral and affective ties to others and committed to an ethically vacuous doctrine of duty for duty's sake. Kantian moral personality, such as it is, is almost entirely negative, shaped by the experience of struggle with its lower desires and impulses. Unlike, say, Aristotle's self-sufficient and happy man, endowed with a rich list of social and intellectual attributes, the Kantian moral agent is said to be the product of a desicated rationalism, with no sense of culture, tradition, or history. "The agent," Iris Murdoch has written in reference to Kant, "thin as a needle, appears in the quick flash of the choosing will."[50]

This conception of Kantian moral personality as ethically and culturally deracinated, though widely held, is mistaken. Every bit as much as Aristotle, Kant was interested in producing the right kind of moral character. But unlike Rawls's rational decision maker or Murdoch's pinpoint of consciousness, Kant taught a morality of respect, respect for the rational moral element both within ourselves and others. The Kantian moral personality is an appropriately democratic one, tailored to the needs of an egalitarian age. The difference between Aristotle and Kant is not that the one had a theory of character and the other didn't, but over just what kind of character it was desirable for a person to have. Judith Shklar has captured this difference nicely in her book *Ordinary Vices:*

48. John Rawls, *A Theory of Justice* (Cambridge, Mass.: Belknap Press, 1971), p. 251.
49. *PR,* par. 133A, p. 253; *Werke* 7:251.
50. Iris Murdoch, *The Sovereignty of Good* (Boston: Ark, 1985), p. 53.

> The real difference between [Aristotle] and Kant is glaringly obvious. Anyone can in principle aspire to become a Kantian good character. It requires no special gifts of intelligence, beauty, wealth, or good luck. . . . This is a thoroughly democratic liberal character, built to preserve its own self-respect and that of others, neither demanding nor enduring servility.[51]

Kantian moral character, then, provides the philosophical underpinnings for a liberal-democratic society based upon egalitarian conceptions of human rights and respect for individuals as such.

Despite his professed admiration for the "loftiness" of Kant's moral outlook, however, Hegel believes it conceals a deeper, darker side. Kant had used the criterion of universality or consistency as a means of distinguishing right from wrong principles of action. But if sheer consistency in willing is the criterion of an action's moral worth, then in principle any action—murder or torture—could be upheld as moral, so long as the agent was able to will it consistently. Universality may be no more than adhering consistently to what one believes, irrespective of the content or purpose of those beliefs or their objective consequences. The result may even be to sanction hypocrisy and immorality by providing no external means of checking the intentions of the agent or, as Hegel puts it, "My good intention in my action and my conviction of its goodness makes it good."[52]

A particularly gruesome example of the way in which Kantian morality may serve as a smoke screen for evil is related by Hannah Arendt in her book *Eichmann in Jerusalem*. In the course of the police examination of the Nazi war criminal in which he was attempting to justify his acts, Eichmann remarked that he was simply acting out of respect for the principle of the Categorical Imperative. When the Israeli judge, struck by this remark, asked him to explain himself, Eichmann replied: "I meant by my remark about Kant that the principle of my will must always be such that it can become the principle of general laws." Arendt then goes on to describe the rest of the exchange:

> Upon further questioning, he added that he had read Kant's *Critique of Practical Reason*. He then proceeded to explain that from the moment he was charged with carrying out the Final Solution he had ceased to live according to Kantian principles, that he had known it, and that he had consoled himself with the thought that he no longer "was master of his own deeds," that he was unable "to change anything." . . . Kant, to be sure, had never intended to say anything of the sort; on the contrary, to him every man was a legislator the moment he started to

51. Judith Shklar, *Ordinary Vices* (Cambridge, Mass.: Harvard University Press, 1984), p. 233.
52. *PR*, par. 140R, p. 99; *Werke* 7:274.

act: by using his "practical reason" man found the principles that could and should be the principles of law. But it is true that Eichmann's unconscious distortion agrees with what he himself called the version of Kant "for the household use of the little man." In this household use, all that is left of Kant's spirit is the demand that a man do more than obey the law, that he go beyond the mere call of obedience and identify his own will with the principle behind the law—the source from which the law sprang. In Kant's philosophy, that source was practical reason; in Eichmann's household use of him, it was the will of the Führer.[53]

This is clearly a grotesque distortion of Kant's moral philosophy, although it allows one to see in particularly stark form the lengths to which acting "for the sake of duty" without any further specification might be put.

Exactly this kind of distortion is evident in the work of a present-day defender of Kantian ethics, R. M. Hare. In his book *Freedom and Reason,* Hare stages an imaginary debate between a Kantian liberal and a Nazi over the mass murder of the Jews.[54] The Kantian hopes to refute the Nazi by showing him that his principles cannot stand the test of universalization and cannot therefore be moral. What if, for example, it was discovered that the Nazi were himself a "non-Aryan"? Would he voluntarily go to Auschwitz? The Kantian expects the Nazi to try to make an exception in his own case and thus convict himself of inconsistency. But, Hare admits, if a Nazi could be found who would suffer death for the sake of his ideals, then all the Kantian could do would be to deplore, not refute, the Nazi's logic.

What Eichmann and Hare share is a belief that ethical behavior consists solely in a willingness to act out of principle. This is why, for Hare, the Kantian is silenced when faced with a truly principled Nazi. What they both overlook, however, is the fact that for Kant, principle alone is not enough to ensure morality unless it is joined to a willingness to treat all persons as beings endowed with dignity simply by virtue of their personhood. As a being capable of moral action, a human being has infinite potential value and deserves to be treated with respect. Under no description, then, could the Nazi logic of destruction ever have satisfied the Kantian test of morality: to treat humanity, whether in one's own person or in that of another, never as a means but always as an end.

While Hegel did not anticipate the kind of bureaucratic rigidification of Kantian ethics that the Eichmann example illustrates, he was alarmed by two equally troubling instances of its misuse. The first stresses the one-sided attention to independence from the will of others, external authority,

---

53. Hannah Arendt, *Eichmann in Jerusalem: A Report on the Banality of Evil* (New York: Viking Press, 1965), pp. 136–37.

54. R. M. Hare, *Freedom and Reason* (Oxford: Clarendon Press, 1963), chap. 9.

or nature itself. The Kantian notion of autonomy has the effect of delegitimizing all social and political institutions that do not flow from our own free will. The result is what Bernard Yack has recently described as a kind of "Left Kantianism," a revolutionary or terroristic morality that preaches liberation from all contexts or situations.[55] Such a morality obliges the Kantian to reject as dehumanizing, alienating, and oppressive everything that does not immediately express man's essential humanity or dignity. Reflecting, no doubt, on the example of the French Revolution, but also on the German romantics like Fries, Hegel was particularly sensitive to the misuses of an "ethic of intention" divorced from an "ethic of responsibility."[56]

> It is one of the most prominent of the corrupt maxims of our time to enter a plea for the so-called 'moral' intention behind wrong actions and to imagine bad men with well-meaning hearts. . . . today [this doctrine] has been resuscitated in a more extravagant form, and inner enthusiasm and the heart . . . have been made the criterion of right, rationality, and excellence. The result is that crime and the thoughts that lead to it, be they fancies however trite and empty, or opinions however wild, are to be regarded as right, rational, and excellent, simply because they issue from men's hearts and enthusiasms.[57]

The second extreme which the Kantian insistence on the good will can take is what Hegel calls the "beautiful soul."[58] Such a person—the extreme conscientious objector might be an example—is no longer able to participate in any actions that do not emanate from the absolute purity of his intentions. Hegel describes Jesus as such a person in the early manuscript "The Spirit of Christianity and Its Fate," but he returns to it again in the *Phenomenology*. The beautiful soul is depicted here as having a devoutly religious form of inwardness. Hegel was here probably thinking of the German Pietist movement in which Kant was involved and which swept northern Germany in the late seventeenth century. This movement expressed itself in terms of a rejection of doctrine and a return to the Bible as the source of all true inspiration. For the Pietist, what was important was

55. Bernard Yack, *The Longing for Total Revolution* (Princeton: Princeton University Press, 1986), pp. 89–133.

56. For Hegel's critique of this kind of political romanticism, see *PR*, pp. 5–7; *Werke* 7:18–20; see also Shlomo Avineri, *Hegel's Theory of the Modern State* (Cambridge: Cambridge University Press, 1972), pp. 119–22.

57. *PR*, par. 126R, p. 85; *Werke* 7:237.

58. *PhM*, pp. 664–68, 675–79; *Werke* 3:481–85, 491–94; for useful treatments, see Judith Shklar, *Freedom and Independence: A Study of Hegel's Phenomenology of Mind* (Cambridge: Cambridge University Press, 1976), pp. 180–96; Hinchman, *Hegel's Critique of the Enlightenment*, pp. 175–84.

not external conformity to religious dogma but the purity of the believer's convictions, and whether they emanated from the heart. More than most contemporary critics, Hegel was fully aware of the religious origins of Kantian ethics.[59]

The problem with the beautiful soul is not, of course, that it is religious as such, but that "it lives in dread of staining the radiance of its inner being by action and existence," and that to preserve its purity "it flees from contact with actuality, and steadfastly perseveres in a state of self-willed impotence."[60] Indeed, Hegel reserves some of his most caustic comments for those hyperconscientious souls who are so concerned with their personal integrity and virtue that they take no part in the real world. This withdrawal into the inner space of conscience is for Hegel irresponsible at best and a mask for narcissistic self-indulgence at worst. It is the cast of mind that Nietzsche was later devastatingly to ridicule in *The Use and Abuse of History,* when he remarked: "But there is also a famous danger in [German] inwardness; the internal substance cannot be seen from the outside, and so may one day take the opportunity of vanishing, and no one will notice its absence any more than its presence before."[61]

CRITIQUE OF NATURAL RIGHTS, IIB: FICHTE

In contrast to Kant's, Fichte's deduction of natural right is less well-known, but it is no less important for an understanding of Hegel's position. Like Kant, Fichte sought to infuse the principles of right with a new idealism that early modern liberalism had lacked; but unlike Kant, Fichte hoped to achieve his goals, not through an open, tolerant, market society, but through a "closed commercial state" where, in his own words, "the police know pretty much what everyone is doing at any time of day."[62] Hegel's

59. For the influence of Pietism on Kant, see Theodore M. Greene, "The Historical Context and Significance of Kant's Religion," *Religion Within the Limits of Reason Alone,* trans. T. M. Greene and H. H. Hudson (New York: Harper & Row, 1960), pp. xii–xiv, xxii–xv; Ernst Cassirer, *Kant's Life and Thought* (New Haven: Yale University Press, 1981), pp. 15–18.

60. *PhM,* p. 666; *Werke* 3:483.

61. Friedrich Nietzsche, *The Use and Abuse of History,* trans. Adrian Collins (Indianapolis: Bobbs-Merrill, 1957), p. 26.

62. J. G. Fichte, *The Science of Rights,* trans. A. E. Kroeger (London: Routledge & Kegan Paul, 1970), p. 386. Here Fichte describes in chilling detail the role of "police law" in his ideal state. Carrying out the logic of Kantian transcendental argument to its conclusion, he argues that the police must oversee not just "*actual violation*" of the laws but "the *possibility* of such violation" (p. 377). For example, the police must be able to detain anyone walking the streets at night without a light, since such actions can only be attempts to avoid police surveillance. As the chief maxim regulating a well-ordered state, Fichte lays down the following: "*That each citizen should be at all times and places, when it may be necessary, recognized as this or that particular person* [by the police]" (p. 378).

depiction of the Fichtean community as a "police state" in which individual activity is regulated—down to and including the painting of citizen's likenesses on their passports for internal security measures—is not, as Georg Lukács has reminded us, simply a cheap shot at some of the more eccentric forms of Fichtean idealism.[63] Rather, it goes to the heart of Hegel's critique of revolutionary politics, with its attempt to synthesize collectivist communitarianism and expressivist freedom. It is the marriage of these two incompatibles that Hegel regards as the core of modern radicalism.

Fichte's *Science of Right* begins, as does Kantian idealism, with an awareness of a radical dualism. The fundamental starting point in philosophy is that between subject and object, the *I* and the *not-I*. For Fichte, this starting point reduces itself to the necessity of a radical epistemological choice. Either we are posited or determined by nature or the world of experience is somehow determined or made by us. The first alternative he describes as "dogmatism" and the second as "idealism." Which of these alternatives one chooses is as much a moral as an epistemological claim, since "what sort of philosophy one chooses . . . is not a dead household object which we can lay aside or take hold of just as it pleases us; rather it is animated by the soul of the man who has it."[64] A little like Jean-Paul Sartre, he believes that the kind of epistemology we adopt is ultimately a matter of ethics—moral choice. We can either choose to acknowledge our freedom or we can try to escape from it, but in either case it is a free human decision.

Fichte then goes on to deduce the basis of right from the transcendental structure of self-consciousness. To be self-conscious is not only to be aware of a world of things; it is to be aware of one's own awareness of things. Self-consciousness is thus characterized by an ability to stand back from one's self and reflect upon one's own states of mind. To be self-conscious, then, is to be both the subject and the object of knowledge, both the knower and the known. And the ability of the mind to perform this kind of double hermeneutic is, for Fichte, a form of action (*Tathandlung*). The mind is not, as in Lockean or Humean empiricism, merely a passive transcription of an independently existing external world. Rather, the mind seeks to grasp, appropriate, and transform reality. There is, then, a fundamentally antagonistic character to the dualism between self and other, in which the self continually strives to subdue or overcome otherness by turning it into a projection of the mind's own essential powers. The telos of activity is, to use Descartes's phrase, the "mastery and possession" of the world. Fichte's

63. Lukács, *The Young Hegel*, p. 292.

64. J. G. Fichte, *The Science of Knowledge (Wissenschaftslehre)*, trans. Peter Heath and John Lachs (New York: Appleton-Century-Crofts, 1970), p. 16.

philosophy is through and through a possessory one; Fichte is virtually the textbook case of what C. B. Macpherson would call the "possessive individualist."

Fichte is, of course, aware that the individual self-consciousness does not exist in isolation. The structure of the mind is essentially social, developing in and through conflict both with nature and other minds. The other mind, the *du,* serves as a mediating link between the *I* and the *non-I.* Indeed, the Fichtean theory of rights begins with the mutual recognition of freedom that is the original property of all minds. This freedom, for Fichte, as for Kant, is not something I merely happen to possess but is central to my well-being as a moral agent. Where Fichte departs from Kant is in seeing freedom less as the capacity for spontaneous choice than in the exercise of worldly mastery and control. Our freedom is thus not restricted but enhanced by our joining in a community of other selves who seek to overcome otherness and to impress their collective designs upon the world through labor and activity. As Susan Shell has written: "Here, then, is one vital source of those later 'industrial armies' and 'heroes of labor,' that transformation of human toil from a classically contemned and Biblically accursed burden into the emblem it for so many subsequently became of human mastery and freedom."[65] The community is less bound up with the need to satisfy material desires or to protect the right of self-preservation than with the metaphysical desire to achieve autonomy and control over one's own and externally imposed nature.

Fichte's theory of community, spelt out most elaborately in his *Closed Commercial State,* is a curious amalgam of socialism, nationalism, and technocratic elitism. Like Rousseau, Fichte advocates a small, homogenous, insular community as a way of providing for a self-disciplined, virtuous citizenry. Yet unlike Rousseau, Fichte defines virtue, not by political participation or in the older Aristotelian language of learning to rule and be ruled in turn, but in participating as a fellow laborer engaged in the collective pursuit of honest toil. In words that would later acquire a sinister ring for their misuse of the Fichtean idea: "Arbeit macht frei." Political participation, for Fichte, is exercised only once, in the decision to enter a community. Thereafter legislation is left a matter of purely technical expertise rather than popular deliberation. In fact, Fichte's desire to leave matters of ordinary politics to "impartial experts" not only points backwards to the Platonic ideal of the philosopher-king but points forward to the modern

65. Susan Shell, "Fichte's Science of Right: An Introduction," paper presented to the 1984 meeting of the American Political Science Association, p. 4.

administrative state. The only strictly political matter that concerns Fichte is finding a means to prevent governmental abuse of power. His answer here is the creation of an ephorate empowered to look after the interests of the citizenry and to remove officials for dereliction of duty. Yet whether this body will have teeth or is merely a court of moral appeal is a matter left ultimately ambiguous.

Hegel rejects the Fichtean formulation of a right for a number of reasons. First, like Kant, Fichte sought to put rights on a more metaphysically secure foundation than had early liberalism. Nevertheless, Hegel recognizes that the radical "decisionism" at the core of Fichte's jurisprudence is unable to establish this. Fichte simply presents the reader with a choice: either to affirm freedom or to deny it. But by making the difference simply a matter of choice, Hegel concludes, neither dogmatism nor idealism is able to refute its opponent. In the end, freedom seems more like a methodological postulate than an ontological necessity. Thus, like Weber later on, Fichte is led ultimately to deny that matters of "ultimate value" have a rational grounding.

Second, Fichte's goal, we have seen, is the abolition of otherness, or the appropriation of the *non-I* by the *I,* or ego. To use the language of present-day critical theory, we have not only a "technical interest" in the overcoming of nature but also a moral or "emancipatory" one. We cannot be free until we see our freedom manifest in the world. But freedom consists less in the conquest of nature for the satisfaction of human desires than in the exercise of mastery over nature as evidence of the drive for autonomy. As he puts it in his book, *The Vocation of the Scholar:* "To subject all irrational nature to himself, to rule over it without restraint and according to his own laws is the ultimate end of man; which *ultimate end* is perfectly unattainable. . . . But he may and should constantly approach nearer to it;—and thus the *unceasing approximation* to this end is his true *vocation* as man."[66]

Hegel's complaint is that the Fichtean drive towards mastery is an essentially infinite and thus impossible moral task. "The highest synthesis," he says in his early essay on Fichte and Schelling, "which the system presents is an Ought [*ein Sollen*]."[67] Unlike Kant, for whom *ought* necessarily implies *can,* Fichte leaves the goal of moral aspiration essentially open-ended, an *unendliches Streben,* or the so-called "bad infinity," as Hegel would later call

---

66. J. G. Fichte, *The Vocation of the Scholar* in *The Popular Works,* trans. William Smith (London: John Chapman, 1848) 1:183.
67. *Werke* 2:68.

it in the *Science of Logic*.[68] Rather than achieving a final reconciliation or synthesis between the ego and nature, Fichte, according to Hegel, is left with the unappetizing conclusion that "striving" alone is the most enduring mark of human dignity and greatness. It is precisely this discrepancy between man's infinite reach and his finite grasp that serves to reaffirm the phenomenon of the divided self that we have seen Hegel sought so desperately to overcome.

Third, Hegel found extremely unappealing Fichte's conception of a close-knit, cohesive moral community. In such a community, right no longer specifies a domain of private freedom, where I am free to pursue whatever my goals may be, so long as they do not infringe on the rights of others. Rather, it specifies an equal right to as many of the primary goods of life as society is able to afford. "This state," Hegel writes, "has the goal of preventing injuries to its citizens more than of avenging them when they have already occurred. . . . it must not only 'prohibit actual injury' under penalty of the law, but also must prevent the possibility of an injury.'"[69] In other words, the state not only serves the negative goal of ensuring equality of opportunity but also the positive one of ensuring equality of result. Every citizen is to be entitled to as many of the actual satisfactions of life as is technically feasible, an ideal of which Hegel says "there is no act nor motion which would not necessarily have to be subjected to a law, taken under immediate control, and observed by the police and the other officials."[70] In such a state, he goes on, "the people [*einem Volk*] is not the organic body of a common and rich life" but is reduced to "an atomistic, life-impoverished multitude."[71]

Finally, Hegel takes exception to Fichte's conception of a body of ephors capable of checking executive abuses of power. For Hegel, such a proposal was utopian or nonsensical, for it would result in a doctrine of dual sovereignty that would in the long run prove unworkable. Indeed, his critique of such a constitutional check on state authority anticipates a number of present-day critics of the separation of powers doctrine. Rather than resulting in limited government, such schemes have produced a dangerous constitutional deadlock, where all authority is paralyzed. He writes: "But such a *perpetuum mobile* whose parts are all supposed to follow one another round in the circle, will, instead of moving, settle at once into complete equilibrium and become a complete *perpetuum quietum;* for pressure and

68. *SL,* pp. 150–54; *Werke* 5:166–71.
69. *Werke* 2:84.
70. *Werke* 2:85.
71. *Werke* 2:87.

counterpressure, coercing and being coerced, are entirely equal, and they stand directly against each other and effect the same reduction of forces."[72]

Throughout his critique of the formal conception of rights, it is clear that the thought of the French Revolution is never far from Hegel's mind. That Fichte was widely regarded as a supporter of the Jacobin policies of Robespierre contributed all the more to Hegel's distaste for Fichte's "police state." Thus, in a passage intended to point out the practical impotence of Fichte's ephorate, Hegel included a thinly veiled reference to Napoleon's coup d'état of the eighteenth Brumaire: "It is known," he writes, "that on the occasion of a government's recent dissolution of a rival and paralyzing legislative force, a man [i.e., Napoleon] who was himself involved in it . . . judged correctly that a council with similar supervisory powers and the will to oppose the government would have been treated just as violently."[73]

HEGEL AND THE FRENCH REVOLUTION: ROUSSEAU

In the *Philosophy of History,* Hegel writes: "We should not therefore contradict the assertion that the [French] Revolution received its first impulse from philosophy."[74] By "philosophy," it is clear that Hegel means the natural rights doctrines of Rousseau and Kant, who had sought to remake the world in accordance with the principles of critical rationality. Reason alone could liberate men from the inherited weight of custom, tradition, and history and allow them for the first time to master the world by submitting it to their own conscious designs and purposes. Unlike previous revolutions, which had sought essentially limited and parochial goals such as the substitution of one ruling class for another, the French Revolution sought to establish political institutions on a universal and secure foundation supplied by the principles of philosophy alone. Even in his later more conservative writings, Hegel could still extol the revolution for carrying out in practice what Enlightenment philosophers had already vindicated in theory:

> Anaxagoras had been the first to say that *nous* governs the world; but not until now had man advanced to the recognition of the principle that thought ought to govern spiritual reality. This was accordingly a glorious mental dawn. All thinking beings shared in the jubilation of this epoch. Emotions of a lofy character stirred men's minds at that time; a spiritual enthusiasm thrilled through the

---

72. *NL,* pp. 86–87; *Werke* 2:473–74.
73. *NL,* p. 88; *Werke* 2:475.
74. *PH,* p. 446; *Werke* 12:528.

world, as if the reconciliation between the divine and the secular was now first accomplished.[75]

While Hegel, as we have just seen, continued to regard the French Revolution, along with the Protestant Reformation, as one of the great watershed moments in modern history, he later came to see it more as a great moral and political tragedy. Like Burke, to whom he has often been compared, Hegel came to see the revolution as the harbinger of an era of "ideological" politics. Rejecting the older Aristotelian conception of politics as prudence (*phronesis*), which found a resonance in Burke's later appeals to tradition and authority, these new advocates, ideologues, or "men of principle" (*Prinzipienmänner*), as Hegel derisively called them, set themselves up as the engineers and architects of the new social order.[76] The revolutionaries, Hegel writes, have destroyed the fabric of traditional politics by a sort of reckless appeal from the *is* to the *ought,* from actually existing but imperfect regimes to the one naturally and universally sanctioned social order. Whereas previous politics presented itself as a play of particular passions and interests, the new politics assumes a higher and therefore more doctrinaire bearing. "[I]t is not private interest nor passion that desires gratification, but Reason, Justice, Liberty; and equipped with this title, the demand in question assumes a lofty bearing, and readily adopts a position not merely of discontent, but of open revolt against the actual condition of the world." And Hegel goes on to say: "At no time so much as in our own, have such general principles and notions been advanced, or with greater assurance."[77]

Hegel traces the tragic, even nihilistic, character of the French Revolution back to the philosophic critique of the ancien régime. In the chapter "Absolute Freedom and Terror" in the *Phenomenology,* Hegel shows how the revolution originated from an effort to overcome the division, or diremption (*Entfremdung*), of culture under the old regime.[78] The old regime, Hegel argues in a manner anticipating Marx, is a culture in alienation or estrangement. By estrangement, Hegel means a discrepancy between *seeming* and *being,* between what a culture says and thinks about itself and what it actually is. Under the old regime, this discrepancy between seeming and being became especially acute as the nobility, whose love of honor and prestige, which had earlier defined the ethical ideals of feudalism, became

---

75. *PH,* p. 447; *Werke* 12:529.
76. *PH,* p. 451; *Werke* 12:533; *PW,* pp. 325–26.
77. *PH,* p. 35; *Werke* 12:51–52.
78. *PhM,* pp. 599–610; *Werke* 3:431–41.

transformed into the spirit of the courtier, the flatterer, and the valet. In Hegel's memorable phrase, the "heroism of service" was replaced by the "heroism of flattery."[79]

Hegel's account of the old regime is clearly indebted to Montesquieu, who saw the sentiments of honor and service as animating principles of the older aristocratic ethos. But Hegel goes beyond Montesquieu in showing how this "noble consciousness" is not a kind of frozen ideal type but is dialectically transformed by the power of wealth and money into relinquishing its position and accepting a life of comfort and enjoyment. The proud aristocrat, this once "haughty vassal" who sought glory and nobility for himself in battle, has become a property-owning bourgeois seeking to accumulate goods and property to insulate himself from the consciousness of death. This contradiction between the "base" (*böse*) or bourgeois consciousness, defined by its fear of death, and the older aristocratic or warrior consciousness, defined by its contempt for wealth and comfort, marks the beginning of the end of the old regime.

The final stage of the denouement is revealed most powerfully by Hegel in his analysis of Diderot's *Le neveu de Rameau,* the text which lays bare and reveals this contradiction in all its duplicity. The work describes virtually the prototype of the prerevolutionary mind, torn between the conflicting ideals of the aristocracy and the bourgeoisie. What emerges from this "disintegrated" consciousness is of course the demand for "absolute freedom" from all previous restrictions and cultural restraints. What Hegel describes here is a kind of contextless freedom, a nihilistic yearning for oblivion or a "freedom of the void" which is often associated with the modern desire for revolution and total emancipation. In the preface to the *Phenomenology,* Hegel describes how this yearning for radical freedom emerged from the process of cultural disintegration that preceded it:

> But it is here as in the case of the birth of a child; after a long period of nutrition in silence, the continuity of the gradual growth in size, of quantitative change, is suddenly cut short by the first breath drawn—there is a break in the process, a qualitative change—and the child is born. In like manner the spirit of the time, growing slowly and quietly ripe for the new form it is to assume, disintegrates one fragment after another of the structure of its previous world. That it is tottering to its fall is indicated only by symptoms here and there. Frivolity and again ennui, which are spreading in the established order of things, the undefined foreboding of something unknown—all these betoken that there is something else approaching. This gradual crumbling to pieces, which did not alter the gen-

79. *PhM,* pp. 527–28; *Werke* 3:378–79.

eral look and aspect of the whole, is interrupted by the sunrise, which in a flash and at a single stroke, brings to view the form and structure of the new world.[80]

The French Revolution looked to Hegel like an attempt to recreate the conditions for social and political harmony which not only the old regime but all postclassical culture had torn asunder. The revolutionaries, acting out of a desire to bring the doctrines of the philosophers down to earth, directed themselves to removing all traces of transcendence or other-worldliness. To bring about this reconciliation of the rational and the real, the radicals sought to recreate the kind of consensus and public-spiritedness evinced by the ancient polis. The polis experience, as we have seen, was based on a devotion to the general will at the expense of private interests and elevated the virtue of the citizen over and above the private man or bourgeois. " [T]his will is not," as Hegel tells us, "the empty thought of will, which is constituted by giving a silent assent, or an assent through a representative, a mere symbol of willing; it is concretely embodied univer-sal will [*allgemeiner Wille*], the will of all individuals as such."[81]

Hegel's reference here to the "universal will" is clearly an allusion to Rousseau's *volonté générale,* which in the *Social Contract* he held to be at the basis of all political right. Like Kant, Rousseau believed that the principles of right could be found not through an analysis of merely empirical facts about human beings but rather in the capacity for free choice and agency, what Rousseau calls (somewhat ambiguously) one of "the essential gifts of nature."[82] For Rousseau, the will must be free of all appetite or empirical determination. It is characterized by the absence of any determination or direction. It follows, then, that since the will is not limited by nature, the problem of politics is to " [f]ind a form of association that defends and pro-tects the person and goods of each associate with all the common force, and by means of which each one, uniting with all, nevertheless obeys only him-self and remains as free as before."[83]

Rousseau's answer to this "difficulty" is that only the general will can provide for this combination of freedom and security in just the right way. The general will is the source of freedom, because since it is the creation of all, no one is coerced to do anything that he has not agreed to do. Each

80. *PhM,* p. 75; *Werke* 3 : 18–19.

81. *PhM,* pp. 600–601; *Werke* 3 : 432.

82. Jean-Jacques Rousseau, *Discourse on the Origins and Foundations of Inequality, The First and Second Discourses,* trans. Roger D. Masters and Judith R. Masters (New York: Saint Martin's, 1964), p. 168.

83. Jean-Jacques Rousseau, *On the Social Contract,* trans. Judith R. Masters (New York: Saint Martin's, 1978), 1 : 6 (p. 53).

individual participates in the creation of the general will and therefore does no more than obey rules that he has set down for himself. Since there are no a priori restrictions on what the general will may in fact will, it therefore satisfies the individual's desire for, or interest in, freedom. Furthermore, the general will is the source of security, because its dictates must be universally and hence impartially applicable to everyone. The general will can promulgate no law covering a single case but, like the Kantian moral imperative, must be universally binding on all. Thus, Rousseau concludes that since no one would will to harm himself, the general will can be safely made the final depository of rights. The general will is, then, the only possible basis for right, since it accords both with the principles of freedom and choice and with the principles of equality and equity.

What really is an act of the general will, then? Rousseau says:

> It is not a convention between a superior and an inferior, but a convention between the body and each of its members. A convention that is legitimate because it has the social contract as a basis; equitable, because it is common to all, useful, because it can have no other object than the general good; and solid, because it has the public force and the supreme power as a guarantee. As long as subjects are subordinated only to such conventions, they do not obey anyone, but solely their own will, and to ask how far the respective rights of the sovereign and of citizens extend is to ask how far the latter can engage themselves to one another, each to all and all to each.[84]

Hegel's rejection of Rousseau's formulation of the general will stems from its claim to stand in judgment of all traditional social institutions and practices. The attempt to realize the general will in the here and now resulted in a "rage and fury of destruction" which had "no inner significance or filling" any more than "cutting off a head of cabbage or swallowing a draught of water." The claim that the general will should be the only legitimate ground of rights would not only abolish all existing institutions and hierarchies but would regard "all differences in talent and authority as being superseded." Nothing would be allowed to exist that is not a product of the general will. Even God, "the empty *être suprême*" of the radicals, is said to hover there "merely as an exhalation of stale gas." The culmination of the revolution, then, is "the sheer horror of the negative," in which all the "determinate elements disappear with the disaster and ruin that overtake the self in the state of absolute freedom."[85]

The argument being made here is that while the general will can abolish,

---

84. Rousseau, *On the Social Contract*, 2:4 (p. 63).
85. *PhM*, pp. 602, 604, 605; *Werke* 3:434, 436.

it cannot create. It can destroy the old regime but cannot build a new one. The idea of the general will is that I am only free when I obey the laws that I have myself created. But since the general will is the outcome of a collective decision, it cannot be decided by me alone. If everyone is to be free, then everyone must at least participate in the decision making. There is no sense there as, say, in Hobbes, of authorizing someone else to do the work for me. The idea of a tacit consent, what Hegel called above "a mere symbol of willing," is insufficient. Freedom is attained for everyone when there is a complete unanimity of wills. But, as Hegel points out, the search for unanimity is a chimera less likely to result in community than in anarchy. Since each will necessarily regards itself as absolute, as the supreme expression of the *volonté générale,* there is no standard short of universal agreement that can guarantee the legitimacy of the outcome. Any halfway measure, such as representative institutions or rule by the majority, would be a violation of my inalienable right to self-legislation, my right to obey laws of my own making. The result is to create a permanent and implacable opposition between the people and their government, which will always appear to them as a particular corporate will, a "faction," interposing itself between them and their true wills.[86]

Rousseau conceives the problem of politics as one of transforming men who are by nature solitary and individualistic into citizens capable of collective and cooperative activities. "What man loses by the social contract," Rousseau says, "is his natural freedom and an unlimited right to what he can get; what he gains is civil freedom and the proprietorship of everything he possesses."[87] The social contract is not, then, merely a juridical device, as it was for Hobbes. It effects nothing less than a moral transformation of human nature. Unlike Hobbes's egoistic calculators, who remain more or less the same after the contract as they were before, for Rousseau, "this act of association creates a moral and collective body . . . receiving from this act its unity, its common self, its life, and its will."[88]

Rousseau conceives the social contract, then, as the substitution of one type of freedom for another. Natural (or what we would call "negative") freedom, the freedom to do as one likes—he calls it "the mere impulse of appetite"—is exchanged for rational or "moral" freedom, the freedom to live by laws of one's own making. Our rights are the exclusive product of the general will which must take the form of public, civil law. But if we ask:

86. *PhM,* p. 605; *Werke* 3:437.
87. Rousseau, *On the Social Contract,* 1:8 (p. 56).
88. Rousseau, *On the Social Contract,* 1:6 (p. 53).

"what is it, exactly, that this rational will wills when it wills?" or "what is the content of the general will?" Rousseau can provide no satisfactory answer. There is the same kind of vacuity about the general will that Hegel thought he observed in Kant's moral imperative, except that it is more dangerous, since Rousseau saw it as directly applicable to politics. The general will, as we have seen, is not "universal" in the Kantian sense. It applies, not to persons qua moral agents, but to citizens, that is, to members of particular communities localized in time and place. The general will, Hegel writes in the *Philosophy of History,* is free when "it does not will anything alien, extrinsic, foreign to itself . . . but wills itself alone—wills the will. This is absolute will—the volition to be free."[89]

The problem with Rousseau's conception of the general will is that it remains too abstract to serve as an instrument for political reform. It elaborates only a set of procedures by which valid laws and institutions can be achieved; it says nothing about what the character of those laws or institutions ought to be. Rousseau obviously thought that the procedure alone was rigorous enough to prevent abuse, but as Hegel was to show, his agnosticism about ends tends to prove dangerously open-ended. Furthermore, Rousseau uses the concept of the general will to show how substantive forms of community are generated. But a community is not the product of a will. Rather, any popular will requires a preexistent community before it can become operative. Rousseau is thus guilty of presupposing what he needs to establish.

THE POLITICS OF VIRTUE

The inability of the French Revolution to recreate a cohesive republican community is thus related to the faulty conception of rights on which it rested. Following Rousseau, the revolutionaries had seen the new French republic as based on an austere, self-sacrificing civic virtue in which private goals would be ruthlessly subordinated to the pursuit of the public good. But, as I have just suggested, this conception of virtue requires certain preexisting laws and institutions to support and sustain it. Where these are lacking, as they are in the postclassical world, this kind of civic ethos can only be created artificially, through an act of will. The question then becomes: what guarantee does the man of virtue, the republican citizen, have that he is really acting for the public good and not simply out of some private interest or scheme? What standard can the will supply against self-delusion?

89. *PH,* p. 442; *Werke* 12:524.

The only standard that the man of virtue can provide of his own moral goodness is, then, his own self-certainty or sincerity. Sincerity thus becomes the essence of moral virtue. But herein lies the difficulty. For if purity of intent is the only criterion of the worth of action, then men must be judged, not according to the outcome of their deeds, but by their subjective convictions alone—by the "law of the heart." Yet the result of this purely subjective conception of virtue was to unleash a relentless search to unmask those hypocrites who pursued their own private ends under the guise of public virtue. As Hegel depicts it, the reign of terror was nothing more than the working out on the public stage of this obsessive concern with inner purity:

> Virtue is here a simple abstract principle and distinguishes the citizens into two classes only—those who are favorably disposed and those who are not. But disposition can only be recognized and judged of by disposition. *Suspicion* therefore is in the ascendent; but virtue, as soon as it becomes liable to suspicion, is already condemned. . . . Robespierre set up the principle of Virtue as supreme, and it may be said that with this man Virtue was an earnest matter. *Virtue* and *Terror* are the order of the day; for Subjective Virtue, whose sway is based on disposition only, brings with it the most fearful tyranny. It exercises its power without legal formalities, and the punishment it inflicts is equally simple— *Death.*[90]

One might, of course, wonder why hypocrisy, what Judith Shklar has called a relatively "ordinary vice," should be responsible for such a wave of violence and fanaticism.[91] After all, hypocrisy is the only vice that pays homage to virtue. Hannah Arendt has argued at length that this desire to root out hypocrisy stems from the revolution's own "favored simile" of itself as tearing the mask, the persona, off a corrupt French society to expose behind it the uncorrupted "natural man."[92] For a theorist like Arendt, for whom politics is a kind of "play acting" where actors become the roles or legal personae that they assume, this search for the natural or authentic man behind the mask is profoundly antipolitical.

The natural man was also an invention of Rousseau, who in the *Second Discourse* had described him as unspoilt, honest, and self-complete; only through society or history does man become corrupt, calculating, and dependent. The object of Rousseau's scorn was, however, a particular species of civil or historical man that he was the first to identify as the modern

90. *PH,* pp. 450–51; *Werke* 12:532–33.
91. Shklar, *Ordinary Vices,* pp. 45–86.
92. Hannah Arendt, *On Revolution* (New York: Viking Press, 1965), pp. 91–104.

bourgeois. The bourgeois was for Rousseau, not an owner of the means of production, as this term was later used by Marx, but in the first place the possessor of a kind of self-love (amour propre) that leads him constantly to live both in and through the opinions of others. The bourgeois, as Allan Bloom has described him, is someone who thinks constantly of others when he is by himself and of himself when he is with others.[93] Unlike *l'homme naturel,* who is fundamentally self-sufficient and drawn to others only through the instinct of pity or compassion, civil or bourgeois man needs others as a means to satisfy his almost limitless appetites. What repels Rousseau is that unlike both the natural man and the classical citizen, who are both directly what they seem to be, the bourgeois is alienated in the sense of the term described above: he is not what he appears to be. He is a dissembler, a role player, and worst of all, a hypocrite.

According to Arendt, the tragedy of the French (and later, the Russian) Revolution stemmed from what could be called the fallacy of misplaced compassion. Just as Rousseau had seen pity as the source of all morality, so did Robespierre and Saint Just regard virtue as the ability to identity oneself immediately with the immense poverty and suffering of the majority of the French people. Virtue thus becomes a purely subjective capacity to sympathize with the plight of others, the *malheureux,* or the wretched of the earth. Robespierre's "republic of virtue" would henceforth turn its "compassionate zeal" on all those suspected of harboring an impure heart or a lack of identification with the nation as a whole. The irony of this situation is that it was precisely those people of superior moral sensitivity who were responsible for a wave of unprecedented ruthlessness and terror. And out of the mistrust of others, the revolutionaries came to mistrust their own motives. Recognizing with Pascal that the heart has "reasons that not even reason can know," the revolution could only end by devouring its own.

> Robespierre's insane lack of trust in others, even in his closest friends, sprang ultimately from his not so insane but quite normal suspicion of himself. Since his very credo forced him to play the "incorruptible" in public every day and to display his virtue, to open his heart as he understood it, at least once a week, how could he be sure that he was not the one thing he probably feared most in his life, a hypocrite?[94]

The failure of the French Revolution to create a cohesive republican order stemmed from its transformation of an essentially private conception

---

93. Allan Bloom, "Introduction," *Emile or On Education* (New York: Basic Books, 1979), p. 5.
94. Arendt, *On Revolution,* p. 92.

of virtue as sincerity into a test of citizenship. While Rousseau and his followers may have set out to politicize the private, they ended up by privatiz-
ing the political. The problem with this immense privatization of the
political, to repeat, is that it provides no external check or reference point
by which virtue can be judged. Consequently, it must be coerced and manipulated, ultimately by terror or, in Rousseau's phrase, one can be "forced
to be free." The failure of the experiment in radical republicanism was not
due to enemies of the people or to those harboring an impure heart, but
rather to a conception of civic virtue wrenched out of all social context.
Rousseau's answer to the question of how this context could be created
was to invoke those semimythical founders or "legislators," like Moses,
Romulus, and Theseus, who founded a people virtually ex nihilo. In the
final analysis, then, when the supporting institutions are lacking, the politics of virtue can only be a pose, and not a particularly attractive one at that.

Hegel's own account of the French Revolution appears to anticipate the
later "law" of revolutionary development. According to this law, a period of
popular energy and enthusiasm is inevitably followed by one of radical terror and revolutionary purity, only to be followed in turn by a call to restore
social order and hierarchy. Thus, Hegel describes how after the abortive
attempt to realize the general will, the period of reaction was bound to set
in. "These individuals," he says, "who felt the fear of death, their absolute
lord and master, submit to negation and distinction once more, arrange
themselves under the 'spheres' and return to a restricted and appor-
tioned task."[95]

What distinguishes Hegel's account of the restoration of state power
after the period of terror and suspicion is that it continues to draw heavily
not only on Rousseau but also on Machiavelli's usage of classical models in
both *The Prince* and *The Discourses.* In an early essay, *The German Constitution,* Hegel recommends *The Prince* especially as Machiavelli's treatise on
how political power is founded and maintained. Rather than moralizing
against Machiavelli as holding up "a golden mirror for an ambitious op-
pressor," Hegel remarks that "Machiavelli's fundamental aim of creating
Italy into a state was misunderstood from the start." When one reads *The
Prince,* not as "a compendium of moral and political principles applicable
indifferently to any and every situation, i.e. to none," but as a response to
"the centuries before . . . and the history of his own times," one will see
him less as a teacher of evil than as a teacher of popular liberty and freedom
from foreign domination. While Hegel admits that many of the actions rec-

95. *PhM,* p. 607; *Werke* 3:438.

ommended by Machiavelli would be "criminal" if carried out by private persons against one another, he still maintains that if such actions are in the service of state building rather than personal advantage one gains "a totally new complexion on the procedure of the prince." Machiavelli's work is in this respect "a great testimony to his age and to his own belief that the fate of a people which hastens to its political downfall can be averted by genius." Unfortunately, he concludes, "Machiavelli's voice has died away without effect."[96]

The same kind of praise can be found in the Jena *Philosophy of Mind,* in which Hegel turns his attention more explicitly to an analysis of the origins of state power. As in the earlier essay, Hegel is here thinking of a Rousseauist legislator or a Machiavellian prince who can found a state by a pure act of will. "All states are founded," Hegel says, "by the sublime acts of great men." Implicitly rejecting any social contract or voluntarist account of the state, Hegel maintains that the principle by which a state maintains its legitimacy in the present cannot be used to explain its origin. The general will is not the cause but the outcome of the state which owes its beginning to force alone. "In this way," he writes, "Theseus founded the Athenian state; also in this way during the French Revolution a terrible power held the state generally. This power is not despotism, but tyranny, pure terrifying power."[97]

Here is where Hegel introduces a concept that would later become central to his whole philosophy of history: the cunning of reason. For while all states have their origins in tyranny, the tyrant unwittingly prepares his subjects for freedom. In educating the people to obey a superior force, namely him, the tyrant makes possible the obedience to law and therefore brings about his own demise. In one of his more strikingly aphoristic passages, Hegel remarks, "Tyranny is overthrown by a people not because it is abominable, beastly, etc., but because it has become superfluous." If the tyrant is wise, he will step down voluntarily, but he rarely does, and he must usually be deposed by force. Such was the case with Robespierre, of whom Hegel says that "power abandoned him, because necessity abandoned him and so he was violently overthrown."[98] It is not, then, because of any intrinsic evil, but because it has simply ceased to serve its function, that tyranny is abolished.

Hegel's reflections on tyranny are the product of neither historical curi-

---

96. *PW,* pp. 220, 221, 222–23; *Werke* 1:555, 557, 558.
97. *JR,* p. 246.
98. *JR,* pp. 247–48.

osity nor mere wishful thinking that some modern tyrant would make Germany into a state. Rather, Hegel's Theseus represents a real and practical way of bringing about a modern rights-based state by means of Napoleon. Indeed, Napoleon was the restorer of the French state after its dissolution in the acid of revolutionary turmoil. While Napoleon is not explicitly mentioned in either the Jena *Philosophy of Mind,* or later in the *Phenomenology,* Hegel does express great enthusiasm for him on a number of occasions, mostly in his private correspondence during this period. Thus, in a letter to his friend Niethammer he says: "I saw the Emperor—this world soul [*Weltseele*]—come to the city for a reconnaissance. It is indeed marvelous to see, concentrated in one point, an individual who, sitting on a horse, overruns the world and conquers it."[99] And in another letter he makes the following observation:

> We speak a great deal about the unification of the various states of the Empire. The principal decision will doubtlessly come from Paris. . . . The German professors of constitutional law are still writing a great number of works on the idea of sovereignty and the meaning of Confederation. The great teacher of constitutional law [*der grosse Staatsrechtslehrer*], however, sits in Paris. . . . After the Württemberg Estates has been dissolved, Napoleon said to one Würtemberg Minister: "I made your master a sovereign, not a despot." The German princes have not yet grasped the idea of a free monarchy, nor have they even attempted to put it into practice—it will be necessary for Napoleon to organize these affairs.[100]

And later Hegel made the following comment upon learning of the introduction of the Code Napoleon into Germany: "The importance of the Code cannot be compared with the importance of the hope that other parts of the French and Westphalian constitutions will be introduced into Germany."[101]

The extent of Hegel's Bonapartism has been a subject of considerable dispute among Hegel's principal interpreters. The most extreme suggestion is that of Alexandre Kojève, for whom the Napoleonic empire makes possible for the first time in history the universal recognition of man as such. Only in the "universal and homogeneous state," as he calls it, can man be fully and completely "satisfied," for only here has the struggle for recognition come to an end. "This state, for the author of the *Phenomenology,* is Napoleon's Empire," Kojève writes. "And Napoleon himself is the wholly 'satisfied' Man, who, in and by his definitive Satisfaction, completes the

99. Letter to Niethammer, 13 October 1806, *Briefe* 1:120.
100. Letter to Neithammer, 29 August 1807, *Briefe* 1:185.
101. Letter to Niethammer, 11 February 1808, *Briefe* 1:218.

course of the historical evolution of humanity."[102] And yet, despite his evident admiration for Napoleon and the new historical era he inaugurated, Hegel sees in him merely an agent for a higher principle which transcends him and of which he is unaware. This principle is the liberal constitutional government based upon the recognition of human rights. But when the basis of this state has been laid, the work of the architect has been made redundant. Like the original Theseus, Napoleon, this modern tyrant, is fated to disappear from the scene which he has helped to prepare. Strictly speaking, it is not Napoleon but Hegel who comes at the end of history, since Hegel puts in conceptual form what Napoleon did. "The phenomenon that completes the historical evolution and thus makes the absolute Science possible, therefore, is the 'conception' (*Begreifen*) of Napoleon by Hegel," Kojève writes. "This dyad, formed by Napoleon and Hegel, is the perfect Man, fully and definitively 'satisfied' by what he *is* and by what he *knows* himself to be."[103]

Kojève overestimates the extent of Hegel's Bonapartism. Hegel was not so much concerned with Napoleon as he was with theorizing about a form of political association based on the substantive attributes of recognition and satisfaction. According to Michael Oakeshott, "Hegel was a philosopher, determined to understand everything in terms of its postulates. . . . And in the *Philosophy of Right* he was concerned not merely to characterize and recommend these [modern European] 'states' but to theorize the mode of association in terms of its postulates and to present it in its place in a philosophy of human association."[104] Precisely what these postulates are must now be examined.

102. Alexandre Kojève, *Introduction to the Reading of Hegel,* trans. James H. Nichols, Jr. (New York: Basic Books, 1969), p. 69.
103. Kojève, *Introduction to the Reading of Hegel,* p. 70.
104. Michael Oakeshott, *On Human Conduct* (Oxford: Clarendon Press, 1975), p. 257.

4 HEGEL'S THEORY OF RIGHTS

THE CONCEPT OF HUMAN RIGHTS AND ITS CRITICS

The concept of rights has recently undergone a revival in political philosophy. This might seem surprising, given that the concept of human or natural rights has until recently been regarded as hopelessly passé, useful perhaps for rhetorical purposes but outside the bounds of acceptable academic discourse. Indeed, the classic statement affirming the status of rights—"We hold these truths to be self-evident, that all men are created equal, that they are endowed by their Creator with certain unalienable Rights, that among these are Life, Liberty, and the Pursuit of Happiness"— is taken by many to be either meaningless or false. If self-evident is taken to mean true by virtue of the terms involved, it is not difficult to show that by no means have these rights appeared to be self-evident.[1]

Recently, though, the tide has begun to turn. We have been told to "take rights seriously" and that all human beings are endowed by virtue of their humanity with a set of absolute and inviolable moral claims that take precedence over all competing reasons or policies.[2] While rights claims, to be sure, are not scientifically demonstrable, they are thought to be morally necessary in the sense that without them we would have no grounds on which to attribute to the person an absolute and irreplaceable dignity. Furthermore, we would have no grounds for opposing policies that treat individuals as no more than an expression of an impersonal social aggregate to be used in any way that serves the collective ends of the state.

As valuable as the concept of rights is, the idea that an appeal to rights automatically "trumps" all other considerations remains questionable. First, it is circular. If a right belongs to us by virtue of a common humanity, it is by no means clear what is meant by the term *human*. If the term *human* is to be a term of distinction, it must mean something more than "born of human parents" (if this were not already a tautology), since we regularly

1. Leszek Kolakowski, "The Idolatry of Politics," *New Republic,* 16 June 1986, pp. 29–36.

2. John Rawls, *A Theory of Justice* (Cambridge, Mass.: Harvard University Press, 1971); Ronald Dworkin, *Taking Rights Seriously* (Cambridge, Mass.: Harvard University Press, 1977); Bruce Ackerman, *Social Justice and the Liberal State* (New Haven: Yale University Press, 1980).

deny rights to such persons as children, lunatics, and criminals. Second, it has been claimed with some justice that to talk of rights is really to talk about rights to certain things—a job, adequate health care, housing, and so on. Such goods are invariably bound up with a person's fundamental needs or interests, so if our interests are satisfied or protected, no further appeal to rights is necessary. Rights are just so much excess baggage derivative of the more primary needs that underlie them.

Third, to say, as certain theorists have done, that an appeal to human rights automatically trumps all other concerns leads to a false dichotomy between questions of rights and social utility. For reasons that we shall see later, Hegel explicitly rejects this dichotomy and trys to show that rights are not only an intrinsic property of persons but that they are useful for fostering a sense of social solidarity and community. In fact, to speak about rights is not to assert a simple proposition but is implicitly to make a complex set of interlocking claims that can be reduced to five parts: who shall enjoy which rights under what circumstances and for what purposes, and which kinds of restraints need to be imposed to make the enjoyment of those rights possible? An appeal to rights necessarily involves an appeal to the social and political institutions and practices that make the protection of rights possible.

The rehabilitation of human rights has gone hand in hand with the revival of the philosophy of liberalism. Indeed, it is probably not too much to say that the idea of rights forms the core of the Western liberal tradition. This is not to imply that the idea of rights has gone unopposed, but that by the end of the eighteenth century, the doctrine of rights had become the dominant strategy for legitimizing political institutions. Henceforth it would be impossible for regimes to legitimize themselves without some recognition of the rights of their subjects, which rights the regime was entrusted to protect and defend. The Declaration of Independence, which sought to derive the "just powers" of government from the consent of the governed, merely put the stamp of approval on what a century before John Locke had declared in the *Second Treatise of Government,* namely, that men are born free and equal in the state of nature, and that it is the purpose of government to secure for its citizens as large a degree of their natural freedom and equality in civil society as is compatible with their mutual safety, security, and protection.

Despite all of this, the concept of rights has remained problematic.[3] Documents such as the American Declaration of Independence, the French

3. For some of the controversies, see D. D. Raphael, ed., *Political Theory and the Rights of Man* (Bloomington: Indiana University Press, 1967); Richard Flathman, *The Practice of Rights*

Declaration of the Rights of Man and the Citizen, and the charter of the United Nations have been more concerned to enumerate lists of rights than to justify their ground. It is hardly any wonder, then, that with the vast proliferation of alleged social, economic, and cultural rights, the concept itself has come under attack from a variety of quarters. There are three dominant strategies for attacking doctrines of universal human rights.

Marxism   In "On the Jewish Question," Marx offered a critique of natural rights theories as being excessively individualistic and egoistic. A right involves claims that individuals make about their own interests; these claims in turn foster a preoccupation with the fulfillment of personal goals and desires rather than broader social objectives. The claiming of rights puts people into competitive adversarial situations in which each person seeks to promote his own interests at the expense of others. Thus, the idea of rights fosters a kind of possessive individualism which leads to the neglect of one's "species being," a vague term which Marx used to characterize the social or situated character of all human activity.[4]

Marx sought to give his critique of rights a sociological dimension. Rights for him were simply the juridical expression of the formal equality that already prevails between agents in a competitive market economy. Rather than being "natural," such rights arise out of, and correspond to, the mode of production under capitalism, where one finds the separation of "civil society" from the state. Doctrines of natural rights were, for Marx, merely efforts to confer a kind of timeless legitimacy on one historically specific form of society. Also, talk of rights was but a form of "ideology" by which the bourgeois class could conceal its true interests behind a cloak of universalism. Not only rights, but all talk of justice, morality, and the like were but "so many bourgeois prejudices behind which lurk in ambush just so many bourgeois interests."[5] The French Declaration of the Rights of Man struck Marx as an especially insidious example of the relation between political doctrine and social interests, with its reference to "the inviolable and sacred right" to property.

In short, Marx condemned policies according people merely "formal" or procedural rights where there still remained widespread social or material

(Cambridge: Cambridge University Press, 1976); A. J. M. Milne, *Human Rights and Human Diversity: An Essay in the Philosophy of Human Rights* (Albany: SUNY Press, 1986).

4. Karl Marx, "On the Jewish Question," *Marx-Engels Reader,* ed. Robert C. Tucker (New York: W. W. Norton, 1978), pp. 34–35, 39, 43, 46.

5. Karl Marx, "Communist Manifesto," *Marx-Engels Reader,* p. 482.

inequalities. His views were not unlike the barb attributed to Anatole France, who said that both the rich and the poor had an equal right to sleep under the bridges of Paris. While the doctrine of human rights represented an advance over feudalism, it still fell short of Marx's ideal of communism in which the juridical order would be transcended altogether. In his *Critique of the Gotha Programme,* he put it as follows:

> This *equal* right is an unequal right for unequal labour. It recognizes no class differences, because everyone is only a worker like everyone else; but it tacitly recognizes unequal individual endowment and thus productive capacity as natural privileges. *It is, therefore, a right of inequality, in its content, like every right.* Right by its very nature can consist only in the application of an equal standard; but unequal individuals . . . are measurable only by an equal standard in so far as they are brought under an equal point of view, are taken from one *definite* side only, for instance, in the present case, are regarded only *as workers* and nothing more is seen in them, everything else being ignored.[6]

Until such time, then, as the means of production can be socialized, men may have need for rights and rules of justice to regulate relations between them, but this remains only a stopgap until the new distributive principle of "from each according to his ability, to each according to his needs" can be institutionalized.

It is impossible here to discuss the Marxist case against rights in any depth, but two points seem especially worth making. First, Marx's critique depends upon some highly questionable assumptions about history as a process. As methodological individualists of various persuasions have shown, history is not a whole or an organic entity but is a series of localized particulars, with at best a set of contingent connections between them. Any attempt to import teleological considerations into history, then, can only be heuristic.[7] And second, Marx's critique of individual rights presupposes both the desirability and possibility of a society such that the need for rules of justice will be dispensable. Marx believed that such a society, based on universal amity and good will, would be possible only once the means of production had been taken out of private hands. Yet this claim is entirely afactual, in the sense that nothing we know about human beings bears upon the case. Marx's plan to abolish rights remains an empty possibility.

Utilitarianism   Another, equally powerful criticism of human rights is that offered by utilitarianism. In its classic formulation by Jeremy Bentham and

---

6. Karl Marx, "Critique of the Gotha Program," *Marx-Engels Reader,* pp. 530–31.
7. See Jon Elster, *Making Sense of Marx* (Cambridge: Cambridge University Press, 1985).

J. S. Mill, utilitarianism argues that an exclusive attention to individual rights leads to the neglect of "collective goods," and that the preferred way of justifying any social policy is through an appeal to the general welfare. The utilitarian rejection of individual rights derives what plausibility it has from the psychological assumption that in their ordinary lives, most people pursue what they feel gives them pleasure and avoid what they feel gives them pain; this being the case, it follows that the state should pursue only those policies that will bring the greatest happiness to the greatest number. As Mill put it in *On Liberty:* "I regard utility as the ultimate appeal on all ethical questions; but it must be utility in the largest sense, grounded on the permanent interests of man as a progressive being."[8]

The case against utilitarianism was given its classic formulation by Kant. According to him, to base moral principles on utility alone is to depreciate the dignity of the individual by turning him from an end to a means for the collective happiness of the whole. A utilitarian defense of liberty, such as that offered by Mill, ultimately leaves the individual helpless before a potentially capricious majority. By pursuing a policy of aggregating preferences, utilitarianism could sanction grievous harm to some if this could serve the "greatest happiness" or "permanent interests" of the majority. The claims not only of the isolated individual but also of minority groups within society were thus ill served by a utilitarian calculus of aggregation.

Relativism   Relativism starts from the premise that there are no inherent standards of rights or justice apart from the prevailing practices that already obtain in organized communities. Relativism is an ancient doctrine which goes back to Protagoras and the Greek Sophists, who used it to show that the conventions and moral norms of the community are independent of, if not opposed to, the stronger antisocial tendencies of human nature. In our own day, doctrines of moral relativism are associated with the so-called dualism of facts and values, first promulgated by David Hume. On this account, from a statement of what is the case there can be no valid inference to what ought to be. It follows, then, that natural laws of the sort established in the sciences are of a logically different order from moral norms that are decided upon or adhered to, but which vary from place to place.[9]

8. J. S. Mill, *On Liberty,* ed. David Spitz (New York: W. W. Norton, 1975), p. 12.
9. The literature on this issue is too large to address here, but for a sample, see W. D. Hudson, ed., *The Is-Ought Question* (London: Macmillan, 1969); John R. Searle, *Speech Acts: An Essay in the Philosophy of Language* (Cambridge: Cambridge University Press, 1970), chap. 8; Fred R. Dallmayr, *Twilight of Subjectivity: Contributions to a Post-Individualist Theory of Politics* (Amherst: University of Massachusetts Press, 1981), chap. 5.

The force of the relativist objection to human rights stems from its alleged insight into the diversity of cultures and ways of life. No one set of moral norms can be right for everyone, always and everywhere. Relativists from Burke and Herder to Oakeshott and Popper have argued that doctrines of universal human rights are simply too abstract to deal successfully with the contingencies of political life. For the relativist, what rights human beings enjoy stem, not from some purported state of nature stripped of all the influences of custom, tradition, and history, but from the ongoing communities of which human beings are a part. One can speak about the rights of Englishmen, Frenchmen, Americans, and so on, but the rights of man is an abstraction, and an illicit one at that.

The relativist critique of natural rights, with its appeal to the concrete particularities of history and tradition, has some undoubted appeal. In particular, it served to dampen the revolutionary appeal from existing, but imperfect, political orders in the here and now to some abstract rational or natural order in the beyond. Such appeals could not but destabilize existing polities, by showing them to fall short of the universal norms of rights and justice. Since any appeal to universal transcendent norms of justice would make us feel at least potentially "homeless" or alienated in the world, it was necessary to recover some sense of the concrete particularity of all rights.

Nevertheless, the claim that all moral claims and concepts are bound to local and particularist traditions had the effect of making it impossible to understand or criticize peoples and cultures other than our own. Relativism, which sought to make men feel more at home in the world, ended by creating an insularity of mind which made cross-cultural comparisons invalid. The result of relativism would be to render us silent before such moral atrocities as Communism, Nazism, and religious fanaticism, because they do not form part of our tradition. The relativist is led ultimately to a kind of moral nihilism or, in the words of one critic, "to the view that every preference, however evil, base, or insane, has to be judged before the tribunal of reason as legitimate as any other preference." [10]

THE SUBJECT OF RIGHTS

However familiar might be the claim that Hegel is a historical relativist for whom the standards of political judgment cannot be understood except as a product of the times, the fact remains that his major work of political philosophy is entitled the *Philosophy of Right*. As the title indi-

10. Leo Strauss, *Natural Right and History* (Chicago: University of Chicago Press, 1953), p. 42.

cates, Hegel was centrally concerned, not simply with the historical question of how the best or right regime is brought about, but with such traditional questions as the right or just ordering of political relationships. The book would seem to be intended as an analogue not only to modern works like Hobbes's *Leviathan* or Rousseau's *Social Contract,* but also to ancient studies like Plato's *Republic* or Aristotle's *Politics.*

Yet the appearance of tradition or continuity with the past is at least partially deceptive. The term "Right" in the title is ambiguous.[11] The German *Recht* can mean either "right" or "law," and the phrase "philosophy of right" has a peculiar ring to it that the phrase "philosophy of law" does not. Nevertheless, Hegel tends to reserve the term *Gesetz* for law in the narrow sense, when referring to civil or positive legal codes. It is preferable, then, to continue thinking of his book as an inquiry into *Recht,* indicating a form of human association in which persons are never treated merely as things, but enjoy a *sittlich* relationship to one another, bound together by relations of reciprocal recognition and respect.[12] *Recht* becomes something like the philosophical range of practical reason as embedded in historically immanent circumstances and institutions. Hegel himself gives credence to this view when he remarks that "[i]n speaking of Right [*Recht*] . . . we mean not merely what is generally meant by civil law, but also morality, ethical life. and world-history."[13]

Still, Hegel's meaning is not so much clarified as complicated, by a glance at the subtitle of the work, namely, *Natural Right and the Science of the State in Outline* (Naturrecht und Staatswissenschaft im Grundrisse). The first term, natural right, seems to point backward to the normative theory of right which has its origins in the philosophy of classical antiquity. But the second term, the science of the state, seems to confirm Hegel's status as a forerunner of legal positivism and the value-free study of politics of the nineteenth and twentieth centuries. It is scarcely any wonder that an early reviewer found Hegel's work to be marred by "great ambiguity, darkness, and misunderstanding."[14]

This distinction is complicated by another one. Hegel distinguishes not only between natural right and political science but also between civil so-

---

11. See Donald Maletz, "Hegel's 'Introduction' to the *Philosophy of Right Interpretation* 13 (1985): 68–69.

12. For this formulation I am indebted to Michael Oakeshott, *On Human Conduct* (Oxford: Clarendon Press, 1975), pp. 259–61.

13. *PR,* par. 33A, p. 233; *Werke* 7:90–91.

14. Manfred Riedel, ed., *Materialen zu Hegels Rechtsphilosophie* (Frankfurt: Suhrkamp, 1975), 1:111–12.

ciety and the state as a further specification of *Recht.* Whereas traditionally these concepts were treated synomymously, Hegel wants to separate out the realm of *bürgerliche Gesellschaft,* or the "economy" which caters to persons seeking the satisfaction of various contingent wants, needs, and desires, from *der Staat,* which refers to relations of authority which some individuals exercise over others, not by virtue of market transactions, but through the right of sufficient reason. While civil society comprehends the activity of the *Bürger,* or bourgeois, who as a private person engages in competitive struggles with others in the marketplace, the state is the realm of the citizen, who is related to others by certain shared ethical understandings or mutual recognition.

A partial clarification of Hegel's meaning is provided by a later addition appended to the preface to the *Philosophy of Right.* [15] Here he returns to the ancient sophistic distinction between nature (*physis*) and convention (*nomos*). There are, Hegel says, two kinds of law: those governing the natural world and those governing the ethico-political world. While the laws governing the natural world merely are what they are, independent of our thinking or willing, the positive laws governing the community and determining its standards of right and wrong, just and unjust, are the result of human art or contrivance. Hegel remarks that the standard for the laws governing physical nature is something "outside us," to which our knowledge adds nothing, but the laws of the community are "posited" (*gesetzt*) by the mind.

The discussion does not stop with the distinction between the things that are by nature and those that are by convention. The mere fact that civil or positive law is made by us does not render it immune from criticism. To the contrary: if these laws do not comply with our sense of what is right or just, a conflict emerges between what is and what ought to be. The conflict between the sheer existence of a law and its right to exist—to obligate—is unthinkable in the natural order. It is, however, a conflict that Hegel attributes to the very ground of right, that is, the human mind. Another way of stating this is to say that while the laws of nature are immutable, the laws of right have a history. Only those things with a history, the human things, can come into conflict or contradiction with themselves. It is the contradictory character of the very ground of right that Hegel, echoing Rousseau, says "seems" to be the source of human "discontent and unhappiness."

---

15. *PR*, pp. 224–25; *Werke* 7 : 15–17; see also Manfred Riedel, *Between Tradition and Revolution: The Hegelian Transformation of Political Philosophy,* trans. Walter Wright (Cambridge: Cambridge University Press, 1984), pp. 57–59.

The task that Hegel sets for himself, then, is the reexamination of the very "fundamentals of right." This reexamination is, he implies, more important now than at any other time in the past. The "ancients," unlike ourselves, respected the law in an immediate, habitual manner. They did not feel the need to ask questions like "why ought I to obey the law?" or "what makes this law binding on me?" They merely obeyed the law on the basis of a naive trust in the goodness or naturalness of custom and tradition. The question of measuring the law against some external standard of right or justice simply did not exist as an option prior to the rise of philosophy with Socrates and the Sophists.

For the "moderns" all of this changes. Beginning with Hobbes, but developed explicitly by Rousseau, Kant, and Fichte, "theories are set over against the existent and are intended to appear as absolutely correct and necessary." Modern theories of right presuppose a distinction between the self and its environment. The ability to make this distinction Hegel regards not only as the decisive advance in self-consciousness but also as destructive of the earlier ethical fabric of society. The implication here is that the modern doctrines of right associated with Hobbes, Rousseau, and Kant set themselves in opposition to the old localist and particularist traditions by appealing to certain putatively universal and necessary features of human beings as such. Furthermore, the modern theories owe their greatest advances to the modern science of nature, which succeeded in demystifying the older mythological and religious idea of the universe.

Hegel's conception of rights is bound up with the nonteleological science of nature which it presupposes as its background. Unlike ancient and medieval writers, who could infer the proper ordering of human relations from their place within the whole, Hegel follows the lead of Hobbes, Rousseau, and Kant in denying that there are any natural ends or purposes there to be discovered. There is no graduated scale of nature in which there is a place for everything and everything has its place. Rather, Hegel assumes the triumph of the principles of modern natural science, which had emptied the world of all telos or meaning and left the moral subject free to construct his own order of right and justice. Nature provides no clues or evidence for how the moral order should be constructed. It is this fact that ultimately renders the term "natural right" so equivocal, since "nature is not free and therefore is neither just nor unjust." [16]

This leads me to my first thesis about rights, namely, that they have their

16. *PR*, par. 49R, p. 44; *Werke* 7:113.

ground (*Boden*) in the individual subject, or *Wille*, who distinguishes himself from the rest of external nature.[17] Hegel's starting point here is the minimal, or "thin," theory of the subject. Hegel's theory of the subject helps to situate his doctrine within the modern individualist and voluntarist tradition that goes back to Hobbes in the seventeenth century. What characterized Hobbes and the whole modern "idiom of individuality" is that politics was seen less as a collective activity aimed at a single end than as an engagement among human beings who are related to one another by ties of legal justice.[18] While Plato and Aristotle regarded man as the "political animal" and thus avoided the question of political obligation altogether, modern voluntarist thinkers from Hobbes onwards could deny the legitimacy of any law or institution that did not derive from the consent (tacit or expressed) of those to whom it applied.[19]

Hegel's concept of right takes the form of a phenomenology of the moral will. The will is simply the way the mind functions when it functions practically, as opposed to theoretically. The first moment or "determination" (*Bestimmung*) of the will is defined by an abstraction from all content, from everything empirical or given. What is left is the purely "negative will," the pure "I" which is characterized by a capacity for freedom. Hegel tries to explicate the freedom or self-determination of the will by an analogy to the sciences of nature:

> Freedom, I mean, is just as fundamental a character of the will as weight is of bodies. If we say: matter is 'heavy', we might mean that this predicate is only contingent; but it is nothing of the kind, for nothing in matter is without weight. Matter is rather weight itself. Heaviness constitutes the body and is the body. The same is the case with freedom and the will, since the free entity is the will. Will without freedom is an empty word, while freedom is actual only as will, as subject.[20]

One might assume from the above that the concept of freedom would result in nihilism, the condition in which anything goes. Hegel even implies as much when he remarks that "only in destroying something does this negative will possess the feeling of itself as existent." He refers further to

---

17. *PR*, par. 4, p. 20; *Werke* 7:46.

18. Michael Oakeshott, *Rationalism in Politics and Other Essays* (London: Methuen, 1962), pp. 249–51.

19. See Stephen Salkever, "Virtue, Obligation, and Politics," *American Political Science Review* 68 (1974):78–92.

20. *PR*, par. 4A, p. 226; *Werke* 7:46.

"the fanaticism of the Hindu pure contemplation" and the "universal equality" pursued by the French Revolution as evidence of the nihilistic goals of this purely negative freedom. It is the freedom identified with arbitrary choice (*Willkür*), rather than with concrete freedom under law. But while negative freedom has produced the "maximum of frightfulness and terror" and as such is a source of contemporary irrationalism, Hegel also maintains that the will has the resources to provide out of itself a new purified order of right and justice.[21]

The need for some kind of self-limitation leads to the second Hegelian thesis about the will's activity. The need for limits is not a contradiction of freedom but is essential to it. Freedom does not imply a world ungoverned by any regulative principles but a world inhabited by subjects capable of supplying these principles themselves. Willing is not, then, an arbitrary activity, but already implies some minimal notion of a meaningful way of life within which willing and choosing can take place. Hegel's point is that willing presupposes a community of wills or rational agents whom we cannot choose to be without. Willing is never an isolated activity but always takes place within the context of a plurality of wills. It is the irreducible plurality of the human condition that makes willing a transaction between subjects, an *I* and a *we* or, as he put it in the *Phenomenology,* between "an I that is a we . . . and a we that is an I."[22]

The subject of rights is, then, the rational will (*vernünftige Wille*) which Hegel characterizes as "self-determining universality."[23] So long as we understand the will to mean "arbitrariness" it is not really free. For reasons not unlike those of Rousseau and Kant, Hegel believed that such a view of freedom generally meant no more than slavery to certain desires or passions of the soul. When the will's content is "immediate," that is, some first-order desire, it is free only "*in* itself."[24] The self-determination of the arbitrary will is a "moment" of freedom but not yet developed rational liberty. The moral will is characterized not just by a capacity for free choice but by deliberation and reflection. While the arbitrary will may be able to pursue various impulses and desires, it has not yet attained control over its impulses and desires. Moral freedom contains the capacity not just to desire but also to reflect evaluatively upon the kinds of things we ought to desire. It contains, in the last instance, the capacity to select and evaluate

21. *PR,* par. 5R, p. 22; *Werke* 7:50.
22. *PhM,* p. 227; *Werke* 3:145.
23. *PR,* par. 11, p. 25; *Werke* 7:62.
24. *PR,* par. 15R, p. 27; *Werke* 7:66.

desires. The will understood as mere negative or arbitrary freedom, then, can never be more than the Hobbesian "last appetite in deliberation."[25]

The question that Hegel must answer to escape these problems is, what is the particular content of the will and to what can it attach itself? The idea that human rights belong to the individual as such appears to ignore the social basis of personality, that we are socially constituted in a variety of complex ways. His answer to this question is that by concentrating on the first aspect of the will—its ability to distinguish and distance itself from all content—his early modern predecessors forgot that willing is also a tele-ological or purposive activity. To will is not merely to declare one's inde-pendence; it is to will something, something with a determinate content. Here Hegel takes issue with Kant and other voluntarists, for whom freedom is equated with self-legislation. The will, for Hegel, is free rather when it wills the proper or appropriate things—when it wills what it ought to will. In Kantian terms, this introduces an irreducible element of heteronomy into Hegel's conception of the will, because to prescribe some proper or appropriate end for the will is to limit its autonomy. But, as we have seen, for Hegel, will without some content is an "empty formalism." He appears here to return to an older position, given its classic formulation by Aris-totle, that every human deliberate action is performed for the sake of some end to be brought about in the future. It is in "the nature of mind" (*die Natur des Geistes*), a phrase with obvious Aristotelian overtones, to express itself in specific institutions and activities.[26]

Hegel's differences with Kant may, at least on this point, be more appar-ent than real. Hegel writes as if the Kantian emphasis on autonomy and self-legislation were equivalent to acting on mere whim or caprice. But this is to misunderstand Kant. As we saw earlier, Kant's conception of the moral life rests on the capacity to universalize or to give our moral principles the force of law. Kant goes so far as to suggest that acting morally is equivalent to acting from the "laws of freedom." This will, of course, appear paradox-ical if we regard freedom and lawfulness not as complimentary but as an-tagonistic to one another. But Kant here follows Rousseau in suggesting that freedom is only achieved under the rule of law. Freedom does not mean the absence of necessity but the recognition of necessity of a moral kind. Moral necessity is, for Kant, the unique human power not just to follow but to

25. Thomas Hobbes, *Leviathan,* ed. M. Oakeshott (London: Macmillan, 1962), chap. 6, p. 54.

26. Charles Taylor, *Hegel and Modern Society* (Cambridge: Cambridge University Press, 1979), p. 76, n. 2

make law. And obedience to the moral law is not a limitation on freedom but a condition for it.

The test of universalization seems to provide the kind of formal impersonality that moral justification requires. What this means is that what I may be morally called upon to do in a given situation is not to be peculiar to my private moods, capacities, or talents but would have to be universally binding on anyone so situated. Only when laws can be made equally and indifferently applicable to everyone do they satisfy the test of universality that Kant took to be central to the moral point of view. Thus, the first and most famous formulation of the universalization principle reads: "Act only on that maxim through which you can at the same time will that it should become a universal law."[27]

Kant's conception of the moral life, then, rests upon the will's ability to universalize the principles of its actions. But universalization, as we have seen, has often been interpreted to imply sheer consistency. And as Hegel argued in *Natural Law,* the principle of noncontradiction alone is insufficient to guarantee the morality of our actions. Indeed, by placing almost exclusive emphasis on the "good will" as the core of moral virtue, Kant perhaps unwittingly helped to promote the impression that his theory was indifferent to questions of ends.[28] What Kant opposed was the view that the moral worth of an action resides in its consequences or results. To argue that morality consists in achieving some specific end or purpose would be to demote the absolute goodness of the good will. The will would be valued as an efficient cause of good actions but not as an end in itself. While Kant was not deaf to matters of expertise and moral competence, he refused to succumb to their charms.

In order to clear himself of the charge of "empty formalism," Kant sought to wed his standard of universalization to a doctrine of "objective ends." Kant's doctrine of ends imposes on us the duty to treat all others with the same respect as we would hope to receive in return. It is not inappropriately regarded as a secularized formulation of the Golden Rule. It is secular because the source of goodness is nothing outside of us but emanates from our rational nature. The conclusion that Kant arrives at, then, is that "man and in general, every rational being exists as an end in himself and not merely as a means to be arbitrarily used by this or than will." Or as

27. Immanuel Kant, *Groundwork of the Metaphysic of Morals,* trans. H. J. Paton (New York: Harper & Row, 1964), p. 88.

28. That Kant was indifferent to ends is a prejudice widely held by the many neo-Kantians (Rawls, etc.) who have invoked him as an authority and by the many others (Sandel, MacIntyre, etc.) who have rejected Kant, but without questioning the validity of the stereotype.

he says later: "Act in such a way that you always treat humanity, whether in your own person or in the person of any other, never simply as a means, but always at the same time as an end."[29]

The difference between Kant and Hegel, then, turns on their respective theories of objective ends. For Kant, the ends of moral action do not indicate some condition in the world not yet in existence but for the sake of which our actions are performed. This is the formula of the older Aristotelian teleology that makes actions instrumental to some good yet to be achieved. To view moral action as a means is, for Kant, already to deny its status as moral. Rather, for Kant the end to be achieved is not something extrinsic to action but is already "there" in us as part of our "rational nature." Treating people as ends mandates treating them with respect—as having intrinsic value or worth. Humans should be treated as ends because we are the only creatures capable of shaping and pursuing ends.[30] While one has to turn to the *Tugendlehre*, the second part of the *Metaphysic of Morals*, to discover exactly what kinds of obligations are entailed by this injunction to treat humanity as an end in itself, we can see already that this might serve as a negative pole for ruling out certain kinds of institutions and practices. For example, murder, theft, slavery, and adultery would all be excluded by Kant's criterion. To treat others as ends means treating them, not as means for the attainment of one's own private satisfactions, but as free and equal partners in a "kingdom of ends," a moral community of free, self-legislating agents.

The ground of the difference between Kant and Hegel is not, as is so often believed, that Kant's theory is deontological while Hegel's is teleological. Their theories are both teleological, but in different senses of the term. While Kant regarded the moral will as part of our "rational nature," as a "self-subsistent end" or a "fact of reason," Hegel regarded it very much as a specific historical accomplishment, something with a more pronounced developmental component to it. The will is not something prior to its actions. Put another way, a person cannot be totally detached from the kinds of commitments he has made. The will is always embedded in real life in an objective world of political and legal institutions which reach their fruition in the idea of the state.[31]

The will that Hegel theorizes in the *Philosophy of Right*, then, is not a homogeneous desocialized self but rather one that achieves its realization,

29. Kant, *Groundwork*, pp. 95, 96.

30. Immanuel Kant, *The Doctrine of Virtue: Part 2 of the Metaphysic of Morals*, trans. Mary J. Gregor (Philadelphia: University of Pennsylvania Press, 1971), pp. 45–46, 51.

31. *PR*, par. 75A, p. 242; *Werke* 7:159.

or "substantive end," only in the state. Now to say that the will becomes rational and free only in the state is, to be sure, hard doctrine. Hegel's infamous remark that the state is "mind on earth" and the "march of God in the world" seems inimical to any conception of individual rights.[32] His *étatisme* allegedly identifies freedom with obedience to the police. But what Hegel means by the state need carry none of these notorious implications. The Hegelian state is above all an organization of laws, a *Rechtsstaat*. Law is what purges the state of caprice and makes possible such modern freedoms as contract and property, career choice, religion, and speech. The result, as we shall see later, is by no means some irrational state worship, but the deepening of a recognition or respect for the wishes and ways of life of others, a manner of behavior that could be called civility.

The core of the modern state is, then, respect for the person, or "free personality," as such. This is very different, for example, from the Greek world, where, according to Hegel's own investigations, the individual had not yet learned to distinguish himself from his environment but lived in an "immediate" condition of trust or faith with his surroundings. As his interpretation of the story of *Antigone* demonstrates, the Greeks simply did not think of themselves as individual subjects capable of choice and deliberation but rather as "accidents" of certain all-powerful substances which had already sealed their fates in advance.[33] It is the exercise of the will, of the critical intelligence, the desire to be in everything that we do, that most clearly distinguishes ancient from modern freedom. The "I will" which accompanies all our actions is for Hegel the *differentia specifica* of modern freedom:

> [E]ven in the beautiful democracy of Athens . . . we cannot help noticing that the Greeks derived their final decisions from the observation of quite external phenomena such as oracles, the entrails of sacrificial animals, and the flight of birds. . . . At that time, self-consciousness had not yet advanced to the abstraction of subjectivity, not even so far as to understand that, when a decision is made, an "I will" must be pronounced by man himself. This "I will" constitutes the great difference between the ancient world and the modern, and in the great edifice of the state it must therefore have its appropriate objective existence.[34]

This leads us to a third thesis concerning the will which helps to distinguish Hegel from others in the individualist and voluntarist tradition. For

---

32. *PR*, par. 258A, p. 279; *Werke* 7:403. The offending phrase actually reads: "es ist der Gang Gottes in der Welt, dass der Staat ist . . ."
33. See George Steiner, *Antigones* (Oxford: Clarendon Press, 1946), pp. 19–42.
34. *PR*, par. 279A, p. 288; *Werke* 7:449.

Hegel, the will is not a "natural" property that belongs to persons as such, as Hobbes believed. Rather, the will is a product of history which belongs only to particular peoples and cultures. Hegel's official account of the transition from the world of "substantive customary morality" to the modern critical, reflective culture turns on the liberation of the will from earlier ethico-political restraints. Whereas the Greeks tended to see themselves as accidents of certain eternal entities, we tend to see ourselves primarily as individuals endowed with equal rights and dignity. Aristotle's statement in book 1 of the *Politics*—that "man is by nature a political animal" and that "he who is without a city [*apolis*] through nature rather than chance is either a mean sort or a being superior to man," like "the 'clanless, lawless, heartless' man reviled by Homer"—is but the classic statement of the substantialist metaphysics underlying the ancient world.[35]

The ancients, in other words, knew nothing of the independence and autonomy of the individual from the community. Thus, in the *Philosophy of Right,* Hegel can say that while in "the states of classical antiquity, universality was present, but particularity had not then been released, given free scope. . . . The essence of the modern state is that the universal be bound up with the complete freedom of its particular members and with private well-being," and that "the universal end cannot be advanced without the personal knowledge and will of its particular members, whose own rights must be maintained."[36]

The difference, then, between the ancient polis and the modern state is that far from recognizing the individual moral autonomy of each of its members, the polis was virtually the textbook case of a tutelary community based on a shared moral understanding and directed toward a specific way of life. This conception of a closed homogeneous society was given its profoundest expression in Plato's *Republic,* which Hegel sees as "nothing but an interpretation of the nature of Greek ethical life." Unlike Socrates, whom Hegel saw as a moral skeptic questioning all traditional values and institutions, Plato sought to close the lid on the Pandora's box opened by his teacher by requiring restraints on marriage, family, and property. While Hegel commends Plato's "genius" for recognizing that "there was breaking into that life in his own time a deeper principle which could appear in it . . . only as something corruptive," his proposal "did fatal injury to the deeper impulse which underlay it, namely free infinite personality."[37]

35. Aristotle, *Politics* 1253a.
36. *PR,* par. 260A, p. 280; *Werke* 7:407.
37. *PR,* p. 10; *Werke* 7:24.

The oppressive character of Plato's *Republic* is typically contrasted by Hegel to the principle of the will or the "infinite personality" that is recognized by the modern state. The person largely responsible for this principle is Rousseau, who in paragraph 258 of the *Philosophy of Right* is congratulated for "adducing the will as the principle of the state" and "not a principle like gregarious instinct, for instance, or divine authority."[38] The reference to Rousseau here is by no means accidental. Hegel frequently singles out Plato and Rousseau as the two thinkers most characteristic of ancient substantialism and modern subjectivity, respectively. What distinguishes the one from the other is precisely the emphasis on the will and individual consent as the core of political obligation. In Plato's *Republic,* "the subjective end simply coincided with the state's will. In modern times . . . we make claims for private judgment, private willing, and private conscience. The ancients had none of these in the modern sense; the ultimate thing with them was the will of the state."[39] And while in his early writings Hegel had depreciated the emphasis on property and choice of purely private goals, he now reverses himself. "In Plato's state, subjective freedom does not count, because people have their occupations assigned to them by the Guardians. . . . But subjective freedom, which must be respected, demands that individuals should have free choice in this matter."[40]

The phenomenon of the will, of individual self-awareness, is the minimum necessary condition for a theory of rights. But unlike earlier theorists of natural rights, who simply assumed that all men everywhere are entitled to rights, Hegel regards the emergence of rights as profoundly problematic. Rights are only predicable of individual subjects, and the emergence of the subject presupposed the death of the ancient world. However, the development of the individual subject took many and varied forms, from the "unhappy consciousness" of medieval Christianity, to the Protestant Reformation, which Hegel calls a "second world historical shape," for declaring man's emancipation from all institutions that do not recognize "our inalienable right" of self-legislation, and finally to the French Revolution and the emergence of a modern market economy. Rights, then, are not simply given, but are part of a larger historical struggle of human beings to achieve, or to become worthy of, respect or recognition. Without some account of the emergence of rights, the concept itself will remain insecure.

38. *PR,* par. 258R, pp. 156–57; *Werke* 7:400.
39. *PR,* par. 261A, p. 280; *Werke* 7:410.
40. *PR,* par. 262A, p. 280; *Werke* 7:410.

THE ORIGIN OF RIGHTS

It is practically a cliché that Hegel rejected the state of nature and social contract theories of his early modern predecessors. Their "abstract" individualism and lack of attention to the dynamic, developmental features of history are their most frequently cited deficiencies. What is less often noted, however, is that Hegel himself used a crypto-state-of-nature teaching to derive his theory of rights. The account of the "idea of right" in the *Philosophy of Right* presupposes the famous "struggle for recognition" given expression in the opening pages of the chapter, "Self-Consciousness," in the *Phenomenology* and his later clarification of this theme in the *Encyclopedia* version of the *Philosophy of Mind*. Every bit as much as Hobbes or any other contractarian, Hegel explains the origins of rights by reference to a putatively natural condition which is one of maximum conflict and insecurity. Political life is not natural to men but a requirement to rectify the inadequacies of nature.

Hegel presents the emergence of rights as originating in the desire (*Begierde*) of two individuals, each seeking some sign of recognition from the other. Hegel infers the desire for recognition from the very nature of self-consciousness. The mind that desires to know everything desires first of all to know itself. This is not to say that the desire for self-knowledge comes temporally first; rather it means that without self-knowledge no other kind of knowledge is really complete. The maxim "know thyself," inscribed on the Greek temple at Delphi, was adopted by several theorists of the modern age. Hobbes invoked it to show that knowledge of the passions that lead to conflict is the most important kind of knowledge, and Rousseau recalled it as a motive to recover our origins before the accidents of history alienated us from our true selves.[41] Hegel invokes self-knowledge as a way to ground his theory of rights. Self-knowledge is not only desirable in itself but is a critical condition without which no other knowledge can be securely based.

But how is this knowledge acquired? Hegel's answer is that we come to know ourselves not through isolated introspection in the manner of a Descartes but only through interaction with others. Our minds are led to reflect back upon themselves only after experiencing those around us. "Self-consciousness," he writes, "exists in and for itself . . . . by the fact that

41. See Hobbes, "Author's Introduction," *Leviathan,* p. 20; Rousseau, *Origins of Inequality,* p. 91.

it so exists for another self-consciousness; that is to say, it is only being acknowledged or 'recognized.'"⁴² The view of the self developed here could be called relational insofar as it sees us as parts of complex systems of mutual interaction which determine our identities.

This desire for recognition is, for Hegel, the quintessentially human desire. Hegel of course understands that the simplest form of desire is the desire to satisfy some basic corporeal need, hunger, for example. But if we acted only to satisfy our biological urges, human existence would never rise above the state of nature. Obviously, then, the satisfaction of basic animal needs for warmth, food, and protection is a necessary but not a sufficient condition for the fulfillment or satisfaction of our truly human needs.⁴³ Like Rousseau in the *Second Discourse,* Hegel is impressed by the elasticity of our desires. We are instinctually underdetermined. While the desire for food may be universal, there is a great deal of room left to determine how we should eat, when, where, and with whom. Furthermore, there is virtually nothing that cannot become an object of our desires. To use a vocabulary which is not Hegel's own (but which does not do violence to his meaning), it is because man has the capacity to desire not only natural objects but nonnatural objects or values as well, that he is able to rise above the level of the animals and become human. Our desires are not the product of sheer instinct but of will and reflection; they are intentional desires in much the way elaborated by H. P. Grice and others.⁴⁴ Alexandre Kojève offers a particularly clear account of Hegel's antinaturalism: "It is human to desire what others desire, because they desire it. Thus an object perfectly useless from the biological point of view (such as a medal, or the enemy's flag) can be desired because it is the object of other desire."⁴⁵ There comes a time when a man is no longer satisfied with the appropriation of external things as the objects of desire but desires the desire of another. This kind of desire can only be satisfied through an association or community with other desires.

Hegel's concern could be put in the following terms. We begin with some object of immediate desire. Such an object is here conceived as part of a means to the fulfillment of some specifiable end. It is the kind of desire attributed to all of us (all of the time) by Hobbes when he wrote that "felic-

42. *PhM,* p. 229; *Werke* 3:145: "Das Selbstbewusstsein ist *an* und *für sich,* indem und dadurch, dass es für ein Anderes an und für sich ist; d.h. es ist nurals ein Anerkanntes."

43. My reading here is very much indebted to Alexandre Kojève, *Introduction to the Reading of Hegel,* trans. James H. Nichols, Jr. (New York: Basic Books, 1969), although my differences with Kojève will be clear.

44. H. P. Grice, "Meaning," *Philosophical Review* 66 (1957): 377–88.

45. Kojève, *Introduction to the Reading of Hegel,* p. 6.

ity is a continual progress of the desire, from one object to another, the attaining of the former, being still but the way to the latter."[46] But unlike Hobbes (and later utilitarian writers), Hegel does not stop here. Human beings not only have desires of various kinds; they have desires to have desires. Our identities are not fixed in stone; we can desire to have identities of a particular sort. Thus, we have the capacity to stand back from our desires and ask ourselves whether they are the desires we want to have. It is this desire to desire, or what Harry Frankfurt has called "second-order desires" that is the distinctive mark of human rationality: "Human beings are not alone in having desires and motives, or in making choices. They share these things with members of certain other species, some of which even appear to engage in deliberation and to make decisions based on prior thought. It seems to be peculiarly characteristic of humans, however, that they are able to form . . . second-order desires."[47]

It is our capacity, then, for entertaining these second-order desires that leads us out of the infinite regress implied by Hobbes, where every desire is simply a means to another desire. For the desire for recognition is a desire unlike others. It is a socially mediated desire insofar as the enjoyment of respect depends upon gaining the approbation of others. Unlike, say, the desire for a new car which can be enjoyed independently of our social worth, the desire for recognition involves a desire that we come to be seen in a certain way, namely, as persons worthy of recognition. The desire to be recognized is not just another desire that we happen to have; it is the core human desire, central to our sense of well-being, our sense of who and what we are. We are beings, Hegel implies, who are not just constituted by a desire for comfort, safety, and security, but who cannot live, or at least cannot live well, if our desire for recognition is not respected by those around us. What we desire above all is to be treated with a sense of decency and respect. Such treatment is necessary for our basic sense of self-respect. As we shall see later, this desire for recognition is the standard by which to judge the adequacy of our political institutions and the quality of our civic life.

The problem, as Hegel describes it, is that at least initially the recognition or respect to which each believes himself entitled is not immediately forthcoming. Each wants to be recognized without in turn having to grant recognition to the other, and this one-sided and unequal state of affairs

---

46. Hobbes, *Leviathan*, chap. 11, p. 80.

47. Harry Frankfurt, "Freedom of the Will and the Concept of a Person," *Journal of Philosophy* 67 (1971):6.

leads men to enter a life and death struggle, not unlike what Hobbes described as a *bellum omnium contra omnes*. It is from this life-and-death struggle (*Kampf*), in which man's passion for honor and prestige is asserted over his fear and terror at the possibility of violent death, that the all-important relationship between master and slave arises. It arises because in the struggle one of the parties is unwilling to go all the way and risk his life for the sake of recognition, thereby submitting to the other, granting recognition without requiring it in turn. In short, the vanquished subordinates his own desire for esteem to his stronger desire for self-preservation. In the exceptionally lucid account he gives in the *Encyclopedia*, Hegel writes:

> But because life is as requisite as liberty to the solution, the fight ends in the first instance as a one-sided negation with inequality. While the one combatant prefers life, retains his single self-consciousness, but surrenders his claim for recognition, the other holds fast to his self-assertion and is recognized by the former as his superior. Thus arises the status of *master and slave*.[48]

Like Aristotle before him and Nietzsche later, Hegel disputes the standard liberal account that regards the origins of society as a consensus of men who are already free, equal, and rational. Freedom, rights, and mutual recognition are the ends for which politics exists; they cannot be presupposed as its cause. For Hegel, civil association has its origins in the difference between the prideful and self-assertive few and the timid and fearful many. Yet even though this may be the origin of human association, like Rousseau, Hegel denies that conquest can ever produce right: "To prevent any possible misunderstandings . . . we must here remark that the fight for recognition pushed to the extreme here indicated can only occur in the natural state, where men exist only as single, separate individuals; but it is absent in civil society and the state because here the recognition for which the combatants fought already exists."[49] Or, as he says later:

> In the battle for recognition and the subjugation under a master, we see, on their phenomenal side, the emergence of man's social life and the commencement of political union. *Force [Gewalt]*, which is the basis of this phenomenon, is not on that account a basis of right, but only the necessary and legitimate factor in the passage from the state of self-consciousness sunk in appetite and selfish isolation into the state of universal self-consciousness. Force, then, is the external or phenomenal commencement of states, not their underlying and essential principle.[50]

48. *PM,* par. 433, p. 173; *Werke* 10:222–23.
49. *PM,* par. 432A, p. 172; *Werke* 10:221.
50. *PM,* par. 433, pp. 173–74; *Werke* 10:223.

Hegel's account of the resolution of this struggle for recognition seems almost like a parody of Aristotle's account of slavery in book 1 of the *Politics*. For Aristotle, slavery was justified because it was the political institution that corresponded most closely to the natural hierarchy or inequality between the body and soul. Just as it is the function of the soul to rule or govern the body, so is it the function of the slave to free from a life of drudgery and toil those few men who are capable of engaging in political activity and philosophy. If nature provides a model or paradigm for our institutions, then slavery has its origins in human nature itself. Aristotle, of course, uses his doctrine of natural slavery to show that not all existing slaves are in fact slaves by nature, as many have been taken prisoners in war. Yet elsewhere he argues that just as the soul and body can work together to produce a well-functioning or healthy individual, so too is there a kind of common interest and even freindship between a master and a slave.

Hegel turns the Aristotelian account on its head. The conceptual basis for slavery is the need of one self-conscious mind to be recognized by another. In the ensuing struggle, the vanquished grants recognition to his lord by the very fact that he is forced to work in his service. The master's enjoyment is predicated upon his freedom from work. However, the recognition which the master now enjoys is not accorded by an equal but by a degraded tool who is merely employed to satisfy his lord's material comforts. The master, ironically, finds himself in the same position as that occupied by Aristotle's "great-souled man," who desires honor and recognition above all else, but finds it unworthy of him once it has been bestowed. The master is somehow greater than any sign of recognition he may receive. Furthermore, rather than having attained a level of contemplative autonomy and self-sufficiency, the master comes to realize his dependence upon the slave for the satisfaction of his desires. He is not, as he believed himself to be, a "being for himself." He is, in fact, a "being for another."[51]

This change in the self-consciousness of the master finds a corresponding change on the part of the slave. Through a strange dialectical twist, it is the fearful slave who becomes the mover of humanity toward a deeper level of self-awareness. The slave had initially accepted his position out of fear of death, but through labor (*Arbeit*) he learns to conquer and discipline this fear and in the process develops a sense of his own worth. Labor is not conceived here as the Biblical curse of Adam but as the basis for all histori-

---

51. See my article, "Goodness, Nobility, and Virtue in Aristotle's Political Science," *Polity* 19 (1986): 5–26.

cal change. Through work the slave transforms nature into a specifically human world, a world of culture (*Bildung*). But this is not all. Through work the slave not only humanizes nature; he humanizes himself as well. His labor educates him beyond the level of instinctual immediacy and prepares him for a life of citizenship as a possessor of rights. Here again Kojève may serve as our guide: "Work is *Bildung* in the double sense of the word: on the one hand, it forms, transforms the world, humanizes it by making it more adapted to Man; on the other, it transforms, forms, educates man, it humanizes him by bringing him into greater conformity with the idea that he has of himself."[52] Indeed, there is an etymological kinship between the German word for culture, *Bildung,* and the word for shape or form, *Bild.* Culture is a process of formation or cultivation of a human being.

The role of labor, then, is central in the transformation of natural man into a moral agent capable of possessing rights. Labor is for Hegel an "expressive" activity where we not only interact with a world of material objects (*Gegenstände*) in a causal way but in the course of that interaction develop our own distinctive capacities, skills, and dispositions. Labor is primarily a means of self-realization, whereby things with no point or purpose come to take on the purposes of their creators. In this respect, Hegel is one not only with Fichte but with the whole modern tradition of natural right, in putting a higher value on making or fabricating, what the Greeks called poiesis, than on acting or doing, praxis.[53] Clearly Marx was not altogether off the mark when he said: "Hegel's standpoint is that of modern political economy. He conceives labor as the essence, the self-confirming essence of man."[54] Or when Hegel says that a thing has no end of its own but "derives its destiny and soul for [its maker's] will," the "redemptive tone," as Alan Ryan has said, is marked.[55]

Two points can now be made. First, unlike Hegel's Marxist interpreters, Hegel considered labor fundamentally an intentional activity. It is an expression of the will or free personality and cannot be reduced to more rudimentary material sources like external pressures or bodily needs. For the Marxist, intentionality is ultimately illusory, whereas for Hegel it is the dis-

---

52. Kojève, *Introduction to the Reading of Hegel*, p. 52.

53. See Manfred Riedel, *Theorie und Praxis im Denken Hegels* (Stuttgart: Kohlhammer, 1965).

54. Karl Marx, "Economic and Philosophic Manuscripts of 1844," *Marx-Engels Reader,* p. 112.

55. Alan Ryan, "Hegel on Work, Ownership, and Citizenship," in *The State and Civil Society: Studies in Hegel's Political Philosophy,* ed. Z. A. Pelczynski (Cambridge: Cambridge University Press, 1984), p. 186.

tinctive mark of the human. Thus, Hegel, unlike a materialist such as Hobbes, explains mastery and slavery as the outcome of a struggle not for self-preservation, a material end, but for recognition, a spiritual one.

Second, Hegel differs from Marx and Kojève in that it is misleading to see the dialectic of master and slave, in the words of G. A. Kelly, as a "regulative idea" guiding all of Hegel's analysis. To see this as "an unqualified device for clarifying the progress of human history" is to risk "anachronistic overtones of the Marxian class struggle." [56] The dialectic of the position of the master and slave is appropriate only for a particular point in human history and cannot be resurrected as a transhistorical principle capable of explaining history as a whole. A passage from the *Philosophy of Right* serves to bring this home:

> The position of the free will, with which right and the science of right begin, is already in advance of the false position at which man, as a natural entity and only the concept implicit, is for that reason capable of being enslaved. This false, comparatively primitive, phenomenon of slavery is one which befalls mind when mind is only at the level of consciousness. The dialectic of the concept and of the purely immediate consciousness of freedom brings about at that point the fight for recognition and the relationship of master and slave. [57]

Even slavery, Hegel adds, is a voluntary phenomenon, for "if a man is a slave, his own will is responsible for his slavery, just as it is its will which is responsible if a people is subjugated. Hence the wrong of slavery lies at the door not simply of enslavers or conquerors but of the slaves and the conquered themselves." [58]

Hegel's resolution to the dialectic of master and slave seems unduly forced. Nevertheless, it provides a convenient transition from the struggle for recognition to the ethical sphere of "universal self-consciousness." Hegel defines this as "the affirmative awareness of self in an other self," which is "the form of consciousness which lies at the root of all true mental or spiritual life—in family, fatherland, state, and of all virtues, love, friendship, valor, honor, and fame." [59] From the context, it is clear that what Hegel calls "universal self-consciousness" here is a close approximation to his conception of *Sittlichkeit,* or ethical life. What Hegel means by this term will be examined more fully in the next section. For now it is only nec-

56. George A. Kelly, "Notes on Hegel's 'Lordship and Bondage'," in *Hegel's Retreat from Eleusis* (Princeton: Princeton University Press, 1978), pp. 31–32.
57. *PR,* par. 57R, p. 48; *Werke* 7:123–24.
58. *PR,* par. 57A, p. 239; *Werke* 7:126.
59. *PM,* par. 436, p. 176; *Werke* 10:226.

essary to emphasize that ethical life means more than the Kantian self-determination of the will. It is something like a common culture made up of distinct but overlapping spheres.[60] For Hegel, there are three such spheres: family, civil society, and the state. Taken together these constitute the ethical order of society. What distinguishes this ethical order is not simply an appeal to some shared moral consensus, but the more ambitious task of relating the will to its proper objects of activity. These institutions, then, are seen not as mere restrictions on the will's activity but as providing the moral context within which freedom is possible. Only from within the concrete forms of ethical life is mutual recognition possible.

THE RIGHT OF RECOGNITION

The point of the foregoing discussion was to show that Hegel's idea of right is not just tautologically posited to make sense of the modern state, but is historically constructed through a process of labor and struggle. Unlike a contemporary legal philosopher, Ronald Dworkin, who lays down a right to equal concern and respect and then goes on to describe the kinds of social and political institutions necessary to sustain that right, Hegel deduces the concept of right from what it means to be a person. Rights derive what meaning they have from the prior emergence of an autonomous self.

The idea of right is only possible where there is some universal conception of the self or personhood which is the designated bearer of right. Hegel traces the concept of personhood back to the Roman Empire, when the essentially modern idea of "legal status" came to take precedence over active citizenship. For the Roman, but not for the Greek, being a free man meant not the freedom to participate in public affairs but the liberty we enjoy under law. Roman *libertas* never meant political participation but rather private security; it was a primarily passive and defensive posture having more to do with institutional protections against the abuse of power than with access to power itself.[61] While the Roman idea was of the legal person having rights against the state, the Greek citizen was regarded as part of a larger ethical whole or totality. Aristotle actually called the city a *koinonia politike,* a political association or community, to comprehend better the nature of the civic tie. A community is not just a society of

60. I borrow this term from Michael Walzer, *Spheres of Justice: A Defense of Pluralism and Equality* (New York: Basic Books, 1983).

61. See Kurt Raaflaub, "Freiheit in Athen und Rom: ein Beispiel divergierender politischer Begriffsentwicklung der Antike," *Historische Zeitschrift* 238 (1984): 529–67; see also Chaim Wirszubski, *Libertas as a Political Idea at Rome* (Cambridge: Cambridge University Press, 1960), pp. 11–15; Hanna Pitkin, "Are Freedom and Liberty Twins?" (unpublished paper).

strangers but of friends or comrades (*heteroi*), whose lives are centered on certain common corporate goals.[62]

All of this is quite different from the modern *Rechtsstaat*. Hegel's conception of the emergence of legal status is noteworthy especially because of its place within the various nineteenth- and twentieth-century theories of political modernization and development. Like Henry Maine, whose classic work *The Ancient Law* saw the development of the modern state in terms of a shift from status to contract, or Ferdinand Tönnies, who characterized the same process as a movement from gemeinschaft to gesellschaft, Hegel sought to account for it as a move from the classical citizen to the modern bourgeois, or *Bürger*.[63] Unlike the citizen, who was what he was by virtue of his membership in a particular community, the *Bürger* is defined precisely by his freedom from all such parochial attachments and traditions. While a citizen is related to his fellows by a shared moral understanding, the *Bürger* is a private individual who engages in competitive struggles with others in the arena of civil society. Thus, underlying the *Bürger's* way of life is a formal equality expressed in the demand for mutual respect set out above. For the *Bürger*, a "man counts as a man in virtue of his manhood alone, not because he is a Jew, Catholic, Protestant, German, Italian, and so on."[64]

The right to recognition, we might say, is not simply a contingent feature of the modern state; it is its inner soul and purpose. Accordingly, one of the rights most crucial to the recognition of personality is the right to property. Property is not just instrumental to the attainment of material ends but is a means of moral self-realization or the development of personality. Not just our moral growth, but our very sense of self, of who and what we are, is dependent upon possessing something that makes this development possible. I cannot know myself unless I can express my will, and I cannot express my will unless there is a medium for such expression. This medium is property. Accordingly, Hegel opposes in the strongest possible manner any attempt to curtail or abolish the right of property. Platonic communism is condemned, therefore, because it "violates the right of personality by forbidding the holding of private property."[65]

Another form of right equally important for the development of personality is the right to free speech and expression of opinion. The right of publicity is concretized in what is called "public opinion" (*öffentliche*

62. Riedel, *Between Tradition and Revolution*, pp. 133–37, 163; R. C. Mulgan, *Aristotle's Political Theory* (Oxford: Clarendon Press, 1977), pp. 13–17.

63. PR, pars. 187, 190R, pp. 124, 127; *Werke* 7:343, 348.

64. PR, par. 209R, p. 134; *Werke* 7:360.

65. PR, par. 46R, p. 42; *Werke* 7:108; see also PR, par. 185R, p. 124; *Werke* 7:341–42.

Meinung).⁶⁶ The right of public opinion is the way in which ordinary citizens are able to enter into the political process by submitting the laws to critical public examination. Because law, as we shall see in chapter 5, is the expression of the common will of a people, it is through the public expression of private opinion that this will is translated into a concrete way of life. To be sure, Hegel is aware that public opinion is not an infallible guide to the determination of law. It is a "hodge podge of truth and error" which "deserves to be as much respected as despised."⁶⁷ However, the right to the free expression of ideas is a central right of the modern state, which "derives its authority not at all from force" but "from insight and argument."⁶⁸

What Hegel calls the right to recognition is not unlike what the liberal tradition has deemed as a right to equal treatment before the law or what has recently come to be called the doctrine of equal respect and concern. Hegel says as much in a passage from the *Encyclopedia*:

> There [in the state] man is recognized and treated as a *rational* being, as free, as a person; and the individual, on his side, makes himself worthy of this recognition by overcoming the natural state of his self-consciousness and obeying a universal, the will that is in essence and actuality will, the *law*; he behaves, therefore, towards others in a manner that is universally valid, recognizing them—as he wishes others to recognize him—as free, as persons.⁶⁹

Note that Hegel is not trying here to deny the natural inequalities between human beings. Like any sensible observer, he is attentive to differences in moral attainment and assumes that these differences have their origin in the agent. He assumes that inequalities in respect to moral excellence must be due to human faults or virtues. Where Hegel departs from Aristotle, however, and joins issue with Rawls is in denying that these actual moral differences carry any weight in the determination of fundamental human rights. The conclusion we reach is that the mutual recognition of one another's rights must take place at the expense of nature, by abstracting or denying all the individual differences between us until we arrive at the pure *I*, the free will or "universal consciousness" which is at the root of these differences. As one would expect, Hegel does not fail to provide an interesting phenomenology of the development of his own human rights doctrine:

66. *PR,* pars. 316–18, pp. 204–5; *Werke* 7:483–86.
67. *PR,* pars. 317R, 318, p. 205; *Werke* 7:484–85.
68. *PR,* par. 316A, p. 294; *Werke* 7:483.
69. *PM,* par. 432A, pp. 172–73; *Werke* 10:221–22.

As regards the historical side of this relationship, it can be remarked that ancient peoples, the Greeks and Romans, had not yet risen to the notion of absolute freedom, since they did not know that man as such, man as this universal "I," as rational self-consciousness, is entitled to freedom. On the contrary, with them a man was held to be free only if he was born free. With them, therefore, freedom still had the character of a natural state. That is why slavery existed in their free states and bloody wars developed in which the slaves tried to free themselves, *to obtain recognition of their eternal human rights* (italics mine).[70]

One difficulty with this right of recognition is that it is every bit as formal and abstract as the deontological ethic Hegel often claims to attack. The idea of personhood is itself based on an abstraction from all the empirical characteristics and attachments we develop in the course of our lives and histories. The result is what John Schaar has called the creation of a sort of "theoretical everyman" having little in common with the flesh-and-blood creatures we encounter in experience.[71] Hegel himself gives further support to this objection in a passage devoted to exposing the alleged "ambiguity" in the term "natural right":

The phrase "Law of Nature," or Natural Right, in use for the philosophy of law involves the ambiguity that it may mean either right as something existing ready-formed in nature, or right as governed by the nature of things, i.e., by the notion. The former used to be the common meaning, accompanied with the fiction of a *state of nature,* in which the law of nature should hold sway; whereas the social and political state rather required and implied a restriction of liberty and a sacrifice of natural rights. The real fact is that the whole law and its every article are based on free personality alone—on self-determination or autonomy, which is the very contrary of determination by nature. The law of nature— strictly so called—is for that reason the predominance of the strong and the reign of force, and a state of nature a state of violence and wrong, of which nothing truer can be said than that one ought to depart from it. The social state, on the other hand, is the condition in which alone right has its actuality; what is to be restricted and sacrificed is just the willfulness and violence of the state of nature.[72]

Hegel's defense of the right of recognition against the charge of unreal abstractness could take one of two tacks. The first could be called the *neutralist* defense. On this line of argument, adopted variously by Kant, Rawls, and Dworkin (in at least some of his moods), rights are valuable, not be-

70. *PM,* par. 433A, p. 174; *Werke* 10:223–24.
71. John Scharr, "Some Ways of Thinking about Equality," *Journal of Politics* 26 (1964):885.
72. *PM,* par. 502, p. 248; *Werke* 10:311–12.

cause they promote any one conception of the good or human flourishing, but precisely because they do not. To suggest that rights are valuable because they promote happiness, the general welfare, or civic virtue is a wholly instrumental defense that would reduce rights to a mere means valuable for the sake of other ends. Such an instrumental defense, it is argued, would be compatible with the abuse or mistreatment of some if this were thought to further the ends of the whole.

Underlying the neutralist defense of rights is, then, a kind of skepticism about our ability to achieve a knowledge of the good. Because, it is argued, opinions about the good are ultimately questions of value and therefore incorrigible, the most appropriate political response is the construction of a constitutional framework that is neutral to substantive questions about which goods we ought to pursue and respects only our right to pursue them. In the language of contemporary Kantian liberalism, the right must take precedence over the good. Since there is no single or comprehensive goal for which we all strive, the optimum solution to the plurality of ends is something like the modern liberal state, or one which professes indifference or neutrality to the ways of life pursued by its citizens.

The neutralist defense fails for two reasons. First, skepticism about the good does not by itself engender respect for rights. Consistent skepticism about the good, of the type adopted by Max Weber, leads not to mutual respect and recognition but to an unconstrained struggle among competing values and ways of life. As Weber put it: "It is really a question not only of alternatives between values but of an irreconcilable death struggle like that between 'God' and the 'Devil.'"[73] Only if the parties in question have made a prior commitment not to be skeptical about rights will the neutralist defense not degenerate into a war of all against all.

The second flaw with neutralism is that on closer inspection it is not really neutral at all. The commitment to a framework purportedly neutral with respect to ends is itself a value. Neutralism cannot, therefore, pretend to be some kind of Archimedean standpoint from which all other values can then be derived. The value that the neutralist defense elevates above all others is, in fact, individual liberty. For the neutralist, the greatest political sin is governmental paternalism, the attempt, as we say, to "legislate morality." Paternalism is ruled out because it violates the sacred right of the individual to choose for himself how to live and to have his choices respected

73. Max Weber, "The Meaning of 'Ethical Neutrality' in Sociology and Economics," in *The Methodology of the Social Sciences,* trans. Edward Shils and Henry A. Finch (New York: The Free Press, 1949), p. 17.

by others. Perhaps the boldest defense of individual autonomy against the claims of governmental paternalism was put forward a generation or two after Hegel by J. S. Mill in *On Liberty*. Here Mill sought to put forward "one very simple principle" which he believed should "govern absolutely" the relation between the individual and society. "That principle," he writes,

> is that the sole end for which mankind are warranted, individually or collectively, in interfering with the liberty of action of any of their number, is self-protection. That the only purpose for which power can be rightfully exercised over any member of a civilized community, against his will, is to prevent harm to others. His own good, either physical or moral, is not a sufficient warrant. . . . The only part of the conduct of any one, for which he is amenable to society, is that which concerns others. In the part which merely concerns himself, his independence is, of right, absolute. Over himself, over his own body and mind, the individual is sovereign.[74]

But note here that unlike contemporary defenders of neutralism who even invoke him, Mill's defense of the minimal state is not undertaken on the ground that it is agnostic to questions of the good but exactly for the opposite reason, namely, that it is likely to promote "sovereign" individuals. For Mill, the sovereign individual is to be preferred because he is a superior type of human being; he is one who is autonomous in his judgments, open-minded but emphatic in argument, quick to assume responsibility for his deeds, and in general ready to try bold new "experiments in living." Furthermore, despite appearances to the contrary, Mill does not even adopt this view out of respect for the inviolability of individual choice. Rather, he adopts it because individual freedom is the value most likely to contribute to human progress, or in Mill's own phrase, to "the permanent interests of man as a progressive being."[75]

The second line of argument, adopted in fact by Hegel, provides a more substantive defense of rights. No government, it is argued here, can be entirely neutral on matters concerning the human good. Every society of which we have experience, no matter how wide its territory or how diverse its population, tends to favor or promote one or at most a few human types, whether this be the soldier, the priest, the aristocrat, or the common man. Recognizing, as we have seen Mill did, that any justification of rights is bound to make certain implicit commitments to some conception of the

74. Mill, *On Liberty*, pp. 10–11.
75. Mill, *On Liberty*, p. 12.

good life, it is best to be as clear as we can about what these commitments entail.

Now one finds this argument expounded by a number of present-day political and legal theorists, including Michael Walzer, William Galston, and Ronald Dworkin (in other moods), all of whom are agreed that the citizen's right to recognition mandates some positive conception, not of neutrality, but of equality. Treating citizens equally cannot be specified independent of some theory of the good, since equality of treatment carries with it some conception of what human beings ought to be. Thus, Dworkin, in a growing corpus of jurisprudential literature, has tried to specify exactly in what sense citizens must be accorded equality. Government, he writes, "must impose no sacrifice or constraints on any citizen in virtue of an argument that the citizen could not accept without abandoning his sense of equal worth."[76] This sense of equality, what Dworkin calls "equal concern and respect," is valuable precisely because it helps to foster a more robust sense of democratic citizenship. Thus, he says that the right to equal recognition implies that "each citizen is a member of a community, and that he can find, in the fate of that community, a reason for special burdens he can accept with honor rather than degradation." And he adds: "This is appropriate only when that community offers him, at a minimum, the opportunity to develop and lead a life he can regard as valuable both to himself and to it."[77]

The suggestion here is that rights are valuable not only because they help to foster such individual values as autonomy and responsibility, but also because they contribute to the shared life of the community. Rights are not seen as contravening the "public space," as a number of romantic antiliberal writers have maintained; rather a commitment to rights may serve to support a common way of life and collective solidarity. From his initial definition of equality as implying equal concern and respect, Dworkin goes on to adduce two respects in which the citizen might come to regard himself as being at least partially constituted by the community to which he belongs. First, the community will be an object of the citizen's attachment if he is able to draw on and contribute to its public virtues: the richness of its culture, the justice of its institutions, the imagination of its education. And second, the citizen will be able to identify himself with the fate of the community "if he has some power to help determine the shape of that future."[78]

76. Ronald Dworkin, "Why Liberals Should Care About Equality," in *A Matter of Principle* (Cambridge, Mass.: Harvard University Press, 1985), p. 205.
77. Dworkin, "Why Liberals Should Care About Equality," pp. 210–11.
78. Dworkin, "Why Liberals Should Care About Equality," p. 211.

Only if these two conditions are met can the deprivations that citizens may be asked to make be borne as sacrifices, rather than tyranny.

Hegel's conception of rights carries none of the democratic, participatory overtones of the above. His early flirtation with radical French democracy had convinced him of the danger of using ancient models for modern problems. Nor did he believe that the populistic democracies of the type advocated by the ultraliberal Fries could serve as a secure basis for rights. Hegel emphatically denies that the respect for individual rights must lead to political democracy. In a passage from the *Philosophy of Right* that is still relevant for its critique of direct democracy, Hegel writes:

> To hold that every single person should share in deliberating and deciding on political matters of general concern on the ground that all individuals are members of the state, that its concerns are their concerns, and that it is their right that what is done should be done with their knowledge and volition, is tantamount to a proposal to put the democratic element without any rational form into the organism of the state, although it is only in virtue of the possession of such a form that the state is an organism at all.[79]

The right to recognition, then, mandates a policy of respect for the individual personality. This policy of respect means more than just a watery toleration or adopting a hands-off attitude toward others. It requires a more robust sense of the moral self-realization or self-development so crucial to Hegelian ethics. Theories of self-development imply that every person has a core of what I would call moral personality, which requires expression. Central to Hegel's conception is that personality is never just given but is always in the making. Personality has the connotation of a person developing into something individual and unique. Each individual, on this account, possesses a core personality, there to be developed. Thus, personality carries with it certain quasi-classical resonances of harmony and balance. As we shall see later, there is an inner teleology to moral growth whereby the life-cycle of the individual moral agent in some sense recapitulates the experience or history of the entire species. Nothing is ever lost or forgotten but is incorporated into a richer conception of the self. For Hegel, as for Freud later on, ontogeny recapitulates phylogeny.

The concepts of personality and moral growth do not, however, imply some kind of unfettered individualism. The development of personality always implies a pluralistic context. Part of developing a personality means recognizing one's duties and obligations toward others. The self which is to be realized must always be a social self. What sort of selves we become will

79. *PR*, par. 308R, p. 200; *Werke* 7:477.

ultimately depend upon what sorts of activities we engage in. In this way Hegel regards the institutions of ethical life—family, civil society, and the state—not just as constraints on our powers of moral self-realization, but as the necessary categorial framework within which our individual powers and capacities can flourish.[80] Without such a categorial framework to give some kind of moral ballast, our lives would threaten to become rootless, anomic, and alienated.

What I have called Hegel's substantive defense of right is, to repeat, indicated in his decision to treat politics as a branch of ethics. Like Plato and Aristotle, he denies the possibility of an independent sphere of morality detached from politics and consequently of an independent science of morality detached from political philosophy. The Hegelian state is not neutral vis-à-vis its citizens. Its goal is the positive one of promoting a form of *Sittlichkeit* in which all citizens can share. The division of ethical life into family, civil society, and the state is a form of social differentiation which seeks to imbue citizens with some sense of esprit de corps, or common purpose.[81] Rather than offer an ethical program in terms of rules and principles, Hegel is concerned to offer a theory of ethical relations. These relations precede the will and provide it with a determinate content and focus.[82]

Many interpreters have seen in Hegel's concept of *Sittlichkeit* an incipient relativism according to which standards of right and wrong can only come from existing conventions. His well-known claims that "every individual is a child of his time" and that a philosopher can no more transcend his age than "an individual can . . . jump over Rhodes" are often taken as evidence for his relativism.[83] Likewise, his identification of *Sittlichkeit* with "absolutely valid laws and institutions," "habitual practice," and "the general mode of conduct" of individuals appears to give it a conservative dimension similar to that of the philosophy of Burke or any apostle of traditionalism.[84]

But this is to misunderstand Hegel. Hegel's theory of *Sittlichkeit* is not just an empirical, sociological description of what institutions happen to exist; it is a rational reconstruction of what institutions must exist if rational freedom is to be possible. For Hegel, the social categories of ethical life are

80. For the concept of a social category, see Klaus Hartmann, "What is a 'Social Category'?" *Idealistic Studies* 1 (1971): 65–72.

81. *PR,* par. 207, p. 133; *Werke* 7:359.

82. For a recent interpretation of Hegel along these lines, see Terry Pinkard, "Freedom and Social Categories in Hegel's Ethics," *Philosophy and Phenomenological Research* 47 (1986): 209–32.

83. *PR,* p. 11; *Werke* 7:26.

84. *PR,* pars. 144, 151, pp. 105, 108; *Werke* 7:294, 301; for the conservative interpretation, see Robert Nisbet, *The Sociological Tradition* (New York: Basic Books, 1966), pp. 54–55.

not just read off the behavior of groups and relations in society, but derive from a normative perspective capable of being understood in a teleology of reason leading to social freedom.[85] Hegel is thus not advocating a return to some kind of premodern traditional society where laws, customs, and conventions are unreflectively taken for granted. He abjures conventionalism of this type. Not every pattern of life, just because it exists, is a form of ethical life. Institutions and practices are not, in Hegel's philosophy, called upon to be judges in their own case. Rather, institutions are judged by their capacity to further and sustain our mutual desire for freedom and respect. In the context of his overall philosophy, *Sittlichkeit* explains how "the actuality of concrete freedom" is possible.[86]

85. Hartmann, "What is a 'Social Category'?" pp. 69–70.
86. *PR*, par. 260, p. 160; *Werke* 7:406.

5 THE HEGELIAN *RECHTSSTAAT*

HEGEL AND PRACTICAL PHILOSOPHY

Traditional commentaries on Hegel's *Philosophy of Right* typically ask whether it is a conservative or a liberal book. Partisans of the conservative thesis, like Rudolph Haym and Karl Popper, have pointed to Hegel's alleged deification of the state, as well as to the role of a bureaucratic executive power in securing social stability.[1] The *Philosophy of Right* of 1820 is seen here as anticipating the Bismarckian Prussia of half a century later. According to this view, Hegel's conservatism is not the romantic nostalgic conservatism of a de Maistre or the later Fichte, but the apologetics of the officially sanctioned German ideology, which later came to regard Hegel as *"unser Nationalstaatsphilosoph."*[2]

Partisans of the liberal thesis have by contrast fixed on Hegel's identification of the state with the rule of law and the generous role he allows to a depoliticized market economy ("civil society") in ensuring individual liberty. He is on this account a—perhaps *the*—theorist of civil association (understood as the rule of impersonal law), as opposed to corporate association (understood as the common pursuit of some substantive goal or purpose).[3] Hegel's own preferences for constitutional government and his support for the liberalizing reform movements of Hardenberg and von Stein have, arguably, more in common with the ideas of such figures as Locke, Montesquieu, and Kant than with those of the enemies of liberalism on both the left and the right. The worst one could say of Hegel here is that his views belie a kind of Whiggish "Eurocentrism" typical of even the most advanced liberal opinion of his day.[4]

1. Rudolph Haym, *Hegel und seine Zeit* (Hildesheim: Olms, 1962); Karl Popper, *The Open Society and Its Enemies: The High Tide of Prophecy* (Princeton: Princeton University Press, 1963).

2. Cited in Sidney Hook, "Hegel Rehabilitated?" in *Hegel's Political Philosophy,* ed. Walter Kaufmann (New York: Atherton, 1970), p. 64.

3. Michael Oakeshott, *On Human Conduct* (Oxford: Clarendon Press, 1975), pp. 257–63.

4. W. H. Walsh, "Principle and Prejudice in Hegel's Philosophy of History," *Hegel's Political Philosophy: Problems and Perspectives,* ed. Z. A. Pelczynski (Cambridge: Cambridge University Press, 1971), pp. 181–98.

Obviously, either of these readings depends in part on a prior understanding of the relation between Hegel's political philosophy and his critical theory as a whole. The conservative thesis tends to subordinate his views on such specifics as the method of representation, the role of public opinion, and the composition of the legislature to a kind of metaphysical historicism. By historicism is meant here not just the dependence of thought upon immediate context but, in the words of Karl Popper, "an approach to the social sciences which assumes that historical prediction is their principal aim, and which assumes that this aim is attainable by discovering the 'rhythm' or the 'pattern,' the 'laws' or the 'trends' that underlie the evolution of history."[5] Leaving aside the objection that nowhere does Hegel even imply that history is a predictive science, the above assertions rest on three premises.

First: *holism*. On this view, individuals have existence only as parts of some larger collectivity or whole. Individuals are here no more than representatives or functions of some social aggregate, whether this be a class, state, nation, or even the historical process as a whole. Thus, the explanation of human behavior has little to do with the motives, intentions, or biographies of particular individuals, but everything to do with the places they are supposed to occupy within the relevant system. Second: *organicism*. If one adopts, as Hegel is here said to have done, an organic conception of the whole, it follows that everything that happens is done for a purpose, so that explanation is satisfied when the underlying cycles, patterns, or laws governing the organism are discovered. Social aggregates are regarded as part of the natural whole and thus as subject to the same repeatable patterns of birth, growth, decay, and extinction as any other. Third: *pragmatism*. Once we uncover the immanent teleology of history, it will be possible not to change it but to adjust to it more successfully. Joined to this metaphysical historicism, then, is a moral pragmatism which regards successful adaptation or accommodation to given experiences as the most desirable course for human beings to pursue. Only when we adopt this pragmatic cast of mind will it be possible to avoid failure, or at least to minimize disappointment.

If the conservative understanding of Hegel subordinates his politics to a metaphysical conception of history, the liberal thesis presumes that Hegel had no systematic philosophy at all. Thus Z. A. Pelczynski, in his influential "Introductory Essay," in the English translation of Hegel's *Political Writings*, treats Hegel's political views as wholly separable from his speculative phi-

5. Karl Popper, *The Poverty of Historicism* (New York: Harper & Row, 1964), p. 3.

losophy. Pelczynski bemoans the fact that Hegel has often been treated as apart from the canon of Western political philosophy precisely because he felt compelled to enclose his views within a Procrustean metaphysical system. "Apparently," he writes, "Hegel thought that only by transposing politics to the metaphysical plane and giving his concepts a speculative underpinning could he establish their truth. It is this quest for absolute proof, this passion for certain knowledge in politics, which constitutes one of the distinctive features of Hegel's political thought."[6]

But even while Hegel may have succumbed to the temptation of providing his views with some kind of metaphysical grounding, intellectual fashions change, and what was once considered a strength is now an embarrassing weakness. Yet rather than condemn Hegel to the dustbin of history, it remains possible to salvage his useful political insights from their speculative wrapping. Thus, Pelczynski writes: "There is, however, no need for students of political theory to wait for a renaissance of metaphysical philosophy. Hegel's political thought can be read, understood, and appreciated without having to come to terms with his metaphysics."[7] And in a footnote, he goes on to compare the fate of Hegel today with that of Hobbes. Just as Hobbes sought to provide his political views on law, sovereignty, and authority with a foundation in a materialistic physics, his political ideas continue to command widespread attention and respect, even while his atomism and philosophy of physics are generally ignored. "Today," Pelczynski concludes, "we tend to ignore Hobbes's atomistic philosophy, while his specifically political ideas continue to be studied with great interest."[8]

This radical bifurcation of Hegel's political thought from his metaphysics has a powerful precursor in the interpretation of Karl Marx. On Marx's account, it is possible to distinguish between Hegel's critical or dialectical methodology and the politically conformist conclusions he draws from it. In the famous afterword to the second German edition of *Capital,* Marx speaks disparagingly of the "mystification which dialectic suffers in Hegel's hands" and adds that the dialectic "must be turned right side up again" in order to "discover the rational kernel within the mystical shell."[9] The "rational kernel" is here an allusion to Hegel's dialectic, while the "mystical

---

6. Z. A. Pelczynski, "Introductory Essay," in *PW,* p. 136.
7. Pelczynski, "Introductory Essay," p. 136.
8. Pelczynski, "Introductory Essay," p. 136, n. 1.
9. Karl Marx, "Capital," *Marx-Engels Reader,* ed. Robert C. Tucker (New York: W. W. Norton, 1978), pp. 301–2; for a masterful discussion, see Louis Althusser, "Contradiction

shell" refers to the system of idealistic metaphysics within which it is supposedly encased. It should be unnecessary to remind the reader that such a distinction would have appalled Hegel, for whom his philosophy represented a single intelligible whole. But this did not prevent the distinction between method and system, canonized in the generation after Hegel's death, from serving as a basis for distinguishing the so-called left and right wings of the Hegelian movement.

Neither of these views can be accepted as adequate. The conservative reading fails for two reasons. First, the institutions described in the *Philosophy of Right* were not the property of the Prussian state, or indeed of any particular state existing in Hegel's time or later. To view them, then, as "anticipating" Bismarck or even Hitler is the worst kind of anachronism. The *Philosophy of Right* is rather based on an idealization of certain progressive tendencies immanent in the politics of Hegel's age and to which he sought to give rational expression. Second, this interpretation tends to conflate methodological holism with authoritarianism or even totalitarianism. While Hegel subscribed to a version of the former, he was not logically committed to the latter. While methodological holism—or metaphysical historicism, as I have called it—may often go hand in hand with totalitarianism, it need not necessarily do so. Hegel's collectivism, such as it is, is ultimately more of the methodological than the political kind.

The liberal reading fails for similar reasons. In the first place, it conveniently overlooks the fact that Hegel rejected the political reasoning associated with such classic liberals as Locke and Tom Paine as typical of the "understanding," a term he used as coeval with the utilitarian calculus of the Enlightenment. Rather than regarding the state as a necessary evil to be endured for the sake of civil peace and the enjoyment of private goods, he sees it as an ethical (*sittlich*) institution which has a kind of dignity and sacred absoluteness of its own. The Hegelian state is an end in itself in the older Aristotelian sense, that is, it is a community of rational beings, membership in which is necessary for moral well-being and self-development. And second, the liberal (and Marxist) attempt to separate out Hegel's politics from his critical theory ends by draining his writings of whatever philosophical interest they may have. The result is to reduce the *Philosophy of Right* to a piece of polemical literature indistinguishable from the work of any political partisan or hack.

It should be clear from what I have been saying that attempts to identify

---

and Overdetermination," in *For Marx*, trans. Ben Brewster (London: Allen Lane, 1969), pp. 89–128.

Hegel by appending some kind of "ism" to his name are all bound to be more or less unsatisfactory. Such attempts are apt to tell us more about the intellectual or psychological needs of his critics than about Hegel's own views. But if Hegel cannot be understood as engaging in the same kind of partisan polemics as any second- or even third-rate thinker, neither is it true that his purported loftiness of vision "isolates him from the world of practical affairs."[10] Philosophy is not for Hegel simply a surrogate for action intended to bring "comfort or aesthetic pleasure, but not the kind of guidance men need in political life." It is rather a form of practice intended to bring out the structure of rationality from within the concrete embodiments and institutions of political life. As odd as it may sound, the *Philosophy of Right,* perhaps the most formidable and austerely written text in the history of political philosophy, was intended as a contribution to practical philosophy. Let me go on to explain.

The clearest indication of the goal of Hegel's practical philosophy is revealed by his discussion of politics as a part of ethical life. In treating politics as coterminous with ethics, he returns in fact to the standpoint of Aristotle, the founder of practical philosophy, especially in his *Politics, Ethics,* and *Rhetoric.* According to tradition, these writings represent Aristotle's distilled teaching about the practical, as distinguished from his teachings in the so-called theoretical and productive sciences—teachings about nature and art, respectively. As originally conceived, practical philosophy dealt with all those domains relevant to the evaluation and direction of action (praxis). Custom (ethos), the household (*oikos*), and the institutions of law and political science (*politike*) were all deemed part of the philosophy of the practical.[11]

Ever since the time of Aristotle, however, the precise relation between the practical and theoretical parts of his canon has been a matter of intense controversy. One strategy adopted widely by modern scholars regards the practical philosophy as crucially dependent upon Aristotle's explicitly theoretical works, the *Physics* and *Metaphysics* in particular. Since classical physics depended upon assumptions of an extrinsic teleology in nature which are now regarded as refuted by modern science, it follows that Aristotle's practical philosophy collapses under its own weight. Such a reading

---

10. Pelczynski, "Introductory Essay," p. 136.

11. See especially Wilhelm Hennis, *Politik und praktische Philosophie: eine Studie zur Rekonstruktion der politischen Wissenschaft* (Berlin: Neuwied, 1963); Hans-Georg Gadamer, *Reason in the Age of Science,* trans. Frederick G. Lawrence (Cambridge, Mass.: MIT Press, 1983); Rüdiger Bubner, *Modern German Philosophy* (Cambridge: Cambridge University Press, 1981), pp. 203–6.

presupposes modern notions about the unification of all knowledge more typical of Descartes than of Aristotle. While the role of teleology in Aristotle remains a vexed question, it is possible that the *Physics* may be a sufficient but not a necessary foundation for the *Politics*.

For those more sympathetic to Aristotle's practical philosophy, another strategy, arguably closer to Aristotle's original intention, has been adopted. Here his practical works are regarded as having considerable autonomy from his theoretical teaching. Whereas theoretical knowledge (*theoria*) aims at universal knowledge of unchanging nature, practical knowledge (*phronesis*) deals with truths that are more localized and contingent, appropriate to men situated in popular assemblies and courts of law. Thus, Aristotle warns his readers that it is impossible to have the kind of exactitude in ethics and practical matters that one would expect to find in mathematics.[12] Unlike Plato, who rejected practical reasoning as sheer opinion (*doxa*), lacking the hard edge of knowledge (*episteme*), Aristotle sought to theorize a realm of human behavior which, precisely because of its greater contingency and variety, is not amenable to the rigors of deductive logic but is better left to current belief and practice. This area of conduct, to which belong questions of the constitutional forms of government, as well as those regarding political education and the human good, follows a logic of its own, best handled by the practitioners of practical philosophy.

But who, exactly, are the practitioners of this philosophy? Here it is important to distinguish practical philosophy not only from the theoretical sciences but also from the specialized arts and crafts (*technai*).[13] The concept of *techne* in ancient Greece meant in general an "art," "craft," or "skill." It implied the orderly, methodical application of intelligence to some problem for the sake of gaining control over future contingencies. There is a close resemblance between the man of practical wisdom, the *phronimos*, and the skilled craftsman. Plato, for example, used the analogy to the crafts as the virtual paradigm for the successful statesman. The concept of *techne* served for him a critical function within the context of Athenian democracy, where every citizen regarded himself as equally an expert. Nonetheless, whatever the similarities between practical and technical knowledge, the differences are even greater.

First, the *technai* are distinguished by universality. "A *techne*," Aristotle

12. Aristotle, *Nichomachean Ethics* 1094b.

13. See Hans-Georg Gadamer, *Truth and Method* (New York: Seabury Press, 1975), pp. 278–89; for a more recent discussion, see Martha C. Nussbaum, *The Fragility of Goodness: Luck and Ethics in Greek Tragedy and Philosophy* (Cambridge: Cambridge University Press, 1986), pp. 94–99.

writes in the *Metaphysics,* "is produced when from many notions of experience a single universal judgment is formed with regard to like objects."[14] By contrast, practical knowledge is context dependent. Its point of departure is not a set of abstract rules or principles but the citizen who is already situated in an ongoing form of life. Practical philosophy, then, assumes that we are shaped by the normative structures and conceptions, the "horizon," of the world in which we have been brought up. Furthermore, while the universality of the *technai* means that they are in principle available to all, Aristotle limits practical knowledge to those who have been well brought up and are thus predisposed to receive it. Thus, he warns that lectures on political science will be lost on those without the requisite experience and upbringing, especially the young.[15]

Second, the *technai* are instrumental. They seek to produce or bring about some limited end that is external to the activity that produces it; if the *techne* is shoemaking, a pair of shoes; if medicine, health; if poetry, a poem; and so on. Practical knowledge, on the other hand, has no goal but right living in general, what Aristotle calls by the comprehensive name of *eudaimonia.* A *techne* is something that we can choose to learn or forget without incurring blame; practical knowledge is more directly related to the actual conduct of life. It is a form of self-knowledge or self-perfection of the agent. While the actions of the craftsman depend upon nothing but the knowledge of his craft, those of the *phronimos* depend upon his state of character. Human well-being requires practical knowledge, not as a means to an end, but as a constitutive part of what *eudaimonia* is. Practical knowledge thus differs from *techne* in that it encompasses both means and ends.

Third, the *technai* are teachable.[16] One feature of a craft is that it can be learned from a book, repeated by rote, and applied mechanically. Practical knowledge is, however, much less amenble to such abstract codification and reproduction. It is less a matter of subsuming particular instances under general rules or laws than of learning to see the exemplary in specific situations. A case in point is Aristotle's treatment of natural law in book 5 of the *Nicomachean Ethics.*[17] Aristotle does not reject out of hand the idea of an absolute and unchangeable law of nature. It is only that such a law, because of its very generality, will be inappropriate to most political situations. Because of the heterogeneity of the human condition, it is impossible to spec-

14. Aristotle, *Metaphysics* 981a.

15. Aristotle, *Nicomachean Ethics* 1095a.

16. Aristotle, *Metaphysics* 981b.

17. Aristotle, *Nicomachean Ethics* 1134b–1135a; see also Leo Strauss, *Natural Right and History* (Chicago: University of Chicago Press, 1953), pp. 159–63.

ify beforehand what types of rules will be applicable to which situations. Aristotle appears to say that there is no single rule which is not subject to alteration because of circumstances. It follows, then, that Aristotelian natural law lacks the quality of absolute commandment or prohibition. There is no Aristotelian equivalent of the Kantian Categorical Imperative or the commandments of the Decalogue. Knowledge of the natural law cannot be taught but only imparted and acquired.

The tradition of practical philosophy that Hegel inherited from Aristotle most decisively influences his treatment of politics in the *Philosophy of Right*. In any event, the influence of practical philosophy did not carry over directly but was mediated by its reception by the humanism of the Reformation. Philipp Melanchthon's commentaries on Aristotle's *Politics*, especially, did much to shape Hegel's understanding of the tradition. The renewal of interest in Aristotelianism—which grew out of the classical humanists' desire to grasp the authentic meaning of ancient texts—became influential as an "academic doctrine of politics taught at the primarily Protestant universities and gymnasia from the sixteenth through the eighteenth centuries . . . without any major alterations of the ancient teaching of practical philosophy and represented by teaching posts for political science." Even up until the time of Kant, such posts were designated by the title "Professio Ethices vel Politices." [18]

The purpose of this approach to political science becomes apparent in Hegel's desire to prepare citizens for the practical conduct of life. Just as the *Politics* and *Nicomachean Ethics* were originally presented as lectures to potential statesmen and guardians of the polis, so were the materials gathered together in the *Philosophy of Right* presented in various forms and over several years to students at the University of Berlin. Unlike his lectures on the philosophy of history, religion, and aesthetics, as well as the monumental history of philosophy, all of which have been compiled exclusively from student notes, Hegel took pains to prepare the *Philosophy of Right* for publication. The purpose of this "manual" or "compendium," as he called it, was to respond to "the need for putting into the hands of my audience a text-book for the lectures on the Philosophy of Right which I deliver in the course of my professional duties." [19]

Scholars, notably Karl-Heinz Ilting, have debated the influence of the Carlsbad Decrees imposing strict political control over the universities on

18. Cited in Joachim Ritter, *Hegel and the French Revolution*, trans. Richard Dien Winfield (Cambridge, Mass.: MIT Press, 1982), p. 165.

19. *PR*, p. 1; *Werke* 7:11.

the publication of the *Philosophy of Right.* Ilting alleges that Hegel's timidity involved him in complicity with the Prussian reaction.[20] Yet whatever the differences between the published version of the text and Hegel's lectures, the *Philosophy of Right* ultimately reveals Hegel's overall commitment to the ideals of the *Rechtsstaat.* His purpose in publishing it was, I believe, to help foster and create a public-minded ruling class, a sort of ideal civil service, fully committed to the values of civility, impartiality, and honorable conduct. The need to put his lectures in textbook form was part of what he hoped would be a long-term educational project which would begin in the universities and spread out from there. While Hegel's belief in the "esoteric" function of philosophy prevented him from thinking that his works would ever become popular, he could reasonably expect that they might prepare for the kind of world where both philosophers and laymen could live in mutual peace and respect.

CIVIL SOCIETY AND THE CORPORATION

There is no need here to rehearse in any detail Hegel's account of the basic features of political life. This has been done more than adequately before by a host of commentators. What is important for us is to try to connect some of the more controversial features of the *Philosophy of Right,* such as Hegel's account of civil society, law, the bureaucracy, the monarch, and war, with his practical goal of achieving harmony and overcoming the contradictions immanent within the liberal state.

One aspect of the Hegelian *Rechtsstaat* that has recently received particular attention is the role allotted to civil society. Hegel strongly opposed the tendencies of modern civil society under the pressures of the marketplace to degenerate into what is often called atomistic individualism. In particular, he opposed a model of society which saw individuals largely as Benthamite utility maximizers unrelated to others except as potential buyers and sellers of commodities. Society is understood in the Benthamite conception as no more than an aggregate of individuals, each pursuing maximum satisfaction. One can, however, overemphasize, as Marxist interpreters usually do, the relation between Hegelian *bürgerliche Gesellschaft* and the modern capitalistic economy. As George Armstrong Kelly has written: "We should put out of our minds the notion that Hegel's 'civil society' has much to do with our own—except in its power to stimulate certain

20. Karl-Heinz Ilting, "Hegel's Concept of the State and Marx's Early Critique," in *The State and Civil Society: Studies in Hegel's Political Philosophy,* ed. Z. A. Pelczynski (Cambridge: Cambridge University Press, 1984), p. 98.

brands of intellectual alienation. Hegel did not foresee the highly developed conditions of capitalism and their industrial results."[21]

In the Hegelian account of ethical life, civil society is the middle term between the family and the state. Civil society, Hegel makes clear, is a distinctively modern phenomenon.[22] It had no foundation in the ancient world, where the "social," as we understand it, did not yet exist. In fact, civil society was still looked upon by Aristotle as identical with the political community (*koinonia politike*). Thus, Cicero could define the citizen (*civis*) by the civic quality of "civility" or "knowledge of civic affairs and prudence." Indeed, the classical identification of the civil with the political continued into the early modern era where, for instance, Locke calls chapter 7 of his *Second Treatise* "Of Civil or Political Society."[23]

While the family is held together by sentiment and ties of romantic love, the state is bound by the impartiality of the civil service and the kind of disinterested altruism that passes for public spirit. Civil society presents itself, by contrast, as a "system of needs," where individuals are free to pursue their own interests, however understood. The modern world is unlike the ancient world, which knew nothing of the distinction between civil society and the state. In contrast, the independence of an autonomous marketplace is "the achievement of the modern world which has for the first time given all determinations of the Idea their due."[24] Not only does civil society contain an increasingly complex division of labor, but it has given rise to a new "science," namely political economy, that takes for its object the study of needs. It is to the lasting credit of this science, which has "arisen out of the conditions of the modern world," to have discovered the laws governing "mass relationships and mass movements in their complexity and in their quantitative and qualitative character." Hegel compares the insights of social theorists like Smith, Say, and Ricardo to the discoveries of Kepler and Galileo, who found an orderly pattern to the solar system, which displays to the naked eye only "irregular movements."[25]

What defines civil society as a civil, as opposed to a political, society is its division into various classes and estates, each with its own distinctive outlook, interests, and ways of life. These estates—the peasantry, the busi-

21. George A. Kelly, "Hegel and the 'Neutral State,'" in *Hegel's Retreat from Eleusis* (Princeton: Princeton University Press, 1978), p. 113.

22. *PR,* par. 185R, pp. 123–24; *Werke* 7:341–42.

23. Manfred Riedel, *Studien zu Hegels Rechtsphilosophie* (Frankfurt: Suhrkamp, 1969), p. 143.

24. *PR,* par. 182A, p. 266; *Werke* 7:339.

25. *PR,* par. 189A, p. 268; *Werke* 7:347.

ness class, and the "universal" class of state functionaries—provide the crucial links, or "mediations," between the "natural society" of the family and the more abstract rationality of the state. Realizing that in the modern world the state has become too large and impersonal to serve as an object for the citizen's immediate affections, such opportunities for civic virtue and community-mindedness as exist will have to come from the institutions of civil society. Especially significant here is the corporation (*Korporation*), which in this context means more than the modern business firm or joint stock company. The corporation is often thought by Hegelians to consist of the old feudal guilds with their hierarchical division into masters, journeymen, and apprentices. There is some truth to this, but it relies on a very narrow interpretation of Hegelian doctrine. Hegelian doctrine applies not only to the restrictive guilds of the Middle Ages but to the whole range of professional associations and voluntary organizations that grow out of the conditions of civil society. The freedom to associate is, for Hegel as for Tocqueville, a fundamental freedom of the modern world.[26]

Corporatism is, in fact, a doctrine that significantly predates Hegel. Originally corporatism began in medieval times, when groups and private associations first sought to acquire legal or rights-bearing status for themselves. These corporate entities, precisely because they represented organized interests and not just shifting coalitions of individual opinions, were held to be the voluntary and spontaneous basis of society. Accordingly, representation was to proceed along corporate lines, expressing these broad functional groupings of society. Corporatist theories later came to be advocated by European conservatives, who, alarmed at the rise of modern industry and the "cash nexus," saw these intermediary bodies as restoring the moral authority and stability that allegedly characterized the medieval world. Some of these same ideas were rehabilitated by the so-called guild socialists in England like G. D. H. Cole, R. H. Tawney, and Harold Laski, whose idea of a "corporate state" was intended to provide organized occupational-industrial groups with a greater say in government. Most famously, however, corporatism came to be identified in this century with Mussolini and his National Union of Fascists, who held it as a way of eliminating social conflict by integrating the people through their work groups into the state, which is nothing other than "the nation itself rendered articulate." And finally, a different picture has been presented by group theo-

26. See Alexis de Tocqueville, *Democracy in America,* trans. George Lawrence (New York: Doubleday, 1969), pp. 189–95, 520–24.

rists like Theodore Lowi and J. K. Galbraith, who have used the term somewhat promiscuously to characterize virtually any intimate relationships between interest groups and the state.[27]

Hegel's corporate doctrine is intended to fulfill a number of functions. First, like Montesquieu before him and Tocqueville later, Hegel saw the corporations as essential to the structure of modern freedom. The freedom to associate, even more than freedom of speech, is crucial to modern freedom. A community requires subordinate and superordinate spheres of influence for the development of diverse human capacities; it requires specific forms of organization with which the individual can identify. These intermediary bodies prevent either excessive centralization from the state above or excessive atomization from the market below. The corporation also provides a context within which a person's skills, abilities, and talents may develop. It is, then, an important source of *Bildung,* where people learn the virtues of cooperation and responsibility from sharing in common enterprises. Membership in a corporation disciplines the inclinations and thus contributes to the advance of moral culture. The corporation introduces a sense of esprit de corps into the "playground" of civil society by means of the sentiments of professional pride and integrity. It provides life with a moral ballast which acts as a kind of second family for the individual who "unless he is a member of an authorized corporation . . . is without rank or dignity [and whose] isolation reduces his business to mere self-seeking."[28]

Second, the corporation has important welfare functions, especially for its indigent members. Hegel was no advocate of the welfare state or the planned economy. These functions, providing for people's substantive wants, were not a part of the state's role. Nevertheless, he opposed the radical libertarian tendencies of his own time (and ours) simply to let people fend for themselves. Hegel recognized the dangers that a large disenfranchised class, or "rabble" (*Pöbel*), would pose for social stability.[29] Civil society produces a class of people who, through no fault of their own, are reduced to penury and thus require a "safety net" to protect them from the vicissitudes of the market. This is where the corporation comes in:

27. The literature on corporatism is immense; for the origins of the doctrine, see Otto von Gierke, *The Political Theories of the Middle Ages,* trans. F. W. Maitland (Cambridge: Cambridge University Press, 1900); on the conservative uses, see Robert Nisbet, *The Sociological Tradition* (New York: Basic Books, 1966), chap. 3; for the fascist appropriation see Hannah Arendt, *The Origins of Totalitarianism* (Cleveland: World Publishing Co., 1969), pp. 258–59; for its use by group theorists, see Theodore J. Lowi, *The End of Liberalism* (New York: W. W. Norton, 1979).

28. *PR,* par. 253R, p. 153; *Werke* 7:395.

29. *PR,* par. 244, p. 150; *Werke* 7:389.

The consideration behind the abolition of Corporations in recent times is that the individual should fend for himself. But we may grant this and still hold that corporation membershp does not alter a man's obligation to earn his living. Under modern political conditions, the citizens have only a restricted share in the public business of the state, yet it is essential to provide men—ethical entities—with work of a public character over and above their private business. This work of a public character, which the modern state does not always provide, is found in the Corporation.[30]

The third function of the corporation is to provide political representation for its members. Hegel opposed the system of direct suffrage, thinking it would lead to atomization and apathy, and instead favored a form of corporate representation in the legislature or estates. The relevant issue here is not geographical milieu but social function. The corporation could serve as a link, or "mediation," between the state and civil society. In this way, the corporations could better defend the aggregate interests of their members by giving them a voice in politics. Hegel is less concerned that the members of the estates be selected by universal suffrage than that they be tied to their constituents by common needs, interests, and experiences. The corporation is conceived, then, as a system of functional representation designed to foster class cooperation and harmony. Since these "circles of association [i.e., corporations] in civil society are already communities [*Gemeinwesen*]," Hegel says, it only makes sense to give them political recognition; only then is it possible to prevent the people from acquiring "the appearance of a mass or an aggregate" and thus "crystallizing into a powerful bloc in opposition to the organized state."[31]

The idea of a corporate state does not sit well, especially since its association with Italian fascism and the authoritarian regimes of Latin America. Here the term has been used to designate a statist ideology in which politicians control and direct both business enterprises and labor movements from above in order to ensure unity, discipline, order, and efficiency. The goal is to control market competition by creating a state-sponsored consensus between different social groups. Hegel's corporatism, however, is closer to what is sometimes called liberal corporatism. Here corporatism is regarded less as direct control from the top than as a system of self-regulation by quasi-autonomous social groups within the context of liberal constitutional forms of government. Such a view may still offend some democratic sensibilities, since it seems to accord primacy to organized groups and the

30. *PR*, par. 255A, p. 278; *Werke* 7:396–97.
31. *PR*, pars. 302, 303R, pp. 197, 198; *Werke* 7:472, 474.

elites within them. But on the whole, Hegel's form of corporatism is probably closest to the contemporary experiences of Scandinavia, France, and Britain, with their highly structured relations between interest organizations and administrative bodies.[32]

THE RULE OF LAW

The rise of the *Rechtsstaat* has often been identified by thinkers of both the left and the right with the emergence of the modern market economy with its new form of instrumental rationality.[33] Kant is often taken to be the paradigmatic expression of this new kind of rationality. In his essay "Theory and Practice," he states with unparalleled clarity the principles underlying the new political order. "The civil state," Kant remarks, "is based on the following *a priori* principles: 1. The *freedom* of every member of society as a *human being*. 2. The *equality* of each with all the others as a *subject*. 3. The *independence* of each member of a commonwealth as a *citizen*."[34] These three principles are based on the insight, central to liberal political thought, that every person is entitled to as much freedom as is compatible with the equal freedom of others. Justice in Kant's official view is concerned neither with happiness nor virtue but with "the sum total of those conditions within which the will of one person can be reconciled with the will of another in accordance with a universal law of freedom."[35]

The central feature of the *Rechtsstaat* is, as the name implies, the rule of law.[36] As we have seen earlier, law for Hegel is, not a limitation on, but a dimension of, freedom. Hegel has both a broad and a narrow conception of law. In the widest possible sense, law (*Recht*) applies to more than civil law but carries with it many of the connotations of the Greek *diké*, or justice, to indicate the proper ordering of social relations. Law here refers not only to what is codified in positive rules but also to the whole system of ethical

32. On liberal corporatism, see Leo Panitch, "The Development of Corporatism in Liberal Democracies," *Comparative Political Studies* 1 (1977):61–90; Gerhard Lehmbruch and Philippe Schmitter, eds., *Corporatism and Public Policy Making* (Beverly Hills, Calif.: Sage, 1982); Jeffrey Lustig, *Corporate Liberalism: The Origins of Modern American Political Theory, 1890–1920* (Berkeley: University of California Press, 1982).

33. Georg Lukács, *History and Class Consciousness: Studies in Marxist Dialectics,* trans. Rodney Livingstone (Cambridge, Mass.: MIT Press, 1971), pp. 95ff; Leo Strauss, *Natural Right and History* (Chicago: University of Chicago Press, 1953), pp. 35–80.

34. Immanuel Kant, "Theory and Practice," in *Political Writings,* trans. H. B. Nisbet (Cambridge: Cambridge University Press, 1970), p. 74.

35. Kant, "The Metaphysics of Morals," in *Political Writings,* p. 133.

36. See Jean-François Kervegan, "Hegel et l'état de droit," *Archives de Philosophie* 50 (1987):55–94.

norms and values, not to mention religious rules and precepts, that inform a culture's way of life. Justice in this sense refers to the institutional ordering of society as a whole.[37]

In the narrower sense, however, Hegel speaks of law (*Gesetz*) to indicate positive legal justice. Thus, he writes that "in positive law . . . it is the legal which is the source of our knowledge of what is right, or, more exactly, of our legal rights [*Rechtens*] . . . the science of positive law is to that extent an historical science with authority as its guiding principle."[38] By indicating the conventional character of the law, Hegel seeks to detach it from the older higher law or natural law tradition. Because modern civil codes are becoming increasingly more rational or public over time, they have made appeals to a higher law unnecessary. Every bit as much as Rousseau, Hegel sought to replace the potentially capricious appeal to transcendent norms with the absolute majesty and dignity of law.

There are two features of law that Hegel emphasizes. First, law must be understood in terms of its form. The form of law is its universal applicability. Laws cannot legislate for particular persons or actions but specify a set of procedures which establish the conditions of human conduct. The rule of law, then, presupposes some minimum or abstract conception of equality among those citizens to whom it is to apply. This formal or legal equality is crucial to Hegel's conception of a "person," a term which designates a capacity for rights. The person, as Hegel understands the term, is essentially a legal entity entitled to disposition over those objects which have become his property. From the legal point of view it is "matter of indifference" whether or how much property a person possesses.[39] All that matters is the individual's abstract capacity to acquire, utilize, and exchange property with other persons. Accordingly, the maxim regulating the behavior of such legal persons is simple: "Be a person and respect others as persons."[40] This maxim is by no means idiosyncratic or capricious but is central to much of the legal reasoning of the West. For whenever we think of persons as the law enjoins, we think of them, not on the basis of their specific accomplishments or character traits, but as formally identical and interchangeable entities related only by the capacity to recognize and understand the rule of law.

37. *PR,* par. 33A, p. 233; *Werke* 7:90–91; see also M. B. Foster, *The Political Philosophies of Plato and Hegel* (Oxford: Clarendon Press, 1935), pp. 110ff.

38. *PR,* par. 212R, p. 136; *Werke* 7:365.

39. *PR,* par. 49, p. 44; *Werke* 7:112–13.

40. *PR,* par. 36, p. 37; *Werke* 7:95.

The rule of law must be categorically distinguished, then, from command. The command theory of law, sometimes attributed to Hobbes, would be for Hegel an oxymoron.[41] Laws are determined by their form, and this form is imposed by our practical rationality. What distinguishes a law is not the sheer fact that it commands but that it embodies the form of a rule.[42] If it did not have the form of a rule it would be impossible to distinguish the rule of law from the power of the greatest thugs. While commands are orders addressed to assignable persons for specific purposes, laws are addressed to an unknown audience and apply equally to everyone who falls under their jurisdiction. Furthermore, while commands frequently take the form of a directive from a superior to an inferior, laws express the will of the subjects to whom they are intended to apply. Laws are not merely external commands which one has to obey but are the collective expression of the citizens' will. "[The laws] are not something alien to the subject," Hegel writes. "The subject is thus directly linked to the ethical order by a relation which is more like an identity than even the relation of faith or trust."[43]

It is not the purpose of law, then, to legislate some high ideal of human excellence or the full development of human capacities. This was something only imperfectly understood by the ancients, who saw law as a tool for moral instruction. For Aristotle, the purpose of law was to educate citizens to a high level of civic virtue, whereas for Hegel, such matters are best left to the private discretion of the individual. The ancients saw the law as a means of determining the particular details of conduct, while we moderns regard the very generality of law as providing scope for personal initiative and freedom. Thus, Hegel criticizes "the legislation of the ancients" for being "full of precepts about uprightness and integrity which are unsuited by nature to legal enactment because they fall wholly within the field of the inner life."[44] The rule of law is based instead on a few essential features common to all individuals, features such as will, reason, and consciousness. The laws are what free men would establish by their own rationality. While Hegel is aware that impersonal law may be a clumsy way of dealing with particular cases, on the whole it is a better guarantee of justice than the concrete or specific self.

41. Thomas Hobbes, *Leviathan,* ed. M. Oakeshott (London: Macmillan, 1962), chap. 26, p. 198: "law in general is not counsel, but command."
42. For a brilliant discussion, see Oakeshott, *On Human Conduct,* pp. 127–30, 261–62.
43. *PR,* par. 147, p. 106; *Werke* 7:295.
44. *PR,* par. 213A, p. 272; *Werke* 7:366.

Second, Hegel has a marked preference for rational or written law. He has no patience with romantics like von Haller and Hugo who prefer the *gute alte recht* to codified law. Like Burke, they appealed to tradition and time-honored custom as antedating attempts to "Romanize" the law. Hegel refuses to accept this primeval identification of the good with the ancestral on the grounds that it fosters a "hatred of all laws and legislation" by conferring legitimacy on whatever has managed to survive. His rejection of traditionalism is based on the argument that traditions, too, must come from somewhere, and that if we examine traditions closely enough we find that they rest ultimately on force. In an ironical conflation of Haller with his archenemy Rousseau, Hegel shows that to confer legitimacy on tradition one must go back to what predates tradition, namely, the "animal kingdom" of the state of nature which is nothing other than the law of the jungle. Traditionalism must conclude, then, with the thesis that might makes right, since "the irrational power of brute force" is the first cause of all traditions.[45]

Hegel's preference for codification is based on the premise that for a law to be a law it must be capable of being known. It can only be known if it is first made public. This might seem obvious, but Hegel's work appeared at a time when efforts to rationalize and publicize law were under heavy attack by jurists and politicians alike. Thus Hegel makes much of the etymological point that the German word for law, *Gesetz,* is related to the word for posit, *setzen.*[46] Positing or making public is the activity by which law is made. To be a law, a law must be formulated in a public system of intelligible rules, so that laws attain not only the conformity but the consent of those subject to them. It follows then that "[r]ulers who have given a national law to their peoples in the form of a well-arranged and clear cut legal code . . . have been the greatest benefactors of their peoples," and that "[t]o hang the laws so high that no citizen could read them . . . is injustice of one and the same kind as to bury them in row upon row of learned tomes, collections of dissenting judgments and opinions, records of customs, etc., and in a dead language too, so that knowledge of the law of the land is accessible only to those who have made it their professional study."[47]

45. *PR,* par. 258R, pp. 158–60; *Werke* 7:402–6.
46. *PR,* par. 211, p. 134; *Werke* 7:361; Butler, *Political Philosophies of Plato and Hegel,* p. 119.
47. *PR,* par. 215R, p. 138; *Werke* 7:368.

THE UNIVERSAL CLASS

One of the most important but also most controversial features of the Hegelian state is the class of civil servants, or the bureaucracy. The defining feature of this class is its impartiality, or in Hegelian terms, "universality." Unlike the other classes or estates of civil society, this class has the business of the oversight of the whole, the public business. Such a class will be recruited not from the older warlike nobility but from the modern middle classes (*Bürgertum*). Only in this class does one find "the consciousness of right and the developed intelligence of the mass of people," which for this reason makes it also "the pillar of the state so far as honesty and intelligence are concerned."[48] The basis for eligibility for the civil service, then, is not heredity but "knowledge and proof of ability."[49]

This conception of a disinterested civil service is crucial not only to the Hegelian state but to the *Rechsstaat* generally. What distinguishes the modern constitutional state from, say, the ancient polis or an oriental despotism is its relative impersonality. The constitutional state is defined precisely by its independence from those who currently hold its ruling offices. It is not the personal property of some individual or class of individuals to be used for their own ends but is more like an arbiter whose existence is independent of all such persons or groups. The modern sense of constitutionalism is apt to put more emphasis on such things as institutional restraints limiting the power of government and less on the individual virtues of statesmen or citizens. Modern constitutionalism took a markedly more skeptical stance toward the alleged ability of men to control their own passions and thus prevent the abuse of power by self-interested elites. The widespread maxim that the rule of men was to be replaced by the rule of law was an indicator of just how much it was believed that institutional arrangements could prevent the tyrannical consolidation of power in the hands of the rulers. Such a conception of the state emerged largely as a response to the older classical idea of the *politeia,* or regime, as identical with its *politeuma,* or ruling class. For the ancients, every regime was defined by, and was thus the property of some ruling group known as the one, the few, or the many, who felt there was nothing wrong with using the regime to promote its own partisan interests. Even the claims for the mixed regime or polity was not a call for a regime above partisanship but a way of balancing off the compet-

48. *PR,* par. 297A, p. 291; *Werke* 7:465.
49. *PR,* par. 291, p. 190; *Werke* 7:461.

ing partisan claims to rule in order to prevent the tyranny of some over others.[50]

The Hegelian *Beamtenstatt,* just like the Hobbesian Leviathan, took its task as lowering the stakes of politics, as well as the temperature of political debate. Unlike the older *Obrigkeitsstaat,* the modern rational state is, at least in theory, elevated beyond political partisanship. It should be noted here that there may be more than an element of self-congratulation in Hegel's elevation of the civil service to the status of preserver of official neutrality. University professors, as well as clergymen and members of the liberal professions, were all considered servants of the state. This is why in the preface to the *Philosophy of Right* Hegel remarks that unlike the ancient Greeks who practiced philosophy in private, in modern times philosophy has an existence in the open in the service of the state. It cannot be established whether this statement implies "servility" to the Prussian government or whether it is simply an empirical observation about the organized study of philosophy in the university, where professors are ex officio civil servants. What is certain is that as a notable representative of this estate, Hegel was aware of his responsibility for the social ethos which would express its values.[51]

There are two obvious objections to Hegel's conception of government by the civil service. The first, suggested by Marx, is that whatever liberal theory may say, liberal practice is something else. In his 1843 *Critique of Hegel's "Philosophy of Right,"* he represents the bureaucracy as pursuing corporate interests of its own, which in fact run counter to those of the community. It is at best a "pseudo-universal" class, whose members pursue their own corporate interests under the guise of protecting the public business. In a series of dazzling metaphors, Marx compares the hierarchical structure of the civil service to the hierarchy of the medieval church: "The bureaucratic mind," he says, "is through and through a Jesuitical, theological mind. The bureaucrats are the Jesuits and theologians of the state. The bureaucracy is *la république prêtre.*"[52] He even goes on to ridicule Hegel's celebration of the meritocratic principle of open competitive examination

50. For a comprehensive view of these differences, see Charles McIlwain, *Constitutionalism, Ancient and Modern* (Ithaca: Cornell University Press, 1940); for a more recent discussion, see Giovanni Sartori, "Constitutionalism: A Preliminary Discussion," *American Political Science Review* 56 (1962): 853–64.

51. See T. M. Knox, "Hegel and Prussianism," in *Hegel's Political Philosophy,* ed. Walter Kaufmann, p. 19.

52. Karl Marx, *Critique of Hegel's "Philosophy of Right,"* trans. Joseph O'Malley (Cambridge: Cambridge University Press, 1970), p. 46.

as the basis for selection. Such a system is "nothing but the bureaucratic baptism of knowledge, the official recognition of the transubstantiation of profane into holy knowledge."[53] Rather than making knowledge and proof of ability the basis for entering the service, Marx says that it is authority and the worship of authority that typifies the true bureaucratic mind.

The bureaucracy is not, then, a neutral but interested actor. In perhaps this one respect, Marx is in agreement with Aristotle that politics *is* partisanship, and that to expect some to rule for the sake of others is to create utopian expectations. The possibility of circumventing interested government and replacing it with an ideal of public service could only result in forcing persons to conceal their interests behind a mask of hypocrisy, which was, as Marx believed, already what constitutional government was all about. Still, whatever his strictures were against the Hegelian *Beamtenstaat,* they did not prevent Marx from using the industrial proletariat as a stand-in for Hegel's *allgemeine Stand.*[54]

The second line of criticism is suggested by Max Weber. Like Hegel, Weber sees history as the progressive development of the principle of reason or rationalization and regards the bureaucracy, the legal system, and the capitalistic economy as but the most important areas of this development. For Weber, not breakdown and crisis, but consolidation and efficiency, are the hallmarks of rationalization. Furthermore, this development is irreversible. Bureaucracy thus appears as a primary cause of the enslavement of modern man. There is a powerful romantic undercurrent to Weber's writings which leads him to see this progress as part of the general "disenchantment of the world," the driving out of the older magical and mythological worldviews by modern scientific and technological ones. Consider, for example, the following passage dealing with the cultural effects of bureaucracy:

> [E]ach man becomes a little cog in the machine and, aware of this, his one preoccupation is whether he can becomes a bigger cog . . . it is horrible to think that the world could one day be filled with nothing but those little cogs, little men clinging to little jobs and striving towards bigger ones . . . [T]his passion for bureaucracy . . . is enough to drive one to despair. It is . . . as if we were deliberately to become men who need "order" and nothing but order, who become nervous and cowardly if for one moment this order wavers, and helpless if they are torn away from their total incorporation in it. That the world should

53. Marx, *Critique of Hegel's "Philosophy of Right,"* p. 51.
54. See Shlomo Avineri, *The Social and Political Thought of Karl Marx* (Cambridge: Cambridge University Press, 1970), pp. 22–24, 48–52.

know no men but these: it is in such an evolution that we are already caught up, and the great question is therefore not how we can promote and hasten it, but what we can oppose to this machinery in order to keep a portion of mankind free from this parcelling-out of the soul, from this supreme mastery of the bureaucratic way of life.[55]

Weber's response to the problems of bureaucracy and the rationalization of life was the "charismatic" leader, who acquires authority not by knowing the rules but by virtue of heroic or nonrational qualities. It is arguable that Weber's elevation of the charismatic authority above the humdrum routine of everyday life shares something with the existentialist depreciation of the "inauthenticity" of the quotidian and the workaday world. Heidegger's later critique of *das Mann*, or mass man, who seeks to escape from the uncertainties of existence by creating vast social and technological superstructures, reads in part like a footnote to Weber. Whether or not Weber's celebration of charisma led him (unwittingly, to be sure) to support fascist ideology, it is clear that Hegel's more "rationalist" orientation never permitted him to entertain such misgivings about the impersonal organization of the state.

THE MONARCH

Hegel's concept of monarchy is clearly one of the most vulnerable aspects of his defense of the constitutional state. To some the Hegelian theory of monarchy will appear as a symptom of Hegel's accomodation to Restoration theories of throne and alter, while to others it will look like a forced attempt to make political realities conform to the speculative categories of the *Science of Logic*. Neither of these views is adequate. Hegel's concept of the monarch is free of the legitimist ideologies of Restoration Europe, such as Novalis's *Christenheit oder Europe*. At the same time, the charge that he tries to "logicize" the essentially contingent features of the politics of his day fails to consider how different the political solution offered by the *Philosophy of Right* is from the politics of 1820 Prussia.

The monarch is, first of all, a functional requirement of a rational constitution. To be sure, what is meant by a "rational constitution" cannot be specified once and for all in some deductive manner, but depends on the historical development of a people's laws, moral sentiments, and manners. What is rational for some may not be rational for others.[56] What Hegel means by developed or perfected rationality will be treated in chapter 6,

55. Cited in J. P. Mayer, *Max Weber and German Politics: A Study in Political Sociology* (London: Faber and Faber, 1944), pp. 96–97.

56. *PR*, par. 274A, pp. 286–87; *Werke* 7:440.

but for now we can say that a constitution is rational if it functions as an organic whole. The metaphor of organicism is one of the oldest (and most overworked) in the history of political thought. The organic model of the constitution is based on an analogy between a state and a living organism. This metaphor is usually invoked to show that constitutions, like any living organism, develop gradually over time rather than being the result of direct or conscious planning and design. It is often linked to attempts to justify social differentiation and hierarchy. Thus, underlying all organic analogies there is a Whiggish belief that even the best-laid plans cannot provide fully for all the contingencies of experience, so that the prudent statesman will forego all large-scale reforms and seek to adjust himself to the circumstances. Hegel is indeed often eloquent in denouncing the plans of those utopians who, in the words of Michael Oakeshott, seek perfection as the crow flies.

In more specific political terms, Hegel's idea about a rational constitution is tied to his conception of the separation and division of powers. In one sense he remarks "the necessity for a division [*Teilung*] of powers within the state" ought to be regarded as "the guarantee of public freedom."[57] The principle of separation or division, as Montesquieu argued, distinguishes the modern constitutional state from both Oriental despotism and the classical republics. But Hegel makes much of the distinction between the doctrine of the separation of powers and his own theory of an inward differentiation (*Unterscheidung*) of constitutional powers. While the former is a "false doctrine" attributing absolute autonomy and independence to each of the powers, the latter depicts them as mutually supporting aspects of the same totality. "The constitution," Hegel writes, "is rational in so far as the state inwardly differentiates and determines its activity in accordance with the nature of the concept. The result of this is that each of these powers is in itself the totality of the constitution, because each contains the other moments and has them effective in itself."[58]

This passage was worth quoting because it says a great deal about Hegel's use of the organic analogy. First, Hegelian organicism can be described as an "expressive totality."[59] Hegel's point is not simply that every complex phenomenon consists of parts which get their meaning or function from their place within the whole. His point is rather the stronger one that each part is somehow expressive of the nature of the entire organism. The parts

57. *PR*, par. 272R, p. 175; *Werke* 7:433.
58. *PR*, par. 272, p. 174; *Werke* 7:432.
59. I borrow this term from Louis Althusser, *Reading Capital*, trans. Ben Brewster (London: New Left Books, 1970), pp. 94, 96–97.

are internally related to one another in a way that makes the whole not a mere aggregation but a structured whole. The model here, as throughout, is drawn from the biological sciences. In the *Lesser Logic* we read: "The limbs and organs . . . of an organic body are not merely parts of it: it is only in their unity that they are what they are, and they are unquestionably affected by that unity, as they also in turn affect it. These limbs and organs become mere parts, only when they pass under the hands of the anatomist, whose occupation, be it remembered, is not with the living body but with the corpse."[60]

But Hegelian organicism is not just a biological postulate. It attempts to answer a real political problem, namely, how to guarantee the unity and integrity of the state. If one insists, as we have seen Fichte do, that the powers remain absolutely separate, the result will either be a general paralysis or the self-destruction of the state. Thus, while the crown, the executive, and the legislature may have an important degree of de jure separation, their continual harmony and cooperation is in fact necessary if the state is to achieve its end, the freedom of its citizens. "Sovereignty," Hegel writes, "depends on the fact that the particular functions and powers of the state are not self-subsistent or firmly grounded . . . but have their roots ultimately in the unity of the state as their single self."[61]

The sovereignty of the state, then, is guaranteed by the interdependence of the three main branches of government. If the monarch is viewed in this light, we can begin to see why Hegel regards it as the rational "apex" of the political constitution. In the first place, the monarch is for Hegel the tangible expression of all the features of the constitution. This is why an elective monarch or an American-style president would not do as a surrogate.[62] The President may be an expression of the popular will, as he is in the American polity, but like earlier exponents of mixed government, Hegel regards the popular will as only one part of the constitution. The monarch must embody in his person the entire constitution, and not just a part. "The power of the Crown contains in itself the three moments of the whole, viz. (*a*) the *universality* of the constitution and the laws; (*b*) counsel, which refers the *particular* to the universal; and (*c*) the moment of ultimate decision, as the *self-determination* to which everything else reverts and from which everything else derives the beginning of its actuality."[63]

60. *LL*, par. 135R, pp. 191–92; *Werke* 8:268.
61. *PR*, par. 278, pp. 179–80; *Werke* 7:442.
62. *PR*, par. 281R, p. 186; *Werke* 7:452–53.
63. *PR*, par. 275, p. 179; *Werke* 7:441.

Hegel's depiction of the monarch here is not just a descent into "mysticism," as Marx would maintain. Hegel's problem is the very real juridical one of finding a place where sovereignty resides. He rejects the idea of a truly popular sovereignty, for reasons similar to those for his rejection of direct suffrage. The "people" are no more than an abstraction when considered outside the framework of their laws and institutions.[64] The constitution is thus more than a mere formal arrangement of offices; it is closer to what the Greeks called the *politeia,* or regime, or what is today sometimes called political culture. It is the entire way of life of a people. The constitution can be compared to the form or soul of the regime, while the citizen body is its matter. There is no people, but only peoples formed by the constitutions of which they are a part. "We are already citizens of the state by birth," Hegel writes. "The rational end of man is life in the state."[65]

The monarchy is necessary, then, only to the extent that it solves the constitutional question of sovereignty. In an argument strikingly similar to that of Hobbes, Hegel says that because the state is a one it must have a one at its head. But the sovereignty of the state is guaranteed, not by the person, but by the office of the monarch. In a sense, his person is indifferent, and this is why hereditary succession is the best means of selection. Unlike the Platonic *kallipolis,* who rules by virtue of certain determinate attributes, like wisdom or virtue, the Hegelian monarch is "in essence characterized as *this* individual in abstraction from all his other characteristics, and *this* individual is raised to the dignity of monarchy in an immediate, natural, fashion," that is, by accident of birth.[66] One need not expect the monarch to be a wise man but only to have a sense of the dignity of the office and "to say 'yes' and dot the 'i.'" And he adds, with a certain undertone of irony: "[M]onarchs are not exactly distinguished for their bodily prowess or intellectual gifts."[67]

Hegel's conception of the monarchy is still the most vulnerable part of his politics. Modern politics seems to have outstripped Hegel here in its solution to the problem of sovereign authority. Modern states have, on the whole, been able to retain their sovereign majesty without the institution of a monarchy. But Hegel might add that it is only by appropriating the trappings of monarchy (think of de Gaulle) that they have been able to do this. His point is that any government requires some ceremonial power to confer dignity on it, and in the modern European state the office of the monarch

64. *PR,* par. 279R, pp. 182–83; *Werke* 7:446–47.
65. *PR,* par. 75A, p. 242; *Werke* 7:159. "Die vernünftige Bestimmung des Menschen ist, im Staate zu leben . . ."
66. *PR,* par. 280, p. 184; *Werke* 7:450.
67. *PR,* pars. 280A, 281A, p. 289; *Werke* 7:451, 453.

does this better than any other. This is not to deny that other persons or other bodies might not perform this function equally well for other cultures at other times, but only that monarchy is the office best equipped to elicit some sense of the majesty and authority of government in the West.

The accusation that Hegel merely rationalizes, and hence legitimates, certain contingent historical institutions, thus conferring a purportedly timeless validity on them, is a more difficult charge to answer. In this vein, Ilting accuses Hegel of "deducing" hereditary monarchy by means of dialectical logic, while Sidney Hook says that Hegel, in some of "the most specious reasoning that ever disgraced a philosopher," tries "to 'prove' by [dialectical] logic that state sovereignty must be embodied not merely in an individual, not merely in a monarch, but in a hereditary monarch."[68] But even to charge Hegel with logical inconsistency is to miss the point. Hegel's method of analysis is not deductive; he in no sense tries to deduce the details of political life from the purely abstract categories of logic. The idea of working out some "ideal theory," such as Marx's notion of "true democracy" or "human emancipation," and then using this theory as a criterion for judging existing institutions and as a norm for future society, is entirely foreign to Hegel's approach. Instead, he attempts to bring out the rationality that is already there within existing institutions and forms of life, including the monarchy. Rationality, as we shall see in chapter 6, is not something that we the philosophical onlookers are required to bring with us to the evaluation process, but is to varying degrees already realized within the world we inhabit. As Duncan Forbes has pointed out in his introduction to the English translation of Hegel's *Lectures on the Philosophy of World History:* "The important thing is that to suppose that there should be strict logical links in the movement of the dialectic is to miss its real meaning and significance and value as a device to enable one to think concretely about the state, freedom, etc. . . . the whole point of Hegel's dialectic as a device of philosophical explanation is that it is *not* a process of rigid logical deduction: it moves freely, it is to be used flexibly, its purpose is to provide insight and understanding of the human condition."[69]

WAR AND INTERNATIONAL RELATIONS

This leaves us finally with the problem of war and international relations in Hegel's philosophy. Here, perhaps more than in any other area, his views

68. Karl-Heinz Ilting, "The Structure of Hegel's 'Philosophy of Right,'" in *Hegel's Political Philosophy,* ed. Z. A. Pelczynski, p. 106; Sidney Hook, "Hegel and his Apologists," in *Hegel's Political Philosophy,* ed. Walter Kaufmann, p. 90.

69. Duncan Forbes, "Introduction," in G. W. F. Hegel, *Lectures on the Philosophy of World*

have been subject to sharp attack. His repudiation of the perfectibilian and optimistic theories of the Enlightenment, as well as his claim that war "preserves the ethical health of peoples," has been enough to brand him as a belligerent advocate of German nationalism and imperialism.[70] In point of fact, however, Hegel's views on war help us to pose in an especially revealing manner a weakness in the liberal theory of political obligation. Here as elsewhere Hegel proposes to test the limits of liberalism.

The problem to which Hegel's account of war is an answer concerns the question raised recently by Michael Walzer: "Why should I die for the state?"[71] If the state is, as men like Hobbes, Locke, and Kant have said, an institution for the protection of private rights alone, then it is not clear why the citizen should ever obey the state's command to risk his life in time of war. If the protection of life, liberty, and property is the raison d'être for the state, then there are surely less costly ways of defending these rights than war. The answer given most often by liberal theory is that one incurs obligations to defend the state because it in turn defends one's property, family, and friends. But this is to risk one's life for the sake of some privately incurred obligation. It has nothing specifically political about it.

Hegel rejects the liberal theory of obligation, saying it founders on a conceptual confusion between civil society and the state: "An entirely distorted account of the demand for this sacrifice results from regarding the state as a mere civil society and from regarding its final end as only the security of individual life and property. This security cannot possibly be obtained by the sacrifice of what is to be secured—on the contrary."[72] What is the basis for this distinction?

"Civil society," as the term was used by Hegel, points to an area of life dominated by what I would call individualism, or what Hegel called "subjectivity." As the unique creation of the modern world, civil society is the outcome of both Christianity and modern natural rights theories which conceive of man not primarily as a political creature but as the possessor of rights which it is the duty of the state to protect. What is unique about

History: Introduction, trans. H. B. Nisbet (Cambridge: Cambridge University Press, 1975), p. xxx.

70. For an early study alleging this, see Hermann Heller, *Hegel und der nationale Machtstaatsgedanke in Deutschland* (Leipzig and Berlin: Neudruck, 1921); for a more sympathetic view, see Shlomo Avineri, *Hegel's Theory of the Modern State* (Cambridge: Cambridge University Press, 1972), chap. 10.

71. Michael Walzer, "The Obligation to die for the State," in *Obligations: Essays on Disobedience, War, and Citizenship* (New York: Simon & Schuster, 1970).

72. *PR*, par. 324R, p. 209; *Werke* 7:492.

civil, as opposed to political, association is that it is brought about through the free play of self-interest, where one treats everybody as a means to one's own ends, or, to paraphrase Adam Smith, where in order to achieve one's own ends one appeals not to one's neighbor's sense of altruism but to his self-interest. Civil society is the world of economic transactions governed by the "invisible hand," where the satisfaction of my needs leads to the satisfaction of the needs of others. Thus, what unity civil society possesses is brought about largely unconsciously and automatically, through the exchange of goods and services in the marketplace. What Hegel opposes is not civil society per se, but those writers who confuse civil society with the aims of politics proper.

Hegel's conception of the state, or the "political state," as he sometimes calls it, is first and foremost an ethical community similar to the Aristotelian *koinonia politike*.[73] By calling the state an ethical community, Hegel means to endow it with something other than the mere use of force or the power to coerce. The state is not an instrument for the achievement of material satisfactions; it is a mode of relating which stresses shared values and common sacrifice at the expense of individual interests. In emphasizing the *sittlich* character of the state, Hegel returns to the standpoint of practical philosophy in indicating that the individual is what he is only by virtue of his participation in some totality wider than himself. One is obligated to the state not because of its superior force but because it is a community of persons united around some shared conception of the good life. The state involves shared standards and principles, which is, I take it, what Hegel means by emphasizing its "spiritual" (*geistig*) character.

In the wider context of his philosophy, war is one of the chief means by which the ethical character of the state is preserved. Hegel arrives at this conclusion through the following syllogism.

1. The state is an ethical unity.
2. States frequently engage in war to preserve their unity.
3. War is a "moment" in the ethical life of the state.

This reasoning will no doubt seem strained, if not outright objectionable, to those brought up on the belief that war is symptomatic of collective unreason. War, it is often suggested, is the breakdown of policy, not its continuation. But in keeping with his general methodological prescriptions to seek the rational in what exists, Hegel refuses to engage in "moralistic" denunciations of warfare:

73. Manfred Riedel, *Between Tradition and Revolution: The Hegelian Transformation of Political Philosophy*, trans. Walter Wright (Cambridge: Cambridge University Press, 1984), pp. 133–37, 171–76.

War is not to be regarded as an absolute evil and as a purely external accident, which itself therefore has some accidental cause, be it injustices, the passions of nations or the holders of power, etc., or in short, something or other which ought not to be. It is to what is by nature accidental that accidents happen, and the fate whereby they happen is thus a necessity. Here as elsewhere, the point of view from which things seem pure accidents vanishes if we look at them in the light of the concept and philosophy, because philosophy knows accident for a show and sees in it its essence, necessity.[74]

The ethical significance of war resides, then, above all in its ability to raise us above the level of mere civil association with its rootedness in material possessions and interests. In times of war, common values and commitments are not only preserved but enhanced. Thus, in the *Phenomenology*, Hegel presents war as the power of the "negative," in which the contingency of the material world is demonstrated. This approach is buttressed by a philosophy of history that views prolonged peace as giving rise to the illusion that the state exists for the sake of civil society. The positive value of war is that it transcends attachment to things by uniting men for the purpose of a common ideal. The most extreme formulation of this position reads as follows:

> In order not to let them get rooted and settled in this isolation and thus break up the whole into fragments and let the common spirit evaporate, government has from time to time to shake them to the very center by War. By this means it confounds the order that has been established and arranged, and violates their right to independence, while the individuals . . . are made, by the task thus imposed on them by government, to feel the power of their lord and master, death. By thus breaking up the form of fixed stability, spirit guards the ethical order from sinking into merely natural existence, preserves the self of which it is conscious, and raises that self to the level of freedom and its own powers.[75]

In a passage from the *Philosophy of Right* in which he refers back to his earlier treatise, *Natural Law*, he remarks:

> War is the state of affairs which deals in earnest with the vanity of temporal goods and concerns—a vanity at other times a common theme of edifying sermonizing. This is what makes it the moment in which the ideality of the particular attains its right and is actualized. War has the higher significance that by its agency . . . "the ethical health of peoples is preserved in their indifference to the stabilization of finite institutions; just as the blowing of the winds preserves the sea from the foulness which would be the result of prolonged calm, so also

74. *PR*, par. 324R, p. 209; *Werke* 7:492.
75. *PhM*, p. 474; *Werke* 3:335.

corruption in nations would be a product of prolonged, let alone 'perpetual peace.'"[76]

These passages should not be taken as glorifying war. They are more an argument about what is, conceptually speaking, involved in statehood. Hegel's understanding of the state should be seen here as walking a middle line between two alternatives. One is the market model of politics identified with classic liberalism. The other is a model, given its canonical expression almost a century after Hegel by Max Weber, which sees the state as controlling the monopoly of violence. For Hegel, we have seen, the state may be founded in an act of violence, as the paradigm case of the struggle for recognition indicates. But violence is not its final end. Thus, the view of Hegel as anticipating the *Machtstaat* is premature. The test of a founder or statesman like Theseus or Napoleon is ultimately the ability to create stable political institutions and sentiments that take the place of force. We can see here exactly how far Hegel is from any kind of hero worship of particular charismatic individuals.

War thus comes to have a specific function within the Hegelian *Rechtsstaat*. While in his early writings Hegel turned to a latter-day Theseus as a way of founding the state, in the *Philosophy of Right* he assumes that the state is already established, that we are already in possession of "the idea of right." It follows that war is no longer a means of founding, but of preserving, states from the internal tensions generated by the marketplace and civil society. War becomes, then, a type of school for the civic education of the modern bourgeois. This is not to romanticize war but to turn it into a means of promoting certain types of civic virtues for citizens who in normal times are used to consulting only their private interests. Only in times of national crisis do virtues such as courage and honor take on meaning:

> Courage to be sure is multiform. The mettle of an animal or a brigand, courage for the sake of honor, the courage of a knight, these are not true forms of courage. The true courage of civilized nations is readiness for sacrifice in the service of the state, so that the individual counts as only one amongst many. The important thing here is not personal mettle but aligning oneself with the universal. In India five hundred men conquered twenty thousand who were not cowards, but who only lacked this disposition to work in close cooperation with others.[77]

This passage tells us something crucial about Hegel's views on modern warfare. For men in heroic societies, courage is one way in which individ-

76. *PR,* par. 324R, p. 210; *Werke* 7:492–93; *NL,* p. 93; *Werke* 2:481–82.
77. *PR,* par. 327A, p. 296; *Werke* 7:495–96.

ual excellence is exhibited. Courage is no doubt necessary to sustain the whole nexus of family and community relations, but it belongs primarily to the individual who excels in battle and conquest as a mark of recognition of personal worth or esteem. In his description of the aristocratic warrior psychology in the *Phenomenology,* Hegel shows that it is not enough to encourage such men to seek release in work, the slave side of the master-slave relation. What distinguishes the warrior from the slave is that work is not enough; he needs to risk his life for the sake of an ethical idea. In this respect, Hegel's description of "courage for the sake of honor" as "not true forms of courage" is an implicit rejection of Aristotle's account of heroic friendship in the *Ethics.* Here Aristotle defines the man of heroic excellence as one who will if necessary die for his friend or fatherland because he seeks the noble above all else and because he prefers a twelvemonth of a glorious life to many years of small successes. He is also a man who will make room for a friend to act, but only because in doing so "he is . . . assigning the greater good to himself." [78]

By contrast to the aristocratic warrior of antiquity, the modern hero, Hegel tells us, is characterized by a type of selflessness. The virtue of modern courage is not that it is done for the sake of personal honor, but that it is in the service of something impersonal, the state. What distinguishes the ancient from the modern warrior is that the former regards war as bound up with ideas of personal honor and excellence, whereas the latter is essentially willing to fight for some more abstract "cause" or ideal in which the self becomes lost. Ancient warfare reminds us of an Achilles or a Hector; modern warfare of a Mazzini or a Trotsky. Whereas ancient courage always entails an element of self-assertion, a desire to get one's proper place with its requisite honors and privileges, the virtue of the modern warrior is precisely his "abstract" character. The virtue of the modern hero is not that he fights to receive his due but that he aligns himself with the "universal."

Curiously, Hegel does not infer from the more abstract and universal character of modern warfare the slide into total war, but rather its opposite. Because of the more impersonal character of modern warfare, he predicts that it will be ultimately more humane and less barbaric than wars fought in the past. In a remarkable passage he even claims that the mechanization of warfare beginning with the introduction of the gun will serve in the future to make war more rational and less the product of purely personal enmity and caprice. "It is for this reason that thought," he writes, "had invented the gun, and the invention of this weapon, which has changed the

78. Aristotle, *Nicomachean Ethics,* 1169a.

purely personal form of bravery into a more abstract one, is no accident."[79] Hegel's suggestion seems to be that with the increased accuracy and destructiveness of modern weaponry, war, by a peculiar dialectical ruse, may prepare the way for its own abolition.

If Hegel is overly sanguine about the future of modern warfare, he makes it clear that war exists not merely because states remain unenlightened about their true interests or because of a natural scarcity of resources. War, he believes, is coeval with politics as such. States, like individuals, define themselves in terms of what they are not, that is, in terms of opposition and struggle. The chapter "Lordship and Bondage" in the *Phenomenology,* is simply the archetypal form of this struggle. Thus, Hegel is especially critical of Kant, and would have been critical of all Enlightenment liberals up to and including Woodrow Wilson, for believing that the reeducation of humanity through the spread of enlightenment or the rearrangement of political institutions will solve once and for all the problem of war. The idea of a League of Nations would seem to him nothing more than a pious hope which fails to get at the root of the problem:

> Perpetual peace is often advocated as an ideal towards which humanity should strive. With that end in view, Kant proposed a league of monarchs to adjust differences between states, and the Holy Alliance was meant to be a league of much the same kind. But the state is an individual, and individuality essentially implies negation. Hence even if a number of states make themselves into a family, this group as an individual must engender an opposite and create an enemy.[80]

It is because he believes that the causes of war are sown deep in human nature that Hegel is skeptical about the possibility of international law. A state cannot alienate its own right to act as a state, which means that it cannot be bound by contract. International law would be binding only if there were some superior power to enforce it. Since there is none, states can be said to exist in a "state of nature" vis-à-vis one another. Consequently, international law, like the Categorical Imperative, remains stuck on the *ought:*

> The fundamental proposition of international law . . . is that treaties, as the ground of obligations between states, ought to be kept. But since the sovereignty of a state is the principle of its relations to others, states are to that extent in a state of nature in relation to each other. Their rights are actualized only in their particular wills and not in a universal will with constitutional powers over them.

79. *PR,* par. 328R, p. 212; *Werke* 7:496.
80. *PR,* par. 324A, p. 295; *Werke* 7:493–94.

This universal proviso of international law therefore does not go beyond an ought-to-be, and what really happens is that international relations in accordance with treaty alternate with severence of these relations.[81]

It is important to note that in describing the causes of war in terms of the irreducibility of the state, Hegel is not concerned to distinguish between the right and wrong of the contenders in any actual political struggle. In keeping with his more historically minded attitude toward natural right, he sees right as embodied in different positions. He recognizes a plurality of different regimes or constitutions, without claiming philosophically to arbitrate between them. Thus, when it comes to explaining the causes of actually existing wars, it is not so much a matter of a clash between absolutes as between contending sets of rights. Hegel thus wants to dispense with the notion of a just war or the notion that there are certain a priori standards of justice independent of the combatants engaged in the struggle. The only court of appeal is history itself, to decide the question of right. One recalls in this context Schiller's dictum, quoted by Hegel at the end of the *Philosophy of Right*—*Weltgeschichte ist Weltgericht*—"the history of the world is the world's court of judgment."[82]

This, I think, brings out the ambiguous character of warfare when considered in the light of Hegel's political philosophy as a whole. On the one hand, war is an integral part of the life of the state. The very multiplicity of states would seem to guarantee the permanence of wars and revolutions. It is the means whereby state sovereignty is expressed, as well as where the "ethical health" of a people, their sense of community and political solidarity, is put to the test. But there is also more to war. As the power of "negativity," war brings out the temporality and finitude of all things, thereby serving a philosophical function. It is here that Hegel appears closest to Heidegger and modern existentialists. His description of modern bravery as sacrifice in the service of a "universal" sounds remarkably close to Heidegger's "resoluteness" in the face of death. In any case, war prevents an excessive rootedness in and attachment to the more mundane interests of civil association. It is the means whereby the state and the specifically political form of obligation can come to assert themselves over the cacophony of private rights engendered by civil society. Indeed, the importance of war for Hegel is necessitated by his attempt to reaffirm not only the particularity of the political perspective but the relative autonomy of the state.

On the other hand, even if the state's right is not bound by any inter-

---

81. *PR*, par. 333, p. 213; *Werke* 7:499–500.
82. *PR*, par. 340, p. 216; *Werke* 7:503.

national agreement or contract, it must answer to a higher principle of right, which is of course nothing other than world history itself. Once we understand history as the final arbiter of matters of war and peace, then the whole Hegelian construction of the *Rechtsstaat* loses its autonomous character. Hegel's political philosophy, like that of both Kant and Marx, culminates in the philosophy of history and finally in the idea of an "end of history." The idea of an end of history means essentially the growing rationalization or Westernization of humanity, founded on the twin principles of the rule of law and Protestant Christianity. The growing rationalism of all aspects of life will, of course, lead to the realization of the modern constitutional state inaugurated by the French Revolution and Napoleon and expressed in the idea of mutual respect for persons as such. But the complete and total rationalization of humankind will also lead to the homogenization or unification of humanity, characterized by an increased agreement over all the fundamental aims of life. The triumph of reason will mean the elimination of the grounds of war and conflict, because there will be nothing left to fight about. It will represent the final triumph of bourgeois civil society, with its pacific and commercial interests, over the political state, which seeks preeminence in struggle and combat. In the final analysis, Hegel's idea of history tends to undercut his insistence on the necessity, and even nobility, of war.

6 HEGEL'S IDEA OF A CRITICAL THEORY

WHAT IS DIALECTIC?

No account of Hegel's political philosophy would be complete without some reference to his so-called dialectical method. Of course even to speak of a dialectical method is already to invite controversy, since it has been claimed that the dialectic is not a method at all but a way of describing the way in which our concepts and categories (*Denkbestimmungen*) give rise not just to a series but to a self-generated series. On this account, the concepts and categories we use in everyday speech are such that they inevitably involve us in paradox and contradiction which call out for resolution. Indeed, if one were to summarize this dialectical procedure in a single phrase, we might say that it seeks to overcome contradiction. Dialectic, as Hegel understood it, is nothing if not an attempt to reconcile the various antinomies and contradictions created by previous thought. As a mode of interpretation, its aim is to reconcile, to mend, and to make whole the various facets of the divided self which I have suggested was Hegel's initial point of departure.

Hegel's own practice of dialectic is related to—is arguably the crowning moment of—the "critical philosophy" that he inherited from Kant. In particular, critical philosophy was a protest against the predominant Enlightenment conception of philosophical method conceived along the lines of the modern science of nature. Central to this new science was its conception of method as reduction, or resolving into parts. For the partisans of scientific methodology, we know something only when we have succeeded in breaking it down into its constitutive elements. Thus, Descartes, in his *Discourse on Method*, turned to mathematics to find the one true basis for securing knowledge. On this new foundation, nothing was to be assented to until it was submitted to the canons of evidence, division, order, and exhaustion. Here Descartes's second rule—"to divide up each of the difficulties which I examined into as many parts as possible, and as seemed requisite in order that it might be resolved in the best manner possible"—is especially important.[1]

---

1. René Descartes, *Ouevres philosophique,* ed. Felix Alquie (Paris: Garnier, 1963), 1:586.

The purpose of this method of reduction was ideally to provide the theorist or scientist with the knowledge of how best to control and predict events. Reduction reveals the simplest elements or universals out of which we can begin to construct theories or hypotheses for purposes of control and prediction. This emphasis on control is not simply an extraneous or contingent feature of scientific method. Rather, it is crucial to the whole scientific enterprise that we understand something only when we succeed in isolating those factors that causally produce it. When applied to social phenomena and history, the result is a generalizing science that sees human beings as fundamentally alike across space and time, and as such, subject to the same natural laws as other phenomena. By following the correct set of scientific procedures, it should be possible, at least in principle, to provide rational solutions to all problems concerning the organization of society, a use of rationality concerned only with finding the most efficient means to attain one's ends.

Descartes's appeal to mathematics as the only basis for philosophical method was intended to put an end to dialectical reasoning, which he associated with the discredited philosophies of Aristotle and the medieval schoolmen. By ruling out theology as an article of faith and by denying history any dignity or utility, Descartes sought to clear the deck for the triumph of science. His project was through and through positivistic, by which I mean admitting science, and only science, as the one true form of knowledge.

The founders of critical philosophy envisaged a research agenda virtually the opposite of that pursued by the proponents of science. In the first place, they realized, following Kant, that while the laws of mathematical physics are both necessary and sufficient for explaining the phenomenal world of nature, these laws necessarily draw a blank when confronted with the facts of moral life. When men are considered, not simply as a part of physical nature, but as moral agents with free will or the capacity for initiation, we see that morality can never be reduced to the kind of knowledge that is appropriate in the field of the sciences. In the second place, from a fairly early stage, the founders of the critical philosophy realized that the institutionalization of scientific method does not belong to an autonomous domain of logic but is part of a broader social and historical process. Science is not only a way of knowing; it is a way of life embedded in a culturally specific set of institutions, a form of *Sittlichkeit,* which it is the task of critical analysis to bring out. As Charles Taylor has argued, such an approach begins from the core assumption that human life, and even the cosmos as a whole, constitutes a unity or totality where every part finds its meaning by virtue of its place within the whole.[2] To know the part means to grasp its place within the whole of which it is a part. The procedure adopted here is not to reduce but to relate, or in the words of E. M. Forster in *Howard's End,* "only connect . . ."

It follows that the critical philosophy must, among other things, attempt to give some account of the place of theory within the whole. It must, in other words, seek to relate ideas and beliefs (what Hegel called the sphere of "subjective mind"), on the one hand, to the institutions and social structures ("objective mind") within which those beliefs are embedded, on the other. These two aspects, the subjective and the objective, necessarily go together. Ideas require language to achieve public recognition, and language is itself a social institution. Likewise, no matter how objective and permanent social institutions may appear, they are complex sets of understandings, relations, and activities. Theory and practice, then, are not two discrete or isolated variables only contingently connected to one another, but are bound by relations of mutual and irreducible interdependence. One might even say that there is a dialectical relation between them, but without further elaboration of what this means it would tell us little.

Before we see how Hegel instantiated this dialectical procedure in his own philosophy, three general features of this method can be noted in advance. First, this method must be immanent or internal to its subject matter. Dialectical theorists reject outright the idea that the thinker can occupy some privileged Archimedean point outside the subject of investigation. For rejecting any dialectical method is often criticized for leading absolute, objective, or apodictic foundation for knowledge to subjectivism, relativism, or even worse. Dialectical thinkers, however, tend to regard their subject matters as constituted by the activity of theorizing itself. Theory is always connected, because the subject matter is in part constituted by the theorist. The theorist does not merely describe a pregiven world of brute fact uncontaminated by reflection; he creates this world out of the various cultural resources of his time as they already exist. The point of a dialectical approach is not just to record and observe but to establish a coherent universe of discourse, which the reader may want either to accept or reject.

A second feature of dialectical method is its dialogical character. Theorizing is an activity taking place not simply within the mind but between

2. Charles Taylor, *Hegel and Modern Society* (Cambridge: Cambridge University Press, 1979), chap. 1.

minds. Thinking is dialogical because it always takes the form of an exchange or a conversation between ourselves, our contemporaries, and our predecessors. What Burke said of well-ordered political regimes is equally true of dialectical theories, to wit, that they are conversations between the living, the dead, and those yet to be born. Our thinking is never the result of isolated reflection but is mediated by a common inheritance or intellectual tradition. Indeed, Hegel's greatest works typically have the character, if not the form, of a conversation with his most illustrious predecessors, the purpose of which is a full recognition of their contributions to the making of our current position. Such works are dialectical in the original sense of that term: they aim not just to refute an opponent but to join in philosophical friendship with one's tradition. The essence of the dialectical attitude is a "constant endeavor to convert every occasion of non-agreement into an occasion of agreement."[3]

Third, the dialogical element is related to the historical dimension of theory. This historical (or historicist) dimension of theory was already anticipated by Kant. Kant set for himself the task of rescuing scientific or phenomenal knowledge from the onslaught of Humean skepticism. He showed how the mind, possessed of certain rudimentary forms of intuition and understanding, is the constitutive ground of experience. Knowledge, on Kant's account, is not simply a passive transcription of reality but takes on an active, creative stance towards it. To a far greater extent than previously imagined, knowledge became a subjective creation, limited only by the prior structuring principles of the mind.

As we shall see in the next section, Hegel accepted Kant's account of the active character of the mind but took this one step further. The very structuring principles of consciousness vary with different historical epochs and cultures. Mind is not a given, preformed once and for all. Rather, the capacities, powers, and abilities that it exhibits at any one time will be different from what they are at any other. And this is not only true of certain peripheral or secondary characteristics of thought but of the deepest and seemingly most permanent features of logic and metaphysics, not to mention political philosophy. All are equally subject to change. From this it would appear easy to argue that all thought is equally culture bound or ideological, in the sense that it is relative to the particular needs and interests of men living under diverse historical circumstances.

To be sure, the incipient relativism of some of these pronouncements

3. R. G. Collingwood, *The New Leviathan* (Oxford: Clarendon Press, 1942), p. 326.

raised serious problems for writers like Hegel and Marx, who tried to show that each distinct historical epoch or culture represents but a moment in the unfolding of some final epoch, the end of history, towards which mankind is collectively evolving. The historical character of mind does not present itself as a random movement from one idea or set of ideas to another with no rhyme or reason. It rather takes the form of a progress whereby the consciousness of human freedom gradually becomes extended to ever larger numbers of people. Whatever doubts Hegel may have expressed about the French ideologues who tried to force their ideas about freedom and popular sovereignty on the world, he recognized their positive contribution to the development of more adequate forms of human culture. History is, then, the process of mankind's progressive emancipation from those forces that inhibit the granting of respect or recognition to other individuals, peoples, and cultures. This process is a slow one and depends upon the assumption that human agents are driven by a powerful common interest in freedom that persists throughout the interplay of their passions and actions. But dialectical theorists tend to see history as a moral unity which consists of the overcoming of deep-seated frustrations and deceptions by ever freer and more rational ways of life and systems of thought.

IMMANENT CRITIQUE AND THE FOUNDATIONS OF PHENOMENOLOGY

Hegel's approach to the dialectic begins with what has traditionally been called "the problem of knowledge," namely the search for a criterion (or criteria) that could establish the truth of our inquiries. When one asserts, as has traditionally been done, that philosophy is a search for the truth about the nature of things, one presupposes the existence of a standard that could validate this truth. Without such a standard, philosophy is thought to be impossible. The search for some such standard belongs properly to the domain of epistemology—the theory of knowledge—which is in turn regarded by modern philosophy as a kind of "first philosophy," a universal inquiry into the necessary presuppositions of knowledge.

Hegel appears to follow the lead of modern epistemology right from the start by concerning himself with the problem of the criterion. The opening sentence of the introduction to the *Phenomenology of Mind* reads like something we might find in philosophers from Descartes to Fichte: "It is natural to suppose that, before philosophy enters upon its subject proper— namely, the actual knowledge [*das wirkliche Erkennen*] of what truly is—it is necessary to come first to an understanding concerning knowledge, which is looked upon as the instrument by which to take possession of the Absolute, or as the means through which to get a sight of it.[4]

Hegel's starting point in the *Phenomenology* seems to be entirely traditional. It is the program of modern epistemology, with its search for a set of guarantees or foundations upon which our cognitions can be secured. According to this tradition, before we can acquire directly this "actual knowledge of what truly is," we must first inquire indirectly into the faculty of knowing. Two possibilities have traditionally been considered. Knowledge has been treated as either an "instrument by which we apprehend reality" or "a medium through which the light of truth reaches us."[5] In either case, the result will be problematic. If knowledge is indeed an "instrument" (*Werkzeug*), it cannot help but reshape the object, the "Absolute," which it seeks to grasp. And likewise, if we consider it only as a passive "medium" (*Mittel*) through which reality is filtered, like light refracted through a prism, it cannot but leave reality different from what it was before. The result of either approach would be to produce a skepticism about the possibility of ever reaching the truth or reality in itself.

From this passage it is perhaps not immediately clear to what or to whom Hegel is alluding. The metaphor of knowledge as a medium is almost certainly an allusion to the empiricist philosophies of Locke and Hume. In contrast to the rationalistic philosophers like Descartes and Spinoza, who sought criteria for knowledge in clear and distinct axioms and definitions, the empiricists tried to trace even the most abstract conceptions, like force or law, back to relatively simple experiences. Thus, Hegel can say "[e]mpiricial philosophy . . . abandons the search for truth in thought itself, and goes to fetch it from Experience."[6] So far is he from abandoning experience for mere speculative, a priori assertion that he terms experience "this principle [which] carries with it the unspeakably important condition that, in order to accept any fact, we must be in contact with it."[7]

Empiricism looks for standards of truth, then, in what appears or what presents itself immediately at hand. What is immediate—what is uncontaminated by reflection and analysis—is more likely to be true. In empiricism we find, then, "the great principle that whatever is true must be in the actual world and present to sensation." Accordingly, "the Empirical School

4. *PhM*, p. 137; *Werke* 3:68.
5. *PhM*, p. 137; *Werke* 3:68.
6. *LL*, par. 37, p. 60; *Werke* 8:107.
7. *LL*, par. 7, pp. 10–11; *Werke* 8:49.

elevates the facts included under sensation, feeling, and perception into the forms of general ideas, propositions, or laws." Hegel even goes so far as to identify the "principle" of empiricism, namely, experience, with philosophy itself. For "no less than Empiricism, philosophy recognizes only what is, and has nothing to do with what merely ought to be and what is thus confessed not to exist." "The main lesson of empiricism," we learn, "is that man must see for himself and feel that he is present in every fact of knowledge which he has to accept."[8]

Hegel's criticism of the Lockean theory of mind as a medium, or a tabula rasa upon which anything can be imprinted, is that it fails to account for how experience can serve as a stable ground for truth. While Hegel congratulates Lockean empiricism for establishing "a far ranging culture [*Bildung*]" which has become "the philosophy of the English and the French, and likewise in a certain sense the Germans," he still faults it for confusing the truth of an idea with its conditions of origin.[9] While Locke's "Historical plain Method," as he calls it in the introduction to the *Essay on Human Understanding,* satisfied for Hegel a "true necessity," it also had the defect of introducing a psychological, or more properly, a psychologistic, element into knowledge. By "psychologism" is meant that Locke assimilates conceptual or logical processes to psychological ones; he translates statements about beliefs into statements about how beliefs are acquired. This method is pointedly relativistic, since it invariably makes truth a function of the inquirer rather than the object being investigated, or in Hegel's phrase, "the matter in question is merely subjective, and somewhat psychological, since [Locke] merely describes the methods of mind as it appears to us to be."[10]

Passing now to the metaphor of knowledge as an instrument, it seems evident that Hegel is referring to the "Critical Philosophy" of Kant. For Kant, as we have seen, the mind is not simply a passive transcription of the world but plays an active part in the structuring of it. Unlike Locke and Hume and more like Vico, Kant argued that we can know the world, not simply because it is there, but because we have made it, or at least contributed to its making. We make the world insofar as the mind possesses a structure by which the manifold of sense data is organized and made coherent. The mind is not, then, simply a blank slate upon which any script

8. *LL,* par. 38, p. 61; *Werke* 8:107–8.
9. *LHP* 3:295, 298; *Werke* 20:208–9.
10. *LHP* 3:299; *Werke* 20:209.

can be written, but always experiences the world as a coherent whole mediated by certain fundamental forms that he called "categories."

Kant's point is that intuitions like space and time and categories like causality are not simply inferable from experience, as the empiricists would have us believe, but are the a priori conditions that make experience possible. These categories and intuitions are clearly not "about" reality, since there is no object in experience that corresponds to them. What they are is something like a framework within which we can begin to make statements and pursue inquiries about reality at all. While it may be possible to imagine worlds very different from the one in which we now live, it is impossible to imagine a world in which things do not exist in space and time or are not subsumable under categories like number, substance, or causality. The purpose, then, of Kant's "metaphysics of experience" is to elucidate those basic features of the mind that make experience shared or shareable, as opposed to utterly private. His basic concern is to show how the world we inhabit is a common world and not simply a congeries of diverse perceptions and experiences, as the empiricists were led to think.

While Hegel remained powerfully influenced by Kant's activist account of the mind, Kant's need for a fixed, timeless, categorial framework upon which knowledge depended did not strike him as a decisive victory over the subjectivism and psychologism of his predecessors. As Hegel tries to show, Kant abolishes skepticism only surreptitiously to reestablish it at a higher level. Because the categories apply only to objects of possible experience, Kant leaves open a realm of unconditioned objects, a "noumenal" realm which must, perforce, lie outside of our understanding. This opens up, then, a radical disjunction between things as they appear to us—as conditioned by the mind—and things as they are in themselves. The result of Kant's "transcendental idealism" is to produce a skepticism about the possibility of knowing the unconditioned, the world of things in themselves (*Dinge an sich*).

Hegel's rejection of the instrumentalist conception of mind brings together his objections to the whole modern epistemological enterprise. So long as we continue to think of knowledge as requiring a fixed categorial framework, we will be trapped in a vicious circle. The theory of knowledge (*Erkenntnistheorie*) as traditionally formulated claimed not to be just one form of knowledge among others but an enterprise concerned with the foundations of all possible knowledge. As such, it claimed a privileged insight into the presuppositions of all knowledge. But Hegel's point is that any such claim about the foundations of knowledge is already a claim to knowledge and thus presupposes what it needs to prove. The result is a claim to investigate the faculty of knowledge prior to knowing. This is well stated in a passage from the *Lesser Logic:*

> Kant undertook to examine how far the forms of thought were capable of leading to the knowledge of truth. In particular he demanded a criticism of the faculty of cognition as preliminary to its exercise. That is a fair demand, if it means that even the forms of thought must be made an object of investigation. Unfortunately there soon creeps in the misconception of already knowing before you know—the error of refusing to enter the water until you have learnt to swim. True, indeed, the forms of thought should be subjected to a scrutiny before they are used: yet what is this scrutiny but *ipso facto* a cognition? [11]

The argument here at least struck Hegel as conclusive. It is directed against the claims of epistemology, or theory of knowledge, to provide unassailable foundations for knowledge. Hegel wants to argue that either (*a*) the foundations are already a form of knowledge, an "actual" cognition, which results in circularity; or (*b*) they need to be justified by a further set of criteria, which results in infinite regress. Still, Hegel denies that the contradictions into which the theory of knowledge falls must necessarily lead to doubt and despair. He suggests rather that "the fear of falling into error" is itself the error:

> Meanwhile, if the fear of falling into error introduces an element of distrust into science, which without any scruples of that sort goes to work and actually does know, it is not easy to understand why, conversely, a distrust should not be placed in this very distrust, and why we should not take care lest the fear of error is not just the initial error. As a matter of fact, this fear presupposes something, indeed a great deal, as truth, and supports its scruples and consequences on what should itself be examined beforehand to see whether it is true. [12]

Hegel's answer to the problems inherent in traditional philosophy is his theory of immanent criticism. By an internal or immanent examination of knowledge is meant one that seeks criteria of validity within existing forms of knowledge. As opposed to the claims of a Kantian "first philosophy" (*Ursprungsphilosophie*), which seeks to delimit once and for all standards of cognitive acceptability, Hegel maintains that these standards are already at hand within existing modes of cognition. Immanent criticism must give up the deeply felt epistemological need to impose its own standards upon the subject matter. Any such external input, what Hegel calls "our addition" (*unsere Zutat*), must be avoided by the philosopher, who is allowed only to

11. *LL*, par. 41, p. 66; *Werke* 8:114.
12. *PhM*, pp. 132–33; *Werke* 3:69–70.

observe (*Zusehen*) consciousness. There is no point, then, in trying to determine a priori rules of evidence for what is to count as knowledge or how
it is to be verified. The idea of an immanent critique, or phenomenological
self-reflection, means rather that we need only test the knowledge against
itself.

The idea that knowledge can be tested against itself is obviously not
a translucent one. It is probably more natural to think that there is some
external measure that makes possible the comparison between our consciousness of an object and the object itself. But Hegel immediately denies
this. Any such standard or "yardstick" (*Massstab*) against which we judge
knowledge is already a form of knowledge, that is, something that has already been posited by consciousness. It is not a matter of judging or com-
paring consciousness to something outside itself, for the simple reason that
the distinction between subject and object, inside and outside, is a distinction posited by the mind. Thus "consciousness, we find, distinguishes from
itself something, to which at the same time it relates itself . . . and the determinate form of this process of relating, or of there being something for a
consciousness, is knowledge."[13] Consciousness is not just an object or an
event; it is an activity that lives in relation to itself. It contains both knowledge of an object and a knowledge of that knowledge. This is not just
a multiplication of distinctions. For Hegel, to know something without
knowing that we know it is at best half-knowledge. Consciousness thus
contains a dual structure: it is both knowledge of something and knowledge of oneself.

The search for some external measure for knowledge is related to a more
general theory of truth as "correspondence" to reality. On this account, a
subject is thought of as having certain beliefs and desires which are said to
be adequate when they fit or correspond to what the world (or the self) is
really like. Hegel wants to show that this picture theory of truth is question
begging, precisely because expressions like "fitting the world" or "corresponding to reality" require some further yardstick by which to measure
the fit. This procedure assumes that we can characterize reality in terms
independent of that reality, an assumption that Hegel denies. One feature
of Hegelian connected criticism is that it is in part responsible for creating
the reality on which it must then pass judgment. There is, for Hegel, no
"out there" to which thought refers, since what we understand as being out
there is a function of thought. "Consciousness," he writes, "furnishes its

13. *PhM,* p. 139; *Werke* 3:76.

own criterion in itself; and the inquiry will thereby be a comparison of it-self with its own self; for the distinction, just made, falls inside itself."[14]

BILDUNG AND NEGATIVE DIALECTICS

Hegel's *Phenomenology* charts the development of the various modes or "forms of consciousness" (*Gestalten des Bewusstseins*) by a process of internal self-examination and reflection. Beginning with rudimentary "self-certainty" or the "natural consciousness," Hegel wants to show how "science" (*Wissenschaft*) is possible. Science should not be understood here just as full or complete knowledge but as the series of stages or steps (*Weges*) leading up to that knowledge. The intellectual adventure of mankind that began with the Greeks is now essentially complete and ready to be grasped by an act of philosophical retrospection. Science is not just the final result but the entire process that went into producing that result. "The series of shapes," he says, "which consciousness traverses on this road, is rather the detailed history of the process of training and educating consciousness itself up to the level of science."[15]

The *Phenomenology* is not, then, merely a theoretical treatise, but a practical or pedagogical one, whose aim is nothing short of the education of consciousness. The German word for education, *Bildung*, in a sense provides the key to Hegel's work. "The *Phenomenology*," George A. Kelly has written, "is [Hegel's] profound vigorous testament to the comprehensiveness of *Bildung*—a word that means not only education, but maturation, fulfillment, joy, suffering, a drenching in the stream of time and an emergence to the plateau of judgment."[16] In this sense, the work has been rightly compared to Rousseau's *Emile*, which leads a youth from an untutored "natural consciousness" to full adult maturity, and also to Goethe's *Werther* and the whole genre of the *Bildungsroman*.[17]

The Hegelian concept of *Bildung* is related to the ancient Greek notion of *paideia*.[18] The emphasis here, as in Plato, is on the cultivation of given talents and the imposing of form on inchoate matter. Indeed, the word carries

14. *PhM*, p. 140; *Werke* 3:76.
15. *PhM*, p. 136; *Werke* 3:73.
16. George A. Kelly, *Idealism, Politics, and History: Sources of Hegelian Thought* (Cambridge: Cambridge University Press, 1969), p. 342.
17. Jean Hyppolite, *Genèse et structure de la phénoménologie de l'esprit de Hegel* (Paris: Aubier, 1946), p. 16; Georg Lukács, *The Young Hegel: Studies in the Relations between Dialectics and Economics*, trans. Rodney Livingstone (London: Merlin Press, 1975), pp. 54. 296.
18. See Werner Jaeger, *Paideia: The Ideals of Greek Culture*, trans. Gilbert Highet (New York: Oxford University Press, 1965), p. xxiii.

with it an ambiguity of meaning—both "image" or "copy" (*Nachbild*) and "model" (*Vorbild*).[19] But there is a specifically Hegelian use of the term as well. *Bildung*, as the term appears in the *Phenomenology*, represents the education of humanity from a state of instinctual immediacy to a mature acceptance of ethical rules. As M. H. Abrams has written, the work is "a biography of the 'general spirit,' representing the consciousness of each man and Everyman, the course of whose life is a painfully progressive self-education, rendered in the plot-form of a circuitous journey from an initial self-division and departure, through diverse reconciliations and ever renewing estrangements, conflicts, reversals, and crises of spiritual death and rebirth."[20]

Truth is a matter of recollection, or what Plato called anamnesis. Only at the end of this journey is science—Hegelian wisdom—possible; such wisdom comes when we are able to recapitulate or, literally, "re-collect" the various shapes of human experience and organize them into a coherent whole. "The goal," Hegel writes, "which is Absolute Knowledge or Spirit knowing itself as Spirit, finds its pathway in the recollection [*Erinnerung*] of spiritual forms as they are in themselves and as they accomplish the organization of their spiritual kingdom."[21]

This, of course, raises the vexed question of whether the *Phenomenology* is a treatise of individual moral psychology or one of the collective development of the species. The answer obviously is both. The protagonist of the *Phenomenology* is Spirit (*Geist*), which is both collective and singular, or "the I that is a We and the We that is an I."[22] It is at one level an anonymous collective entity, "the general spirit" (*der allgemeine Geist*), but at another level it is always the identity of a particular person or group. The moral task of the *Phenomenology* is to lead the individual, step by step, through the various stages of consciousness culminating in the present standpoint:

> The task of conducting the individual mind from its unscientific [*ungebildeten*] standpoint to that of science had to be taken in its general sense; we had to contemplate the formative development of the universal individual [*das allgemeine Individuum*], of self-conscious spirit. . . . The particular individual, so far as content is concerned, has also to go through the stages through which the general mind has passed, but as shapes once assumed by mind and now laid

19. H. G. Gadamer, *Truth and Method* (New York: Seabury Press, 1975), p. 12.

20. M. H. Abrams, *Natural Supernaturalism: Tradition and Revolution in Romantic Literature* (New York: W. W. Norton, 1971), pp. 229–30.

21. *PhM*, p. 808; *Werke* 3:591.

22. *PhM*, p. 227; *Werke* 3:145.

aside, as stages of a road which has been worked over and levelled out. . . . Science lays before us the morphogenetic process of this cultural development in all its detailed fullness and necessity, and at the same time shows it to be something that has already sunk into the mind as a moment of its being and becomes a possession of mind.[23]

The *Phenomenology* begins with the natural or empirical *I,* the individual consciousness, aware only of itself and the objects immediately at hand, and shows how this *I* is transformed into a collective subject. This collective subject that Hegel calls *Geist* is in reality nothing other than humanity or mankind in general. By humanity Hegel does not mean merely the aggregate of human beings existing at any one time, but a moral conception of a type of individual who sees himself expressed in others and others in himself. We shall return later to the question of how humanity—this collective noun—can act, think, or feel, given that it is an abstraction based on the concrete empirical attributes of individual agents. But this is to some extent to misinterpret Hegel. Humanity is for him less an agent than a telos, less an actor than an object of human aspiration. The *Bildungsprozess* stands complete when the *I* finds in itself expressed all the capacities and attributes of the species. When this stage is reached, we will have attained science, or what Hegel calls "absolute knowledge."

It is, then, "this dialectic process which consciousness executes on itself" that Hegel terms "experience" or "history."[24] This process is not an easy one; it is marked by estrangement, division, and alienation along the way to unity. But by trying to present the various shapes of experience from within, as they have appeared in history, he feels himself able to avoid the problems of the theory of knowledge. Since any form of experience will contain its own standards of adequacy, rationality, and the like, it is only necessary to compare it against itself to see whether it is as it ought to be. Hegel even suggests that it is not "we," the philosophical onlookers, who do the testing to see whether the experience in question measures up to *our* criteria of adequacy, but rather the experience that does the testing itself:

> The essential fact, however, to be borne in mind throughout the whole inquiry is that both these moments, notion and object, "being for another" and "being in itself," themselves fall within that knowledge which we are examining. Consequently, we do not require to bring standards with us, nor to apply *our* fancies

23. *PhM,* pp. 89–90; *Werke* 3:31–33.
24. *PhM,* p. 142; *Werke* 3:78.

and thoughts in the inquiry. . . . in this respect, too, since consciousness tests and examines itself, all we are left to do is simply and solely to look on.[25]

Hegel's response to the traditional problem of knowledge might at first blush appear to raise more difficulties than it solves. If he seriously believes, as he clearly does, that there is no external standard beyond consciousness by which to judge and evaluate our knowledge claims, then we would be forced to accept existing cognitions at their face value. The result of Hegel's immanent critique would seem to yield an uncritical relativism, where we would have to accept existing forms of thought and ways of life without question. We would seem to have lost whatever critical purchase we might have hoped to achieve.

It is arguable that Hegel's apparently innocuous "we," who only "look on" while consciousness tests itself, carries with it a freight of normative baggage. On one reading, Hegel's purely "phenomenological" or "descriptive" method is not a method at all, but an antimethod. There is no royal road to science; it is a matter of experience or a process of action. But if Hegel rules out the traditional answer that philosophy can supply a criterion for distinguishing true from false notions of experience, then the result would be "a chronicle tracing a formless flow of phenomenal content." Having avoided the Scylla of foundationalism, Hegel would seem to have fallen into the Charybdis of relativism, a paradoxical, if not impossible, position.[26]

The objection, then, to Hegel's rejection of traditional epistemology is that it rules out the possibility of providing any truly critical insights or judgments. Indeed, the suggestion that we only understand something, not when we test it against some absolute standard of beauty, truth, or justice, but when we attempt to grasp it from within, in terms of its own self-imposed standards of adequacy, is central to the whole tradition of interpretive hermeneutics from Schleiermacher to Collingwood and Gadamer.[27] On this account, the aim of interpretation is to recapture the thought of the past as it was understood or intended by those for whom it had meaning. We can do this through an act of sympathetic reenactment where we try, so to speak, to step into the shoes of another and see the world as he might have seen it. Only when we succeed in rethinking or reproducing the

25. *PhM*, p. 141; *Werke* 3:77.
26. Kenley Dove, "Hegel's Phenomenological Method," *Review of Metaphysics* 23 (1970): 629.
27. The best works are Hans-Georg Gadamer, *Truth and Method*; R. G. Collingwood, *The Idea of History* (Oxford: Clarendon Press, 1956); Charles Taylor, "Interpretation and the Science of Man," *Review of Metaphysics* 25 (1971): 3–51.

thoughts of another in terms that would be intelligible to him can we avoid the more egregious forms of presentism or ethnocentric prejudice. Thus, by relativizing or historicizing the view of knowledge adopted by modern philosophy, it would seem that Hegel is only able to engage opposing systems of thought or forms of life in their own terms.

Hegel's response here would be to say that while we must begin by understanding a previous or alien form of life in its own terms, that this is not where we must end. The hermeneutic recovery of meaning is not the telos of the *Phenomenology*. The point is not simply to understand the thought of another as it was intended to be understood but to test it for internal symptoms of stress, weakness, or contradiction. Hegel's phrase for this testing, "the labor of the negative" (*Arbeit des Negativen*), beautifully expresses his intention.[28] The activity of self-examination and reflection is laborious because it is hard and unremitting. It is negative because it progresses by ruling things out, by discarding what cannot be adapted and accommodated, by rejecting things. The aim of Hegel's critical dialectic is not to reaffirm familiar knowledge but to destroy the comfortable certitudes of life. To "do away with the character of familiarity" is what counts, for the reason that "whatever is familiarly known is not properly known, just for the reason that it is familiar."[29]

The process of testing knowledge against itself implies, then, a kind of "negative dialectic" in which existing forms of consciousness are shown to contain the seeds of their own destruction. That each form of consciousness will be shown to be inadequate or self-contradictory is necessary for the possibility of dialectical development. It is precisely the negative or contradictory character of consciousness that allows us to traverse the long road from the immediacy of "natural consciousness" to the heights of Hegel's own elevated perspective. Hegel had no illusions that the road traveled by consciousness will be an easy one. "This pathway has a negative significance," he writes. "The road can be looked on as the path of doubt, or more properly a highway of despair [*Weg der Verzweiflung*]."[30] The process of destruction and dissolution that accompanies "the process of training and educating consciousness itself up to the level of science" involves adopting an essentially negative or antagonistic attitude to what exists quite different from the claims of sympathetic reenactment mentioned above. Indeed, the procedure of "unmasking" the various forms of self-deception, delusion, and mystification that consciousness suffers along this road looks

28. *PhM*, p. 81; *Werke* 3:24.
29. *PhM*, p. 92; *Werke* 3:35.
30. *PhM*, p. 135; *Werke* 3:72.

very much like the kind of *Ideologiekritik* practiced later by Marx, Lukács, and the members of the Frankfurt School.[31]

THE SKEPTICAL MOMENT

Hegel's own practice of dialectic owes a great deal to earlier thinkers, especially the ancient skeptics to whom he attributes the discovery of negative or critical thinking.[32] The importance of skepticism for Hegel's idea of dialectic can be verified by the fact that he returns to it again and again throughout his major works. At times he uses the term in an academically precise sense to indicate a specific tradition of thought dating back to Pyrrho of Elis and extending up to the time of Sextus Empiricus.[33] In this sense skepticism represents a highly developed style of argumentation organized around a number of different modes or "tropes." The famous Ten Tropes of Aenesidenus is but the most famous instance of the skeptical rejection of the possibility of knowledge by the ancient Pyrrhonists. Most of these tropes were used to illustrate the necessary conflict of impressions or opinions over various subject matters. According to the skeptics, people's opinions just ineradicably differ, or are *azetetos,* not subject to further inquiry or examination. The world is as it appears at the moment of its appearance. Rather than searching for some kind of special standard or criterion by which to judge the validity of these impressions, skepticism sought to demonstrate the unsatisfactory character of all such criteria. Because criteria are themselves inherently controversial, there is no way of deciding absolutely between them.

From the equal authority accorded to all criteria, it follows that the only defensible response is the suspension of all belief (*epoche*). But far from resulting in a state of anxiety or uncertainty, this *epoche* was supposed to bring about a moral transformation of the subject. For when we withhold assent to all beliefs, what follows is a condition of *ataraxia,* or imperturbability, the peace and tranquility of soul that comes from not worrying any more about truth and falsity. Of course, even in antiquity a lively de-

---

31. See Raymond Geuss, *The Idea of a Critical Theory: Habermas and the Frankfurt School* (Cambridge: Cambridge University Press, 1981).

32. For Hegel's interpretation of ancient skepticism, see Lucio Colletti, *Marxism and Hegel,* trans. Lawrence Garner (London: New Left Books, 1973), pp. 68–85; J.-P. Dumont, *Le scepticisme et le phénomène* (Paris: J. Vrin, 1972), pp. 75–79.

33. The most complete catalog of ancient skeptical beliefs can be found in Sextus Empiricus, *Outlines of Pyrrhonism,* trans. R. G. Bury, 4 vols. (Cambridge, Mass.: Loeb Classical Library, 1933–49); for some critical studies, see Victor Brochard, *Les sceptiques grecques* (Paris: J. Vrin, 1932); Leon Robin, *Pyrrhon et le scepticisme* (Paris: Presses Universitaires de France, 1944); Mario dal Pra, *Lo scetticismo greco* (Bari: Laterza, 1975).

bate ensued over whether the withholding of assent was not already a positive value and thus a contradiction to the skeptic's way of life. The skeptics' response was to avoid as much as possible any active involvement in the world and to live quietly in conformity with appearances and social conventions. Far from undermining political authority, as is sometimes alleged, there is a pronounced conservatism in ancient skepticism that tends to support the status quo.

Elsewhere, however, Hegel speaks of skepticism in a much broader sense as synonymous with philosophy as such. All genuine philosophy is skeptical in the original sense of the term: moral questioning, or skepsis, sought to break the validity of purely traditional values and institutions by introducing the element of self-consciousness or rational deliberation into the legitimation of society. It was only by submitting the natural or pre-philosophic consciousness to continuous examination that philosophy was able to break once and for all with the traditional world of myth, magic, and religion. Hegel even goes so far as to compare the emergence of philosophy in the ancient world with "the so-called Enlightenment of modern times" in which "thought and general principles" criticize everything "not in conformity with these principles."[34] What Hegel means by "enlightenment" in this passage is not simply the eighteenth-century movement identified with the names of Voltaire, the Encyclopedists, and Kant, but more generally, the activity of relentless criticism of all institutions and beliefs that do not accord with our practical rationality. In this sense, skepticism is both an agent of liberation from the narrow and particularistic perspective of the polis and also the harbinger of a new and potentially destructive form of social dislocation and alienation.

Hegel's appreciation of the role of skepticism frequently takes the form of a contrast between the ancient and modern versions of the doctrine. In an early work, *On the Relationship of Skepticism to Philosophy* (1802), he takes to task the skepticism of the neo-Kantian G. E. Schulze, whose *Aenesidemus* (1792) provided him with a pretext for such a contrast. To speak of neo-Kantian skepticism might seem a contradiction in terms, especially since Kant is often seen as restoring the confidence in reason that Hume and the British empiricists had done so much to undermine. On Hegel's view, however, Kant's limitation of the mind only to what could be known in and through experience did no more than continue the skeptical attack on reason. According to "the latest skepticism," the mind is constituted by certain categories and intuitions that determine the form of our

34. *LHP* 1:356; *Werke* 18:410.

perception or, in other words, provide a transcendental framework within which perception is possible. The result, as we have seen, is to create a barrier between things as they appear—as structured by the mind—and things as they are in themselves. By restricting knowledge to the phenomenal world, Kant sought to insulate natural science and analytical thinking from skeptical attack while denying us access to the noumenal realm of morality and religion.

The problem with this latest skepticism, then, is that it extends doubt only to our ability to grasp the "supersensible," while leaving the world of ordinary experience more or less untouched. While modern skepticism, following the lead of Descartes, may claim to doubt everything, its hidden goal is to establish firmer grounds for certainty. Hegel does not raise this objection for the sake of reviving the older pre-Kantian metaphysics, but because it reveals a hidden dogmatism underlying modern skepticism, "with its certainty about the facts of consciousness." Thus Hegel remarks that the "positive side" of this skepticism consists in the fact that it "does not go beyond consciousness" and attributes "undeniable certainty" to "the existence of what is given within the compass of our consciousness."[35] Likewise, it affirms that "nothing of what experience teaches can be an object of skeptical doubt."[36] This judgment is confirmed later in the *Encyclopedia,* where Hegel refers to this modern skepticism, "which partly preceded the Critical [i.e., Kantian] Philosophy, and partly sprang out of it," as consisting only in "denying the truth and certitude of the supersensible, and in pointing to the facts of sense and immediate sensations as what we have to keep to."[37] Underlying and vitiating modern skepticism is an unwitting positivism which accepts the given as such.

In contrast to modern skepticism, the ancient variety is upheld as "in its innermost heart at one with every true philosophy." "Skepticism," Hegel writes, "is in no way directed against philosophy, but against ordinary common sense [*gemeinen Menschenverstand*] . . . against the ordinary consciousness, which holds fast to the given, the fact, the finite . . . and sticks to it as certain, as secure, as eternal; the skeptical tropes show common sense the instability of this kind of certainty."[38] And he goes on to remark that while skepticism is not identical with the whole of philosophy, it is a necessary preliminary to it. "It can be seen as the first stage for philosophy; for the beginning of philosophy must, of course, be elevation above the

35. *Werke* 2:220.
36. *Werke* 2:223.
37. *LL,* par. 81, p. 119; *Werke* 8:176.
38. *Werke* 2:240.

truth which ordinary consciousness gives, and the presentiment of a higher truth."[39] And at one point he even explains the birth of skepticism by reference to the discovery of history among the Greeks, for whom "the increasing range of acquaintance with alien peoples" had the effect upon "the dogmatic common sense of Europeans down to that time" of shaking "their indubitable certainty about a mass of concepts concerning right and truth."[40]

On the surface it might appear as if the neo-Kantian skepticism of Schulze were more in touch with ancient Pyrrhonism, since the latter held impressions derived from experience to be incorrigible. Hegel's response is that the ancient "skeptics declared all perception to be mere semblance [*Schein*]," and that one "should assert the opposite of what one has said about the object according to its appearance."[41] It is precisely the more radical character of ancient skepticism, "which is directed against everything limited and thereby against the heap of the facts of consciousness," that Hegel approves. It is this "noble side" of ancient skepticism to which he returns more than twenty-five years later in a pointed contrast with Hume. "The skepticism of Hume," he says in paragraph 39 of the *Encyclopedia*, "should be clearly marked off from Greek skepticism. Hume assumes the truth of the empirical element, feeling and sensation [*des Gefühls, der Anschauung*] and proceeds to challenge universal principles and laws, because they have no warranty from sense-perception. So far was ancient skepticism from making feeling and sensation the canon of truth, that it turned against the deliverances of sense first of all."[42]

The virtue of skepticism is, then, contrasted, not to philosophy as such, but to "dogmatism" or "common sense." In this context, these are technical terms used by the ancient skeptics to describe their adversaries; for Hegel dogmatism means something like what we call positivism. Dogmatism takes for granted the autonomy and objectivity of the world of facts and things. For the dogmatist, as for the young Wittgenstein, the world is the totality of facts or things waiting to be given propositional form. The standpoint of skepticism shows this dogmatic certainty to be illusory: it shows that the world is not what it seems to be, or that we can attribute contradictory predicates to things. Because it accepts the Heraclitean principle that everything is in motion, skepticism refuses to regard any description of the world as absolutely true. Truth is made relative to the inquirer. Hegel even

39. *Werke* 2:240.
40. *Werke* 2:242.
41. *Werke* 2:224.
42. *LL*, par. 39, p. 64; *Werke* 8:112.

cites the remark of Diogenes naming Homer as the founder of skepticism for speaking of the same thing from different points of view.[43]

The same attitude toward the inadequacies of common sense and the rigid concepts of the understanding (*Verstand*) are found again in the *Phenomenology.*[44] The opening chapter of the text, on the dialectic of sense certainty, seeks to destroy the naive belief in the objectivity of the world. Here Hegel describes the experience of consciousness as asserting the truth of what presents itself immediately to the senses. An *I* is presented immediately with a *this* or a *non-I* of whose existence it is certain. Hegel here appears to agree with Locke and the empiricists that we can feel before we can think. It is the feeling of certainty, of something immediately "here and now"—this table, this pen, this chair—that provides the basic experience or ground of conviction. The attitude that Hegel attributes to the natural consciousness is not unlike the program of the logical positivists, who sought foundations for scientific judgment in "brute data" or "atomic facts" untouched by reflection. Hegel's point is to show that, when submitted to analysis, even this feeling of certainty exhibits complex and contradictory features that lead us to doubt.

If we look at this experience from the standpoint of the object, we discover that everything has at least two properties: a here and a now, space and time. To say merely that something "is" is not enough; we will want to know what it is, and to ask the "what?" question is to raise the possibility of multiple descriptions. Thus, the *this* to which my attention is directed is now a house, but if I turn away it becomes a car, that is, a nonhouse. Similarly, the *now* is night, but no sooner am I aware of this than it becomes day. The objective world which initially appeared the most stable shows itself to be contradictory. The same process of dissolution occurs if we regard this experience from the standpoint of the subject. For while I may appear to be constant and secure, my perceptions are dependent upon the changing states of my body. Food which may seem appetizing when I am healthy will appear nauseating when I am ill. If certainty depends upon the unity of the self, the question becomes, which self? the *I* that is healthy or sick, hot or cold? The idea that there is some unitary self behind my perceptions turns out to be an illusion just as great as the alleged reliability of the external world.

43. *Werke* 2:227.

44. My reconstruction of the following argument owes a great deal to Charles Taylor, "The Opening Arguments of the Phenomenology," in *Hegel: A Collection of Critical Essays,* ed. Alasdair MacIntyre (New York: Doubleday, 1972), pp. 151–87; Herbert Marcuse, *Reason and Revolution: Hegel and the Rise of Social Theory* (Boston: Beacon Press, 1955), pp. 103–6; Hyppolite, *Genèse et structure,* pp. 81–99.

Hegel's point is that as soon as this mute experience is made to prove itself—to verify its certainty—it is immediately thrown into doubt. Proof requires language, concepts, which by their very nature point beyond immediate singular experiences. Even to speak of tables, chairs, and pens is to universalize—to establish general rules for ordering and classifying experiences. Like the older Wittgenstein and the later linguistic philosophers, Hegel believes that experience takes place in language. Since language performs many functions apart from bare "ostensive definition," to interpret experience is to change it. Thus, the conception of some kind of original prelinguistic experience which forms the grounds of certainty is as much a fiction as Rousseau's depiction of the state of nature in the *Discourse on Inequality*. And just as Rousseau understood the impossibility of returning to an original pristine state of innocence, so did Hegel try to avoid "the fallacy of immediacy," the attempt to uphold unmediated experience as a touchstone of truth, a fallacy which becomes evident simply by articulating it.

The same skeptical attack upon the objectivity of the world is taken up later in the *Phenomenology*. In the chapter, "Skepticism," Hegel congratulates the ancient skeptics for adopting an essentially "negative attitude toward otherness." Under their influence, "thought becomes thinking which wholly annihilates the being of the world with its manifold determinateness."[45] Pyrrhonic skepticism is extolled not only because it makes "the objective as such to disappear" but because "what vanishes is what is determinate . . . no matter what its nature or whence it comes." By contrast to stoicism, skepticism is a "thoroughgoing dialectical restlessness," a "melee of presentations derived from sense and thought." It is further described as "an absolutely fortuitous embroglio, the giddy whirl of perpetually self-creating disorder." And he states again that skepticism demonstrates "the aimless fickleness and instability of going to and fro, hither and thither" from one extreme to another.[46]

Many of these thoughts reappear in less imaginative language in the Berlin *Lectures on the History of Philosophy*. Here Hegel presents skepticism as "the art of dissolving all that is determinate, and showing it in its nullity." It is "the demonstration that all that is determinate and finite is unstable."[47] Unlike modern skepticism, which "more resembles Epicureanism" for its acceptance of the empirically given, "the older skepticism is . . . founded on an elaborately thought out annihilation of everything which is held to be true and existent, so that everything is made transient."[48] He depicts "the

45. *PhM*, p. 246; *Werke* 3:159.
46. *PhM*, pp. 248–49; *Werke* 3:161.
47. *LHP* 2:329, 330; *Werke* 19:358.
48. *LHP* 2:332; *Werke* 19:360–61.

essential nature of skepticism" as consisting in "the disappearance of all that is objective, all that is held to be true, existent or universal, all that is definitive, all that is affirmative." Hegel even quotes Sextus's maxim to "affirm nothing," to withhold assent from all determinate propositions, for nothing can be either true or false in itself. Since everything depends upon context, it follows that "all conceptions are alike in trustworthiness or untrustworthiness."[49]

It is, then, largely the negative, critical, and destructive qualities of skepticism of which Hegel approves. Yet for all his respect for the ancient dialecticians, his praise should not be mistaken for endorsement. Skepticism is a first step, but only a first step, in philosophy. Accordingly, "the skeptic mistakes the true value of his result, when he supposes it to be no more than a negation pure and simple."[50] The virtue of skepticism, as we have seen, consists in its "negative attitude" toward being, which means that it shakes up the complacency of everyday empirical thinking. The maxim "affirm nothing" is a useful corrective to the dogmatism of common sense. But exactly because it remains a purely "subjective" withholding of assent, the liberation engendered by skepticism is empty; it produces no positive result. It is hardly surprising, then, that the only virtue admired by the ancient skeptics was the purely formal one of *ataraxia,* imperturbability in the face of experience.[51] There is, then, at the heart of skepticism a sort of inability to learn from experience. "In skepticism," Hegel writes, "we now really have an abrogation of the two one-sided systems [i.e., Stoicism and Epicureanism] that we have hitherto dealt with; but this negative remains a negative only, and is incapable of passing into an affirmative."[52] And, as he adds later on: "Skepticism deduces no result, nor does it express its negation as anything positive."[53]

The cast of mind evinced by skepticism is, then, not unlike that of modern nihilism. For when we lose our certainty that the objective world is fixed or stable, the result is that "self-consciousness itself loses its equilibrium and becomes driven hither and thither in unrest, fear, and anguish." The consequence of this purely subjective liberation from the "unconscious servitude in which the natural consciousness is confined" turns out to be the affirmation of a kind of resoluteness in the face of hopelessness, in

---

49. *LHP* 2:340.
50. *LL,* par. 81, p. 119; *Werke* 8:176.
51. *LHP* 2:333.
52. *LHP* 2:310–11.
53. *LHP* 2:371.

which thought is cured "of having a content such as this established in thought."[54]

Hegel's critique of skepticism turns out to have important political implications as well. The empty subjectivism of which skepticism is accused is itself a response to historical conditions. In his early essay, "The Positivity of the Christian Religion," Hegel expresses concern for the demise of public virtue and the corresponding rise of purely inward-looking cults of spirituality. Christian otherworldliness was one such response to the decline of the ancient republic, while the abstract negations of Stoicism and skepticism were another. Hegel explicitly depreciates concern with private happiness and individual salvation as symptomatic of political decadence. Thus, in the *History of Philosophy*, he remarks that skepticism "flourishes in the Roman world because . . . in this external, dead abstraction of the Roman principle [i.e., formal law] the spirit has flown from an existence here and now, that could give it no satisfaction, into intellectuality." Under the Roman emperors there were, no doubt, individually good men, but "they only considered the satisfaction of their individual selves and did not attain to the thought of giving rationality to actuality through institutions, laws, and constitutions." Since Hegel, as we shall see, consistently maintains that to be adequate, philosophical forms of rationality must find concrete embodiment in collective life, for him this retreat into the inner citadel of the mind, while understandable, is nevertheless regrettable. "Skepticism thus belongs to the decay both of philosophy and the world," is Hegel's final judgment on the question.[55]

THE LOGIC OF DETERMINATE NEGATION

Hegel's dialectic is, as we have seen, tied to his rehabilitation of the ancient skeptics. Perhaps more than anyone else, Hegel was responsible for uncovering the earliest examples of the speculative use of dialectic in the later dialogues of Plato, especially the *Parmenides*, the *Sophist*, and the *Philebus*, at a time when they had all but been consigned to interpretive oblivion by Hegel's contemporaries. To be sure, Hegel's manner of reading these texts is not that of a modern scholar. His concern throughout is less with philological or historical accuracy than with resurrecting certain aspects of ancient skepticism as permanent features of dialectical reasoning. Whereas contemporary philosophers like Kant regarded the use of dialectic as an "ad-

54. *LHP* 2:341; *Werke* 19:369.
55. *LHP* 2:372; *Werke* 19:402.

ventitious art" productive of only spurious knowledge, Hegel praised the ancients for their intuitive awareness that reality cannot be neatly parceled up on the basis of fixed categories of thought, but must be grasped in all of its fluidity and movement.[56]

The rejection of dialectic by his contemporaries Hegel takes to be typical of the method of the "understanding," or *raisonnement,* a term best translated as "ordinary deductive reasoning based on hypothetical premises." Hegel's rejection of *raisonnement* need not imply a rejection of reason as such, but only a kind of analytical thinking that identifies rationality with the mastery of a universal method which can be applied indifferently to any subject matter.[57] But for Hegel such a method can never yield conclusive results, precisely because it is a method, that is, something external to its subject matter and thus arbitrarily posited. The method of immanent critique, or dialectical analysis, by contrast, enjoins us to abstain from all external contributions of our own, the *unsere Zutat,* and give ourselves over instead to the internal unfolding of the subject matter. This act of philosophical restraint is what Hegel means by the famous phrase "the toil of the concept" (*die Anstrengung des Begriffs*).[58] Yet for all his praise of the ancient dialecticians, Hegel treats their greatest works as exercises without result. Their love of paradox characteristically led to a state of *aporia:* perplexity, doubt, wonder. The ancient inquiries concluded where they needed to begin.

The problem with ancient skepticism is that it was insufficiently developmental or progressive. It could destroy, but it could not create. While Hegel regarded the purely negative or destructive character of ancient skepticism as an advance over the naïveté of the natural consciousness, it remains an incomplete advance. His own dialectic might be called by contrast a positive skepticism, since it tries not only to negate but to affirm. Hegel himself refers to it as a form of "determinate negation," as ironical as this sounds. The logic of determinate negation is the principle of development which exhibits the movement from one category or form of consciousness to another. It constitutes a method for moving from one stage to another that is not externally imposed. A determinate negation, unlike the abstract negations of skepticism, is not merely oppositional or adversarial. To ne-

56. For Hegel's appreciation of the ancient dialecticians, see Hans-Georg Gadamer, "Hegel and the Dialectic of the Ancient Philosophers," *Hegel's Dialectic,* trans. P. Christopher Smith (New Haven: Yale University Press, 1976), chap. 1; Jacques d'Hondt, ed., *Hegel et la pensée grecque* (Paris: Presses Universitaires de France, 1974).

57. *PhM,* pp. 117ff.; *Werke* 3:56ff.

58. *PhM,* p. 116; *Werke* 3:56.

gate, as Hegel shows, is always to negate something, something with a determinate content or limit. To state a negative judgment is not simply to deny what is; it is to state something other than what is. Otherness is not a mere negation of being but an assertion of a relation between things. Negation implies, then, a relational view of reality—that things must be understood both in terms of what they are and what they are not. Only when we understand something in terms of the complex of relations that limit or determine it can we be said to understand it.

Hegel's point here, like that of Spinoza, is that all negation is in fact a form of determination or affirmation (omnis determinatio est negatio), that every form of consciousness is the product of a critique or negation of some previous form of thought.[59] Hence all historical change arises out of the negation of some previous negation. As he puts it in the introduction to the *Phenomenology*: "When once . . . the result is apprehended as it truly is, as determinate negation, a new form has thereby immediately arisen."[60] Or as he puts it later in the *Science of Logic*: "Because the result, the negation, is a specific negation it has a content. It is a fresh concept but higher and richer than its predecessor for it is richer by the negation or opposite of the latter."[61] The result of this process of determinate negation is a continual deepening and enrichment of both life and thought, which becomes increasingly more comprehensive and coherent over time.

The logic of determinate negation has both a critical and a constructive aspect. It is critical because it does not merely accept what a body of thought, a philosophical system, or even an entire culture says about itself, but is concerned to confront that thought, system, or culture with its own internal tensions, incoherences, and anomalies. It is constructive because out of this negation or confrontation we are able to arrive at ever more complete, comprehensive, and coherent bodies of propositions and forms of life. There is, then, a dynamic developmental structure to the Hegelian determinate negation by which human arrangements become progressively more adequate as result of their tensions and contradictions being exposed and brought to light. All science, just like all society, is the result of a cumulative process of negation, whereby both life and thought are tested, not against some externally imposed criterion of adequacy, but against their own self-imposed standards of truth. The true system of thought, like the rational form of life, does not stand over and against the others like a "life-

59. *SL*, p. 113; *Werke* 5:121.
60. *PhM*, p. 137; *Werke* 3:74.
61. *SL*, p. 54; *Werke* 5:49.

less universal," but grows out of a progressive deepening and enrichment, where nothing is ever lost or wasted but is overcome and preserved in a newer, more comprehensive whole. This is the famous Hegelian *Aufhebung,* in which lesser and more inadequate forms of life are both annulled and preserved in the higher ones.[62]

The concept of *Aufhebung* is the centerpiece of the Hegelian dialectic, if any concept is. This concept carries with it the implication of "overcoming" or "resolving" contradictions. In a useful passage from the *Lesser Logic* Hegel stresses the peculiar German usage of this term:

> . . . we should note the double meaning of the German word *aufheben* (to put by, or set aside). We mean by it (1) to clear away, or annul: thus, we say, a law or a regulation is set aside; (2) to keep, or preserve: in which sense we use it when we say: something is well put by. This double usage of language, which gives to the same word a positive and negative meaning, is not an accident, and gives no ground for reproaching language as a cause of confusion. We should rather recognize in it the speculative spirit of our language rising above the mere "either-or" of understanding.[63]

What this passage avers is that a contradiction is overcome or resolved— it is *aufgehoben*—when its constituent elements, while retaining their difference and distinctiveness, are shown to be compatible, or at least consistent, with one another. As we shall see in chapter 7, this need not commit Hegel to accept the truth of contradictory assertions. It is more a recognition of the fact that either individuals may entertain beliefs or desires from which contradictions can be derived, or groups of individuals may entertain various beliefs such that any one of them may be true, though it is logically impossible that they all could be. The concept of contradiction need not be taken in the strictly logical sense. It is the view that the concepts that constitute practical reality are better understood not as static or objective but as constituted by tension, opposition, and competing perspectives. To say that a concept or set of concepts is contradictory means that it contains opposed features or predicates that cannot be unitarily or homogeneously defined.

A criticism frequently leveled against Hegel's conception of determinate negation is that it is unable to engender any positive content or development.[64] It is alleged that Hegel fails to provide any convincing account of how the crucial transitions from one phase of spiritual or intellectual life

---

62. *SL,* pp. 106–8; *Werke* 5:113–15.
63. *LL,* par. 96A, p. 142; *Werke* 8:204–5.
64. Dieter Henrich, *Hegel im Context* (Frankfurt: Suhrkamp, 1971), pp. 95ff.

follow from one another. Hegel answers this charge by claiming that for every concept with its mutually contradictory moments, there is another which contains both of these moments, albeit without contradiction, and which is at the same time implicit in them. What Hegel claims to have discovered is the third term or the excluded middle which had been banished from the canons of logical reasoning.[65] This middle term is able to reconcile both previously conflicting aspects of a concept such that they are no longer in contradiction with one another. Thus, contradictions are no longer regarded as rigidly opposed but are "sublated" in the precise Hegelian sense of the term: "*To sublate* [*aufheben*] has a two-fold meaning in the language: on the one hand it means to preserve, to maintain, and equally it also means to cause to cease, to put an end to. . . . Thus what is sublated is at the same time preserved; it has only lost its immediacy but is not on that account annihilated."[66]

We can now begin to see that the concept of *Aufhebung* is profoundly consistent with Hegel's larger political project of restoring unity and harmony to a broken world. *Aufhebung* carries with it the quasi-theological function of reconciliation (*Versöhnung*) with fate or destiny. Such reconciliation, "to recognize reason as the rose in the cross of the present," is the goal of Hegelian philosophy.[67] To reconcile means to restore a fractured unity, to heal, to mend or otherwise make whole. The process of restoring harmony involves three states: (*a*) an initial condition of "immediate" or "undifferentiated" unity; (*b*) a period of differentiation, division (*Trennung*), or alienation: the first negation; (*c*) the establishment of a higher differentiated unity or reconciliation: the negation of the negation.

Furthermore, this process of restoring unity may occur at several different levels of experience. It may occur, first, at a cosmic or theological level, in the form of a separation and subsequent reconciliation between the finite and the infinite, the human and the divine. An example of this is indicated in the form of religious experience, where the Greek and Roman civic religions gradually gave way to Christian beliefs about a transcendent deity, only, Hegel hoped, to be reunited in turn by a revivified Christianity emerging out of the ashes of the French Revolution. Second, it may occur at the historical level, where a traditional set of institutions and social practices undergoes a period of intense scrutiny, as, for example, Socrates and the Sophists did at Athens, only to be reestablished at a higher level. And

---

65. *SL,* pp. 438–39; *Werke* 6:73–74.
66. *SL,* p. 107; *Werke* 5:114.
67. *PR,* p. 12; *Werke* 7:26–27.

finally, at the level of individual moral development, Hegel shows how the attitudes and beliefs naively accepted in childhood undergo increased pressures and strain during adolescence, only to reemerge in a mature form in adulthood.[68]

In each of these cases, Hegel depicts the process of unity-separation-reconciliation as one of the gradual expansion of human self-awareness or self-consciousness. At each stage in the process, a belief, attitude, or social institution that was once held on trust is submitted to skeptical cross-examination and shown to be inadequate. This examination entails both a separation and an estrangement but also provides an opportunity for an increase in our powers of rationality and moral autonomy. What was once accepted as a brute fact is now raised to a higher level of self-consciousness or, in Hegel's peculiar language, what was once a "being in itself" becomes a "being for itself." Thus, in submitting both ourselves and the world to this kind of reflective examination, we gradually become aware of what we both potentially and actually are.

I want to conclude by raising two objections to this conciliatory function of the Hegelian *Aufhebung*. First, Hegel sticks to the belief that following a period of estrangement there will come one of reconciliation and synthesis. This reconciliation with reality he regards as the practical or pedagogical function of philosophy, as well as a sign of moral maturity. But it is not clear, except as a necessity of logic, why this period of reconciliation is likely to occur at all. At a practical level, the skeptical shattering of traditional customs and shared beliefs is more likely to lead to the intensification of feelings of estrangement and anomie than to the acceptance of fate. Furthermore, the increase in our powers of self-reflection and autonomy is more likely to lead to the cultivation of eccentricities and personal peculiarities than to a revivified sense of community. There is arguably nothing more to connect the first and second negations of this process than mere wishful thinking.

Second, Hegel insists that this reconciliation or overcoming of contradiction is a logical process, something that occurs in thought. But as Hegel's Marxist critics never tire of pointing out, the real, that is, the material contradictions are never resolved, only comprehended. Hegel, it is alleged, never succeeded in making the crucial transition from theory to practice. His famous adage that philosophy is "its own time apprehended in thoughts" merely confirms the ex post facto character of all philosophy.

Here, I think, Hegel is more easily defended. Hegel did not believe that

68. *PM*, par. 396, pp. 55–64; *Werke* 10:75–86.

the philosophical or conceptual understanding of reality leaves it untouched. Reality is changed by being apprehended. As was suggested earlier, reality is in part made up of our interpretations, so that to change our interpretations of the world is to change the world. Our concepts do not merely reflect reality; they enter it and leave it different from what it was before. The crude contrast between interpreting the world and changing it does little to illuminate the complex relationship between theory and practice. To interpret the world is necessarily to change it, since our interpretations are not a superstructure built on top of reality but are part and parcel of the reality to which they refer. Hegel's idealism, such as it is, teaches only that there is no transcendental *ding-an-sich,* no ineffable substrate of experience beyond reason, and that to search for something prior to the concepts and categories we use to interpret experience is a futile enterprise.

7   REASON AND HISTORY

REASON AND UNDERSTANDING

It was suggested in chapter 6 that Hegel's dialectic grew out of the critical philosophy inaugurated by Kant. Critical philosophy was contrasted to naive or "dogmatic" philosophy in its determination to take the validity of no philosophical principle for granted but to submit everything to ruthless criticism. "We often hear complaints," Kant wrote in the preface to the *Critique of Pure Reason,* "of shallowness of thought in our age and of the consequent decline of sound science." But he went on to add "I do not see that the sciences which rest upon a secure foundation . . . in the least deserve this reproach," adding, "[o]ur age is in especial degree, the age of critique [*Kritik*], and to criticism everything must submit."[1]

The special aim of the critical project was to serve as a propaedeutic, or introduction, to metaphysics proper. It was in essence a methodology for exposing the fallacies and errors that had dogged philosophy in the past. In particular, critical philosophy aimed at determining the limits and powers of the human intelligence as an activity operating on its own. Reason, then, was not merely the subject but the object of critique. Critique was nothing short of the limitation of pure reason by pure reason. Kant tried to elucidate his point by means of an architectural metaphor. The concept of critique meant "to lay down the complete architectonic plan . . . to guarantee . . . the completeness and certainty of the structure in all its parts."[2] Critical philosophy, then, belongs to the "transcendental" part of knowledge, since it is concerned with the possibility of philosophy as a system. "Such a critique," Kant wrote, "is therefore a preparation, so far as may be possible for an organon."[3]

The chief substantive finding of critical philosophy was that knowledge was limited to the operation of what Kant called "the understanding." The

1. Immanuel Kant, *Critique of Pure Reason,* trans. Norman Kemp Smith (New York: Saint Martin's, 1965), Axi note (p. 9).

2. Kant, *Pure Reason,* B27 (p. 60).

3. Kant, *Pure Reason,* B26 (p. 59).

understanding is that faculty of the mind which, in cooperation with the senses, provides knowledge of the phenomenal world. Left to its own devices, the understanding would confine itself to empirical investigations of the type pursued by natural scientists. The problem is that the understanding is frequently diverted from its true task by the higher faculty of reason, which is typically concerned with what lies beyond experience or with what (to use a modern colloquialism) makes experience "meaningful." Indeed, Kant even remarks that as human beings we are subject to a "natural and inevitable illusion" that is "inseparable from human reason," namely, thinking that we can gain noetic insight into such nonempirical existents as the soul, the intelligibility of the world as a whole, and God. Such ideas, Kant believed, were no doubt connected to certain needs of men as practical agents, but like many empirically minded philosophers today, Kant denied that the understanding can do more than draw inferences and engage in chains of deduction.

Hegel thought that Kant's attempt to limit knowledge to the operations of the understanding alone failed for two reasons. First, as we have seen, the general object of critical philosophy was to establish certain a priori limits on knowledge. But if knowledge is limited to the realm of phenomena, how do we know that? Is knowledge of the limits of knowledge itself derived from experience? And if not, how is that knowledge to be secured? The answer is that Kant was caught in a web of his own making. The theory of knowledge is a castle built in midair. It tries to justify and delimit what is to count as knowledge, but is incapable of justifying itself. It was the inability of the theory of knowledge to ground itself that ultimately led Hegel to abandon the whole enterprise of epistemology—to refuse to play the "justification game."

Second, the claim of Kantian critical philosophy to take nothing for granted remained for Hegel an unredeemed promise. The Kantian distinction between reason and understanding was itself a traditional one that Kant took over from the methods of traditional logic. He tended to accept uncritically Aristotelian principles of inference and acceptance, especially the principle of noncontradiction. In his effort to free thought from this final orthodoxy, Hegel could be considered the completer and perfecter of critical philosophy.

In the course of his treatment of dialectic, Hegel frequently contrasted his approach to the method of the understanding. The understanding, as Hegel conceived it, is characteristic of the formal logical procedures developed by Aristotle and subsequently adopted by most later philosophers. It is the type of thought presupposed in mathematics and modern natural science, but it is also at the root of common sense and our ordinary ways of thinking. Indeed, the understanding is at work whenever we make simple (or even complex) judgments about identity and difference.

There are a number of distinct features of the understanding that are worth emphasizing. First, Hegel tells us that the understanding "sticks to fixity," by which he means that rather than analyzing our categories, concepts, and modes of consciousness as developing in a logical manner, it treats them as isolated and distinct from one another.[4] Understanding, then, is the sphere of analysis that delights in breaking things down into their component elements. Furthermore, underneath this analytical procedure there is a barely concealed dogmatism with its demand for clarity and exactness.[5] An example of this demand for clarity would be the work of many modern social scientists, who frame their research so the results can be expressed in mathematical formulas that suggest explanatory or predictive powers akin to those of the natural sciences. Hegel's point is that by limiting itself only to what can be expressed in formal mathematical terms, the understanding is led to distort the world, either by forcing it into quantitative patterns of thought or by neglecting what resists quantification.

Second, the understanding relies ultimately on presuppositions that are left unproven. It deals with its subject matter from a restricted point of view and can admit no other. To some extent, Hegel regards this as a necessary and hence indispensable part of thought. "The man who will do something great," Hegel says, citing Goethe, "must learn to limit himself . . . for a person in a given situation to accomplish anything, he must stick to one definite point, and not dissipate his forces in many directions."[6] There is a kind of orderliness and discipline brought about by the understanding that Hegel regards as one of the great achievements in thought. But if the understanding represents an advance in thought, it also represents a refusal to think. Since its presuppositions must be taken as beyond question, the understanding is never capable of rising outside of its own restricted perspective or horizon. The Hegelian critique of the understanding here is not unlike the Platonic-Aristotelian critique of the various "ways of life," which may exercise considerable competence in their own terms but cannot finally account for their own presuppositions.

Third, Hegel identifies the understanding by its use of finite, as opposed to infinite, categories. In describing the categories of the understanding as

---

4. *LL,* par. 80, p. 113; *Werke* 8:169.
5. *LL,* par. 32A, pp. 52–53; *Werke* 8:98–99.
6. *LL,* par. 80A, p. 114; *Werke* 8:170.

finite, Hegel means that they are "cut off from their connection, their solidarity" with each other such that "each was believed valid by itself and capable of serving as a predicate of the truth."[7] Understanding fails to grasp
the mutual dependence of the categories of thought. It is thus unable to
grasp the whole (*das Ganze*) or the totality of things. For Hegel, the infinite
is nothing other than the totality grasped in its systematic interconnected-
ness. What distinguishes, then, the "metaphysics of understanding" from
the "idealism of speculative philosophy" is that the former is "dogmatic because it maintains half-truths in their isolation," while the latter "carries out
the principle of totality and shows that it can reach beyond the inadequate
formulations of abstract thought."[8]

The defects of the understanding already point to the higher capacity of
dialectical reason. If the understanding takes things apart, it is the function
of reason to unite and reconcile them. Reason grasps the necessary connections between our concepts and categories that are beyond the understanding's competence. But Hegel goes beyond this. Reason is not just a synthetic
capacity; it is distinguished from ordinary thought by its capacity to absorb
contradiction.[9] In the course of his discussion, he makes two startling
claims. First, he states that everything is inherently contradictory, and second, that speculative philosophy, or reason, is marked by an ability to hold
fast to contradiction. Before proceeding further, we must see what these
remarks entail.

CONTRADICTION

Hegel's conception of contradiction has caused considerable distress among
his chief interpreters because it expresses his insight less as a part of his
practical philosophy than as a substitute for Aristotle's "laws of thought."
In a famous passage from the *Logic,* he maintains that contradiction is as
essential to reality as identity. An *X* not only is what it is but contains
within itself the potential or possibility of becoming something else, or
not-X. In a passage that would become central to the future development of
dialectical materialism, Hegel writes: "Everything is inherently contradictory, and in the sense that this law in contrast to the others expresses the

7. *LL,* par. 28, p. 48; *Werke* 8:94.

8. *LL,* par. 32A, p. 52; *Werke* 8:99.

9. For useful discussions, see André Sarlemijn, *Hegelsche Dialektik* (Berlin: Walter de
Gruyter, 1971); see also Robert Pippin, "Hegel's Metaphysics and the Problem of Contradic-
tion," *Journal of the History of Philosophy* 16 (1978): 301–12; Thomas J. Bole, "Contradiction in
Hegel's Science of Logic," *Review of Metaphysics* 40 (1987): 515–34.

truth and the essential nature of things."[10] While formal logic had claimed that the law of identity expressed in the formula $A = A$ is the essential determination of things, Hegel claims that the law of contradiction is even more important, because "as against contradiction, identity is merely the determination of the simple immediate, of dead being; but contradiction is the root of all movement and vitality; it is only insofar as something has a contradiction within it that it moves, has an urge and activity."[11] Generally, the possibility of contradiction in thought or reality is taken as "a contingency, an abnormality and a passing paroxysm of sickness," but here too Hegel points out that "[s]omething is therefore alive only in so far as it contains contradiction within it, and moreover is this power to hold and endure the contradiction within it."[12]

These passages, and others like them, have given rise to considerable consternation. According to the laws of formal logic, a self-contradictory thing or thought is alleged not to be a thing or thought at all. Without some stable ground of identity, no ideation would be possible. In fact, the two instances of self-contradiction in things that Hegel gives as evidence, namely, locomotion and natural development, can be explicated without the ascription of formally contradictory predicates. This has led interpreters to adopt one of two strategies in dealing with this problem. Those like J. N. Findlay and Deiter Henrich assert that Hegel could not have meant contradiction in the strict logical sense but only as indicating various kinds of conceptual tensions. Others, like Klaus Hartmann, have argued that Hegel both meant and demonstrated the possibility of logical contradiction in thought.[13]

Hegel was clearly aware of the unorthodox nature of his remarks. Nevertheless, there are ways of conceptually unpacking Hegel's views on contradiction that I hope neither dilute them entirely nor involve logical absurdity. It is possible to distinguish three conceptions of contradiction in Hegel's writings, which are not often kept separate. The first is a logical or metaphysical conception of contradiction, according to which everything is contradictory in the sense of inherently changeful. This is clearly contradiction in the strongest sense of the term and is said to have its origins in Heraclitus's saying that "one cannot step into the same river twice."

10. *SL*, p. 439; *Werke* 6:74.
11. *SL*, p. 439; *Werke* 6:75.
12. *SL*, p. 440; *Werke* 6:76.
13. J. N. Findlay, *The Philosophy of Hegel* (New York: Macmillan, 1966); Dieter Henrich, *Hegel im Context* (Frankfurt: Suhrkamp, 1971); Klaus Hartmann, "Zur Diskussion: Zur neuesten Dialektik-Kritik," *Archiv für Geschichte der Philosophie* 55 (1973):220–42.

Second, there are what may be called social or structural contradictions within a prevailing social order. An example of this kind of contradiction would be in Hegel's analysis of regime transformation in the *Phenomenology*. Here a regime, say the Greek polis or the ancien régime in France, is forced to give way when it is no longer capable of sustaining the variety of forces that gave rise to it. Thus, the polis came to grief when it was no longer capable of absorbing the contradiction between its old traditional laws, based on a spontaneous, unreflective devotion to the common good, and the challenge to that order represented by Socrates, for whom the continual questioning of all law remained the highest human imperative. The same kind of contradiction can be seen at work in prerevolutionary France, where the regime was not able to sustain the conflict between the devotion to throne and altar, on the one hand, and the growing demand for human rights and respect, on the other. When both sides were pushed to their limits, one side had to give.

Third, it is possible to speak of moral or psychological contradictions. These are not simply instances of confused or incoherent thinking of the kind that could be exposed in an introductory logic textbook. Rather, these are contradictions that obtain between personal or class beliefs and ones objective interests. Examples of this kind of contradiction would be Hegel's account of the master-slave dialectic or the antinomies experienced in Kantian morality. In each case, what a person is comes into conflict with what he ought to be, and the resulting awareness of this contradiction creates a sense of dissatisfaction that ultimately leads to change.

Hegel's views on contradiction are controversial mainly because he has often been thought to be putting forward his theory at an ontological or metaphysical level such that all our basic concepts and ideas and the reality to which they refer contain formally contradictory attributes. Indeed, what Hegel refers to as "the self-determination of the concept" is often held—at times even by Hegel himself—to serve as an alternative logic different from the canons of ordinary thought, with its rules of *modus ponens* and so on. Further, he even presents this as a distinction between the analytical thinker who accepts the fixed and static character of all concepts and the creative dialectical thinker who recognizes their mutually contradictory attributes, and he leaves the reader in no doubt that while the latter is able to comprehend the former, the converse is not the case. As numerous interpreters have pointed out, such a sweeping theory would have the effect of rendering any kind of discourse impossible. For if contradictions infected even our most basic concepts and categories, then it would be impossible to communicate anything at all on pain of falling into unintelligibility. The result of Hegel's dialectical analysis would be dumb silence in the face of the inadequate character of all thought and reason.[14]

It might be argued here, as Charles Taylor has done, that what Hegel calls a "law" is really more a poetic vision than a strict proof.[15] The frequent use of terms like "life," "movement," and "vitality" attests to the continuing hold of German romanticism and vitalism even on Hegel's mature thought. Where Hegel differs from the romantics is perhaps less in his insight than in his manner of expressing it. The ultimate contradictoriness of reality must be expressed, not in terms of poetry and feeling, but through rigorous conceptual necessity. Hegel is contemptuous of romantic poets like Novalis and Schleiermacher, who he feels prefer "edification" to "insight" and "ferment and enthusiasm" to "the march of cold necessity."[16] Indeed, the dialectic of concepts in the *Logic* is nothing more than Hegel's attempt to give conceptual expression to this insight.

Taylor, whose account is generally sympathetic to Hegel, tries to salvage Hegel's theory by patronizing him. Hegel's "vision" is said to fail because it would never convince an opponent. Leaving aside the difficulty that this could be said of any philosopher, thus making all philosophy equally false, Taylor goes on to say: "One would be more tempted to accord [Hegel's arguments] the status that some moderns give Aquinas's proofs of the existence of God: they cannot be seen as irrefutable demonstrations, designed to convince the sceptic, but more as expressions of what the believer believes."[17] It is not clear who the "moderns" in this passage are, although it is fair to say, I believe, that Taylor accords to Hegel's vision roughly the same status as he would accord a great metaphysical novel or piece of lyric poetry. The appropriate reference frame would be more like Proust's *A la recherche du temps perdu* than Kant's *Critique of Pure Reason*. In any event, he subscribes to the same view of Hegel's theory of contradiction as the logical positivists do, for whom such metaphysical propositions are neither true nor false but "literally nonsense," an expression of the believer's convictions but utterly lacking any rational or epistemic validity.[18]

Taylor's claim that Hegel's vision is more poetry than philosophy is too strong; it throws out the baby with the bathwater. It is true, perhaps, only

---

14. Findlay, *The Philosophy of Hegel*, pp. 73–74.

15. Charles Taylor, *Hegel and Modern Society* (Cambridge: Cambridge University Press, 1975), pp. 67–68.

16. *PhM*, p. 72; *Werke* 3:16.

17. Taylor, *Hegel and Modern Society*, p. 67.

18. See A. J. Ayer, *Language, Truth, and Logic* (Harmondsworth: Penguin, 1975), chap. 1.

if we take contradiction in the strong sense to imply that "everything is inherently contradictory." However, as I suggested earlier, the theory of contradiction can be useful if we consider it not only as an ontology but as having moral-psychological and social-structural components. To use a somewhat different vocabulary: Hegel's account of contradiction in the *Science of Logic* tends to "reify" the not-inconsiderable achievements of the *Phenomenology* by turning a historical and genetic theory into a timeless and metaphysical one. But whatever Hegel's intentions may have been, it is possible to distinguish between his use of contradiction in the two works under consideration.

In the *Logic,* Hegel tends to speak of contradiction as implying formal, logical contradictions in thought. However, in the *Phenomenology,* a concept is said to be contradictory if it reveals opposed or competing tendencies. Consider, for example, the concept of equality. Our idea of equality, which at first appears simple and unitary, reveals itself upon examination to be remarkably complex. Equality seems to entail treating people similarly. But similarly in what respects? Some people, notably liberals, assume that equality applies only to equal treatment before the law: there should be no built-in legal or hereditary barriers between people. Others, especially socialists, argue that for equality to be meaningful, it must apply to a wider range of social and economic circumstances, so that legal equality is a fiction unless it is undergirded by more substantive social or economic forms of equality. Thus, equality, like all morally and politically interesting concepts, reveals a number of competing and even opposed tendencies that do not allow reduction to some single unitary meaning.[19]

Hegel's account of the contradictory or dialectical character of our concepts has a contemporary analogue in the later philosophy of Wittgenstein, and especially in his idea of a "family resemblance." Wittgenstein, like Hegel, was interested in how our concepts shade off and blend into one another around the edges, and did not try to fix them with permanent and possibly arbitrary meanings. To explain this idea, he analyzed what the word "game" means by trying to show that the meaning is not to be found in some single characteristic feature that all games have in common. When we look, for example, at all the various kinds of games—board games, parlor games, Olympic games, and so on—what we find is no essential characteristic in which they all partake, but rather "a complicated network of similarities overlapping and criss-crossing: sometimes overall similarities,

---

19. For the multiple ways in which this term can be used, see Douglas Rae et al., *Equalities* (Cambridge, Mass.: Harvard University Press, 1981).

sometimes similarities of detail."[20] This complex network of partially over-lapping similarities and differences was called by Wittgenstein a "family re-semblance." And indeed, the various characteristics of any complex notion are related to one another in the same way as "the various resemblances between members of a family: build, features, colour of eyes, gait, tempera-ment, etc., etc. overlap and criss-cross in the same way."[21] Perhaps no member of the family will have all the shared features. Some of these char-acteristics are even mutually contradictory, so that no one member can have them all. But it is this many-sided, one could say dialectical, character of our concepts that shade off into one another that is one of Hegel's most profound and original insights.

Furthermore, if it is possible to speak of our concepts as being contra-dictory, it is also possible to speak of social or structural contradictions in reality. This is even more problematic than speaking of conceptual contra-ditions. Critics of dialectical argument, like Karl Popper in his essay "What is Dialectic?" have argued that while contradictions may exist in our theo-retical accounts of reality, it is impossible that they are embedded in reality itself. Our theories may be flawed, but not the reality to which they refer. Scientific progress consists in the gradual elimination of contradictions from our theories until they come ever nearer to approximating the nature of reality itself.[22]

Popper's rebuttal derives what validity it possesses from an analogy be-tween the natural sciences and the social sciences. It assumes that the social sciences are related to their subject matter in the same way that the natural sciences are to theirs. But this is false. Social theories, we have seen, are constitutive or expressive of social reality in a way that theories in the natu-ral sciences are not. Social theories do not stand outside or above the real-ity they seek to describe, explain, or evaluate. They are a part of that reality, so if the theory is flawed or contradictory, so too will be the reality in which it is embodied. Thus, it is not only possible but even necessary to speak, as Daniel Bell has done, of the "cultural contradictions of capitalism" as struc-tural features of our environment.[23]

Even if it is possible (as I believe it is) to vouchsafe the legitimacy of the Hegelian theory of contradiction, it is considerably more difficult to argue

20. Ludwig Wittgenstein, *Philosophical Investigations,* trans. G. E. M. Anscombe (New York: Macmillan, 1968), par. 66, p. 32.

21. Wittgenstein, *Philosophical Investigations,* par. 67, p. 32.

22. Karl Popper, "What is Dialectic?" *Mind* 49 (1940):403–26.

23. See Daniel Bell, *The Cultural Contradictions of Capitalism* (New York: Basic Books, 1976).

that there is some kind of necessity linking the various concepts and modes of consciousness Hegel describes. He is not just claiming to set out a list or history of our concepts in some kind of empirical manner. Hegel is not engaged in anything like the contemporary school of *Begriffsgeschichte.*[24] His claim is a stronger one, namely, to determine exactly what kind of necessity is involved in our use of concepts. The conception of necessity with which Hegel operates is not a causal or mechanical necessity but is closer to a kind of contextual necessity between respective sets of categories and forms of consciousness. He treats this conception of necessity as virtually synonymous with the famous dialectical method, which he describes as follows:

> [B]y Dialectic is meant the indwelling tendency outwards by which the one-sidedness and limitation of the predicates of understanding is seen in its true light . . . the Dialectical principle constitutes the life and soul of scientific progress, the dynamic which alone gives immanent connection and necessity [*immanenter Zusammenhang und Notwendigkeit*] to the body of science.[25]

Before we turn to the question of what kind of necessity is involved here, a preliminary difficulty must be addressed. Hegel's idea of necessity is often thought to apply not to ordinary empirical reality but to some deeper, more fundamental ontological reality. On this account, Hegel is thought to have championed some kind of superscience that investigates the true reality or essence of things behind the illusory or superficial appearances treated by empirical studies. This sphere of hyperreality can supposedly only be investigated by a method that has successfully eluded interpreters up to this day.[26]

This interpretation is false. Hegel's conception of necessity does not apply to some deep structure underlying the surface of things which is not amenable to ordinary empirical methods of investigation. Rather, this structure is nothing other than the global network of appearances. Appearances should not be seen here in opposition to reality; appearances are not mere illusion. Reality produces appearances, and appearances have reality. Appearances are those modalities of consciousness within which human

24. For a discussion, see Reinhart Koselleck, "*Begriffsgeschichte* and Social History," *Futures Past: On the Semantics of Historical Time,* trans. Keith Tribe (Cambridge, Mass.: MIT Press, 1985), pp. 73–91; see also Melvin Richter, "Conceptual History (*Begriffsgeschichte*) and Political Theory," *Political Theory* 14 (1986):604–37.

25. *LL,* par. 81, p. 116; *Werke* 8:172–73.

26. This (mis)interpretation is due in part to F. H. Bradley, *Appearance and Reality* (Oxford: Clarendon Press, 1893); see also Popper, "What is Dialectic?"

activities take place at any given moment, and reality is nothing more than the sum total of these activities. To attribute to Hegel a conception of Reality (with capital *R*) as something qualitatively distinct from the world of everyday appearances is a fiction. Appearance and reality are better understood as related, not as illusion to truth, but as part to whole. Thus, when Hegel contrasts "the one-sidedness and limitation of the predicates of understanding" to his own dialectical principle, this should not be understood as corresponding to an empirical and nonempirical science, respectively. It is rather the difference between a particular person observing phenomena from his own perspective and the totality of interrelated perspectives that is not tied to any particular person.[27]

RATIONAL NECESSITY

We have now arrived at one of the most difficult problems of the entire Hegelian philosophy. Hegel speaks of the process of determinate negation as embodying a certain "logic" or "necessity." But what kind of logic and what kind of necessity? By necessity Hegel clearly does not mean the kind of external relations of cause and effect, antecedent and consequent, customarily sought by scientific investigations. But if he does not mean material causality, it is sometimes argued that he must be operating with some conception of logical necessity according to which there are certain relations of entailment based on the very meanings of words, that to know the meaning of "isosceles triangle" is to know the meaning of words like line, angle, degree, and so on. Yet if this is the conception of necessity invoked by Hegel, it is difficult to see how this could account for the various transitions in moral, intellectual, and historical development mentioned earlier, all areas which exhibit greater or lesser degrees of contingency, as well as context.

Among interpreters there is considerable disagreement. Even an otherwise sympathetic interpreter such as J. N. Findlay can say that Hegel's "main mistake" was to attribute to the dialectic "*a kind of deductive necessity,* different from, but akin to, that of a mathematical system, whereby we shall find ourselves forced along a *single* line of reasoning, culminating in 'the Idea,' and then leading back to our point of origin" (italics in original).[28] At the other extreme, Michael Rosen has argued that Hegel's logic completely

27. My interpretation here was suggested by Jon Elster, *Making Sense of Marx* (Cambridge: Cambridge University Press, 1985), p. 125; he (incidentally) credits Jean Hyppolite for this view.

28. Findlay, *The Philosophy of Hegel,* p. 78.

breaks with earlier conceptions of inference and evidence. The kind of logic he advocated is "hyperintuitionist," or noninferential. "[A]ll attempts to understand dialectic as a non-standard or non-Aristotelian logic seem to me quite misguided," he avers. "[S]ubstituting a non-standard for a standard logic only puts one set of rules of inference in place of another. But Hegel's objection is to the whole inferential procedure itself."[29]

Neither of these interpretations strikes me as adequate. Findlay's attempt to read into Hegel the search for a deductive necessity along mathematical lines does not recognize Hegel's clear-cut distinction between the dialectical method and the method of *Raisonnieren,* or the understanding. In the sharpest manner possible, Hegel sought to distance himself from the mathematico-deductive procedures of pre-Kantian metaphysics. Rosen's attempt, however, to view Hegel as a "hyperintuitionist" not only runs aground of Hegel's explicit strictures against romantic intuitionism, but would result in turning Hegel's philosophy into a form of solipsism. If Rosen were right that Hegel was trying, not just to substitute one form of logic for another, but to abolish "the whole inferential procedure itself," there would be no intersubjective manner of certifying any of his statements as true. While Hegel, as we shall see in the final section of this chapter, rejects the standard conception of truth as correspondence, or "inner picturing," he is very far from abandoning some notion of intersubjective verification.

When dealing with Hegel's statement that "[t]he completeness of the forms of unreal consciousness will be brought about precisely through the necessity of the advance and *the necessity of their connection* with one another [die Notwendigkeit des Fortganges und Zusammenhanges selbst ergeben]" (italics added),[30] three possibilities suggest themselves. First, Hegel's statement regarding the necessity of his dialectical link-ups may mean no more than a kind of hermeneutic or logographic necessity. On this account, the categories and concepts we employ acquire their meaning not in isolation but as they are related to others which they presuppose, such that "every part of the [text] must be necessary for the whole," and "the place where each part occurs is the place where it is necessary that it should occur."[31] This is the necessity implied by the so-called hermeneutic circle, in which one can only understand a whole text in relation to its parts, and its parts in

---

29. Michael Rosen, *Hegel's Dialectic and its Criticism* (Cambridge: Cambridge University Press, 1982), p. 75.

30. *PhM,* p. 137; *Werke* 3:73.

31. Leo Strauss, *The City and Man* (Chicago: University of Chicago Press, 1964), p. 53.

relation to the whole. Necessity should be taken here not in the strict sense but in a relatively loose sense of not arbitrary or not accidental. The whole can be said to be governed by this kind of necessity if it simply makes sense or hangs together in the broadest possible manner. The problem here is that this sense of necessity is too loose to satisfy Hegel's more stringent criteria.

This leads to a second kind of necessity, which may be called practical necessity.[32] Practical necessity is concerned with those events or states of affairs that it is within our power either to produce or prevent. This sense of the term is clearly tied to a much older usage in which to discover the cause of something meant to provide grounds for ascription of praise, blame, guilt, or responsibility, as when we ask "who caused the war to break out?" On this account, to discover the necessity for something means to disclose (*a*) the initial condition or state of things known or believed to exist by some agent or group of agents, and (*b*) the desire or will on the part of those agents to bring about a change in this state of things, on the basis of their intending or meaning to do so. If either of these two conditions is absent, the necessity in question cannot be of the practical sort. The crucial factor here is that the cause is under human control. If we are not in control, as when we act in a hypnotic trance or ascribe responsibility for our actions to "fate," "karma," or "destiny," then we are no longer speaking of a case of practical necessity. This is a case, to repeat, where a human agent chooses to bring about some state of affairs different from what it is now, on the basis of his understanding of his situation and his forming an intention to change it.

There is, however, a third, and more distinctively "Hegelian," meaning of the term which might be called rational or teleological necessity. By "teleological" is meant that history as a whole expresses a sort of force or cause that must be distinguished from the purposeful plans or deeds of individual actors. In this sense, one can say that history taken as a whole, the totality of human deeds, expresses a plot, plan, or purpose which no one individual may have intended, but which is rational nonetheless. History is teleological because it allows the thoughtful observer to discern its end, which is nothing other than the actualization of the idea of freedom.[33] Of course to say that history embodies a teleology of freedom implies a notion of development, or some distinction between what a thing is in its unrealized or merely "potential" condition and what it is in its fully developed or "actual" state. The distinction, an old one going back as far as Aristotle,

32. R. G. Collingwood, *An Essay on Metaphysics* (Chicago: Regnery, 1972), pp. 290–95.
33. *PH*, pp. 17–19; *Werke* 12:30–32.

implies some contrast between an X as it happens to be and what that X could be if it realized its telos, or essential purpose.

Hegel often reverts, as we have seen earlier, to organic analogies to elucidate this developmental scheme. The "idea"—in the sense of the fully realized form—of a child is a mature adult, while the idea of an acorn is an oak tree; the one contains the other if no natural catastrophes occur to prevent it from coming to completion.[34] More characteristically, Hegel sees this teleology as manifesting itself in historical, not biological, terms. "The successive moments of the Idea [of freedom]," he writes, "manifest themselves as distinct principles."[35] These principles exist in turn as distinct national cultures (*Volksgeister*), which Hegel defines as "every aspect of [a people's] consciousness and will, its entire constitution, morals, legal system, and ethics; its science, art, and mechanical skills."[36] On more than one occasion he credits Montesquieu with the insight that the "spirit" of a people is the product of its antecedent history, customs, laws, and habits. But rather than regarding history, as did Montesquieu, as the pleasing development of individual national spirits, each with its own unique culture, taste, and tone, Hegel was inclined to regard it as the process where the "world spirit" would reveal humanity as one, or—in Reinhart Koselleck's elegant phrase— history as the development of a "collective singular."[37]

Hegel's belief that there is a rational necessity in history implies that the world as a whole expresses an "ultimate purpose" (*Endzweck*).[38] This conception of purposiveness is stated forcefully at the outset of the *Philosophy of History,* where we read that "reason rules the world, and consequently . . . world history too is a rational process."[39] Such a statement is apt to strike the modern reader as bizarre, not least because it seems to treat rationality as the subject, not the predicate, of action. This is surely the kind of criticism that Feuerbach and the young Marx had in mind when they accused Hegel of investing a human attribute, rationality, with certain mystical or pantheistic properties. They regarded Hegel, like Spinoza, as a "God-intoxicated man" for whom speculative idealism had taken the place of revealed religion. The proper way of understanding the place of reason is therefore to "invert" what Hegel had to say so that what had been the predi-

---

34. *PhM*, pp. 75–76; *Werke* 3:19.

35. *PH*, p. 47; *Werke* 12:66.

36. *PH*, p. 64; *Werke* 12:87.

37. Reinhart Koselleck, "Historia Magistra Vitae: The Dissolution of the Topos into the Perspective of a Modernized Historical Process," *Futures Past,* p. 29.

38. *PH*, p. 16; *Werke* 12:29.

39. *PH*, p. 9; *Werke* 12:20.

cate is now the subject and what had been the subject is now the predicate. Following the sensualist empiricism of the eighteenth-century French and English materialists, they came to see reason as the dependent variable determined by the more fundamental passionate and emotional needs of men.[40]

To be sure, there is ample evidence to support this theological reading of Hegel. Like Aristotle, he tends to speak of rationality in elevated tones as participating in something divine, or perhaps of being even the divinity itself. H. G. Gadamer has noted that the ascription of a rational character to all reality "places him squarely within the tradition of Greek nous-philosophy, which begins with Parmenides."[41] However, Hegel's relation to the ancient "nous philosophy" should not be overstated. Unlike the Aristotelian nous or the Platonic *eidos,* Hegelian *Vernunft* is not given once and for all but develops gradually over time. It contains an internal dynamic structure of its own that gives it a historical character quite foreign to anything the ancients would have understood. Reason is, then, above all activity. "The very essence of spirit is action," Hegel writes. "It makes itself what it essentially is; it is its own product, its own work."[42]

To grasp the character of Hegelian rationality it is necessary to divest ourselves of certain modern preconceptions about the subordinate status of reason that treat it as an instrumental activity with no inner dynamic or telos of its own. For Hegel, reason is not primarily a calculative faculty used for getting from here to there, as it was for Hobbes and Hume. It is above all a teleological activity aimed at pursuing its own self-chosen ends.[43] Reason is not, then, a means for maximizing certain values (pleasure, happiness, utility) whose desirability derives from other sources. Rather, it prescribes both an organized hierarchy of ends and the motivational means to attain them. In Platonic language, Hegel conceives reason as an "erotic" activity moving toward the fulfillment of its own goals. To say that "reason rules the world" is not to say that individuals act to maximize their preferences, but that there is some kind of general shape, plan, or pattern to history without

40. An excellent account of this "transformative criticism" can be found in Shlomo Avineri, *The Social and Political Thought of Karl Marx* (Cambridge: Cambridge University Press, 1970), pp. 8–40; Joseph O'Malley, "Introductory Essay," *Karl Marx's Critique of Hegel's "Philosophy of Right,"* (Cambridge: Cambridge University Press, 1970), pp. ix–lxiii; see also Louis Althusser, *For Marx,* trans. Ben Brewster (London: Allen Lane, 1969), pp. 35–36, 72–73, 89–94.

41. Gadamer, "Hegel and the Dialectic of the Ancient Philosophers," *Hegel's Dialectic,* trans. P. Christopher Smith (New Haven: Yale University Press, 1976), p. 13.

42. PH, p. 73; *Werke* 12:99: "Der Geist handelt wesentlich, er macht sich zu dem, was er an sich ist, zu einer Tat, zu seinem Werk."

43. PhM, p. 83; *Werke* 3:26: ". . . dass die Vernunft das zweckmässige Tun ist."

which there would be no means of organizing the empirical substance of inquiry into a meaningful whole. Obviously, much depends here on what is meant by the term "meaningful whole," but whatever else it is, it must be clear that reason is not the unique possession of individuals but is a common property of the species.

Hegel's argument for a rational or teleological necessity in history is based on the assumption that human agents are driven by a powerful common interest in their own freedom, or, in the words of a recent interpreter, that "whether they recognize it or not . . . everyone exhibits a certain tropism for rationality, and this tropism persists through the interplay of a person's own impulses and desires."[44] Hegel's own argument is drawn from an analogy to individual actions. Just as individuals and even lower organisms express purposiveness, it would seem unreasonable to deny it to the whole.[45] To the casual observer, the spectacle of human events is disordered and chaotic, with no relation between individual intentions and final outcomes. Furthermore, those for whom "universal purposes, benevolence, and noble patriotism" have been primary motives have invariably come to grief.[46] History would appear to be nothing more than a "slaughterbench" engendering a "revolt of the good will."[47] And what Hegel says is true of ordinary actors holds also for those leading figures he calls "world historical individuals," men like Alexander the Great, Caesar, and Napoleon, who have sought to bring about major epochal change. While these historical figures act, to the best of their knowledge, out of their own volition, they are in fact fulfilling the telos of a kind of historical rationality that is somehow encoded in them.

It is to explain the apparent anomaly between individual motives and objective consequences that Hegel enlists the idea of a rational necessity at work in history. While it has become fashionable to reject this idea as part of a residual theodicy in which apparent evils are explained (and justified) in terms of the good consequences that come from them, some such notion is important for any theory that wants to accord a role to unconscious motivations in history.[48] Thus, Ernst Bloch has traced the notion's origins to Adam Smith's "invisible hand" and Bernard de Mandeville's fable of the bees, while Jon Elster has more recently compared it to the persistence of

---

44. J. J. Drydyk, "Who is Fooled by the 'Cunning of Reason,'" *History and Theory* 24 (1985): 163–64.

45. *PH*, pp. 9–10, 17–19; *Werke* 12: 20–21, 30–32.

46. *PH*, p. 20; *Werke* 12: 34.

47. *PH*, p. 21; *Werke* 12: 35.

48. Taylor, *Hegel and Modern Society*, p. 100.

functionalist explanations in the social sciences.[49] Elster distinguishes between a "weak" and a "strong" functionalist paradigm. The weak (and therefore unobjectionable) model simply states that an institution or pattern of behavior may have consequences which, although unintended by the actors who bring them about, still confer some benefit on them. However, Hegel is said to have subscribed to the strong functionalist thesis, according to which all institutions and behavioral patterns have a function that explains them. The problem is to explain how something that occurs earlier in time can be explained by something posterior to it.

The latter view cannot legitimately be attributed to Hegel. While his conception is that nothing in history can exist in the long term that blocks or inhibits our interest in freedom, he is also deeply concerned with the subjective motives, intentions, and purposes by which that interest is secured. Put another way: while the ends of reason may be given, the way we achieve those ends is not. Only in retrospect, that is, historically, can we know how this end is achieved. Whether it is achieved peacefully or by "conflict," "destruction," "danger," "opposition," or "harm," is by no means irrelevant to the outcome.[50] Thus, Hegel is unlike proponents of strong functionalism in that for him, human beings not only serve purposes; they also have purposes. While he may frequently speak of human agents as "instruments" of some larger historical cause or destiny, Hegel regards as inadequate any theory that abstracts from the elements of inwardness, choice, and intention that human actions display.

It is this relationship between intentional actions and their unintended consequences that Hegel tries to grasp in his concept of the "cunning of reason" (*List der Vernunft*): "It is not the general idea that is implicated in opposition and combat, and that is exposed to danger. It remains in the background, untouched and uninjured. This may be called the *cunning of reason*—that it sets the passions to work for itself while that which develops its existence through such impulsion pays the penalty, and suffers the loss."[51] And in a related passage from the *Logic*, Hegel shows how reason operates not as a dominant end, which regulates and controls the means from an external standpoint, but as an immanent end, which emerges dialectically out of the means:

49. Ernst Bloch, *Subjekt-Objekt: Erläuterungen zu Hegel* (Frankfurt: Suhrkamp, 1972), pp. 234–35; Jon Elster, "Marxism, Functionalism, and Game Theory: The Case of Methodological Individualism," *Theory and Society* 11 (1982):454–55.

50. *PH*, pp. 33–34; *SL*, pp. 746–47; *Werke* 12:49–50; 6:452–53.

51. *PH*, p. 33; *Werke* 12:49.

That the end relates itself immediately to an object and makes it a means, as also that through this means it determines another object, may be regarded as *violence* [*Gewalt*] in so far as the end appear to be of quite another nature than the object. . . . But that the end posits itself in a *mediate* relation with the object and *interposes* another object *between* itself and it, may be regarded as the *cunning* of reason.[52]

What Hegel means by a rational necessity is, then, the ability to discover some meaning, point, or order behind the apparently random chaos of events. To elucidate this point, Hegel compares the field of history to the solar system, and the philosopher to Kepler.[53] Just as Kepler's knowledge of mathematics enabled him to explain planetary motion in terms of a few simple laws, so does knowledge of history reveal a set of lawlike regularities immanent in human affairs. But while Kepler and the other founders of the modern scientific enterprise sought to expel any sense of human interest or "significance" from nature, Hegel took the final purpose of history to be a distinctively moral one: the realization of freedom. By freedom is meant here not merely negative or bourgeois liberty but rather humanity's awareness that it is both separate from and sovereign over nature, where nature indicates both our external environment and our internal drives and inclinations. Freedom is thus rational freedom, since it requires not merely the absence of impediments to actions but a certain kind of knowledge or self-awareness that, as we shall see in the next section, Hegel called absolute knowledge, or the "science of wisdom."

We can now begin to see that Hegel's conception of rational necessity engenders a paradox. History, as Hegel hopes to show, must take the form of a rational theodicy in which evil can be explained in terms of the good that comes out of it. Failure to determine this good reflects not so much on the events as on the observer's ability to discover their purpose. History can accomplish its goals through using the base side of human nature: "Passions, private aims, and the satisfaction of selfish desires are . . . most effective springs of action. Their power lies in the fact that they respect none of the limitations which justice and morality would impose on them; and that these natural impulses have a more direct influence over man than the artificial and tedious discipline that tends to order, self-restraint, law, and morality."[54]

The paradox is not merely that good consequences can result from self-

52. *SL*, p. 746; *Werke* 6:452.
53. *PH*, p. 64; *Werke* 12:87.
54. *PH*, p. 20; *Werke* 12:34.

ish or self-serving actions. That actions have unintended consequences had been explored already in the writings of Smith and de Mandeville. The paradox is that even on Hegel's own terms it is difficult to see what the comprehension of rational necessity is supposed to do for the moral agent. On one level, it is supposed to enable the agent to believe that his good efforts will not go for nought. On another level, however, Hegel's assurance that other people's selfish actions may unwittingly turn out to have good results may only serve to undermine one's confidence in the need for morality. One might be justifiably alarmed at what appears to be such a blatant counsel of irresponsibility. Rather than encouraging the virtuous to persist in their good efforts, Hegel's belief in a rational necessity tends to absolve the agent of all moral responsibility. The result is that as individual moral actors, Caesar and Napoleon may be blameworthy for the harm they cause, but as agents of history, they are praiseworthy for helping to further higher moral purposes.

There are evident difficulties with Hegel's ascription of an objective teleology to human actions. First (and perhaps most difficult) is the belief that nothing can persist that perpetually frustrates the ends of reason. Such a view assumes an apparently benign faith in historical progress which the experiences of the twentieth century have done much to undermine. In this context, the empiricist's demand for refutability or falsifiability is perfectly in order. It is hard to see how genocide on a massive scale, concentration camps, and nuclear weapons serve our collective interest in freedom and rationality. Of course, one could argue that the experiences of Nazism in Germany and Fascism in Italy, Spain, and Japan made possible the emergence of more liberal rational regimes which would not otherwise have been forthcoming. But at most one is entitled to say that things have just turned out that way; there was no necessity for them to do so.

In any case, the idea that history embodies some kind of progressive rationality or movement toward a "better world" seems to have become largely a matter of faith. The search for "objective meanings" in history is now seen to be part of the Enlightenment's goal of a universal science aimed at the prediction and control of the future. At the very least, the Enlightenment's belief that further advances in scientific knowledge will lead to the amelioration of human suffering and therewith to the emergence of stable and democratic regimes has been shown to be vastly overstated. It is arguable that the modern advances in scientific rationality, far from ensuring the conditions for political decency, have in fact made possible for the first time in history a barbarism of a previously undreamt of scale. Consider the following passage from a refugee from Nazi Germany:

As decent and sober a thinker as Immanuel Kant could still seriously believe that war served the purposes of Providence. After Hiroshima, all war is known to be at best a necessary evil. As saintly a theologian as St. Thomas Aquinas could in all seriousness argue that tyrants serve providential ends, for if it were not for tyrants there would be no opportunity for martyrdom. After Auschwitz, anyone using this argument would be guilty of blasphemy. Indeed, Hiroshima and Auschwitz seem to have destroyed any kind of Providence—the newer, immanent kind no less than the older, externally superintending kind. After these dread events, occurring in the heart of the modern, enlightened, technological world, can one still believe in the God who is necessary Progress any more than in the God who manifests His Power in the form of a super-Providence?[55]

Another problem with the Hegelian idea of a rational necessity in history is that it appears to be a wholly a priori construction which does not pay sufficient attention to the facts. Hegel, it can be argued, makes use of historical materials only insofar as they illuminate his moral and political scheme, but no further.[56] Additionally, it is alleged that the necessity of which he speaks works, not at the level of the empirical data, but at some deeper underlying supersensible reality. But how do we gain access to this reality? If it is not available to the commonsense understanding which merely stays at the level of *empeiria,* how can we plumb the depths of historical reason? Indeed, Hegel often leaves himself open to this charge by suggesting that history is nothing but the progressive instantiation of the categories of logic. The ancient Greek world, for instance, corresponded to the category of substance, while the modern constitutional state, with its recognition of rights, corresponds to the stage of difference or, more properly, identity in difference.

One answer to this problem is that suggested by Kant. Kant, against whom Hegel developed his ideas about a teleology of reason, argued for a sharp disjunction between internal (moral) and external (natural) tele-

---

55. Emil Fackenheim, *God's Presence in History: Jewish Affirmations and Philosophical Reflections* (New York: Harper & Row, 1972), pp. 5–6.

56. The alleged "logification" of history is probably truer of Fichte than Hegel. While formally similar in a number of respects, Fichte's argument distinguishes absolutely between the empirical and the philosophical historian. While the former is a "mere collector of facts," an "annalist," the latter is able to go about his business "paying no respect whatever to experience, and thus absolutely a priori." The general outline of history can be known "without the aid of history at all" since history is but the phenomenal revelation of the Idea. The philosopher is thus a consumer of history who uses it "only so far as it serves his purpose." See J. G. Fichte, *Characteristics of the Present Age,* in *The Popular Works,* trans. William Smith (London: John Chapman, 1848) 2:2–3, 139, 144–46. Nowhere does Hegel ever suggest that the philosopher of history can theorize independently of the facts.

ologies. Kant's moral teleology, as we saw earlier, derives from our status as rational beings. Being rational means, for Kant, having the capacity to universalize the principles of our actions or to give our actions the form of law. But the capacity to universalize, while a necessary, is not a sufficient, condition to guarantee the morality of our actions. To guarantee that our principles are truly moral—"categorical" rather than "hypothetical" imperatives, to use Kant's language—they must be tied to certain objective ends, the chief of which is the injunction that we always treat others as ends and not means. Thus, beginning from a minimalist conception of rational agency, Kant claims to be able to derive immanently or internally a doctrine of objective ends that is binding on all persons. Furthermore, such an immanent teleology is held by Kant to be constitutive of the moral point of view, for without it morality would be "destroyed."

At the same time, however, Kant developed another conception of teleology which is a rival of the first. According to this other view, when it comes to regarding ourselves not as moral agents but as historical actors or even as part of nature as a whole, it is necessary to make use of some notion of purpose, but one imputed by us, the observers. The idea of a purpose in nature is conceived by Kant as a "reflective" rather than a "constitutive" judgment. A reflective judgment is distinguished from a constitutive judgment in that it has no ontological import. The idea of a purposiveness in nature is not something that can be "known" by us, in the strict sense, but is more like a working hypothesis of the type to which biologists and other scientists frequently appeal. It is a regulative or "heuristic principle" necessary for helping us make sense of some phenomenon, but it does not carry with it any strong commitment about what the phenomenon is really like.[57]

The notion of an external teleology is developed in the chapter, "The Ideal of Pure Reason," in the first *Critique*. Here Kant denies that the idea of purpose is "constitutive" of our knowledge of nature. Nature, Kant says, is a self-contained system that can be known entirely by the laws of mechanical physics. It is possible to conceive of natural events as operating purely under mechanical laws. But while nature may operate according to the laws of mechanical causation, our knowledge of nature does not. Scientific investigation is a purposive activity that cannot dispense with questions about the meaning or significance of that activity. Thus, scientific activity virtually requires us to ask questions about the ground of the unity of nature and thereby about the existence of an external creator of nature. Kant summarizes his position as follows: "The law of reason which requires us to

57. Kant, *Pure Reason,* A664/B692 (p. 546).

seek for this unity, is a necessary law, since without it we should have no reason at all, and without reason no coherent employment of the understanding, and in the absence of this no sufficient criterion of empirical truth." [58] By calling the concept of purposiveness in nature a reflective judgment, Kant intended to underscore that it is tied to certain needs of human beings as practical agents, especially the need to think that the world forms a systematic unity or coherent whole. Without thinking this, he feared, we might slip into the abyss of nihilism. "Reason," Kant remarks, "has only one single interest," and this is to effect the systematic unity of the knowledge of nature. [59]

Kant's purpose in distinguishing between intrinsic and external teleologies has a twofold function in his thought. In the first place, the distinction is important to maintain the autonomy and independence of the moral realm. For if Kant thought it possible to discover an immanent teleology in nature, he would have been forced to deny that moral rationality has any distinctive logic of its own. Man would be forced back into the determined order of nature. That morality occupies its own sphere, over and apart from that of nature, is well expressed in a passage from the chapter the "Antinomy of Pure Reason" in the first *Critique*:

> That our reason has causality, or that we at least represent it to ourselves as having causality, is evident from the *imperatives* which in all matters of conduct we impose as rules upon our active powers. "*Ought*" expresses a kind of necessity and of connection with grounds which is found nowhere else in the whole of nature. The understanding can know in nature only what is, what has been, or what will be. . . . When we have the course of nature alone in view, "*ought*" has no meaning whatsoever. [60]

Second, Kant's notion that the idea of purposiveness in nature is a kind of "heuristic principle" needed to guide inquiry is not to say that it is a mere fiction or a quasi-Platonic "noble lie." The idea of a natural purpose, while not scientifically demonstrable, is not something that we are simply free to deny. Natural teleology is a matter of what we might call rationally justified belief, or what Kant himself preferred to call "moral theology." It is a principle about the truth of which we can never say "it is certain," but only "I am certain." [61]

Hegel's answer to Kant's regulative employment of purposiveness is not

58. Kant, *Pure Reason*, A651/B679 (p. 538).
59. Kant, *Pure Reason*, A666/B694 (p. 547).
60. Kant, *Pure Reason*, A547/B575 (pp. 472–73).
61. Kant, *Pure Reason*, A829/B857 (p. 650).

difficult to guess. With Kant, he complains, the idea of purpose becomes a "wholly formal merely regulative unity" that does not "possess a constitutive character as do the categories."[62] Like Kant, he continued to regard teleology as an idea of reason, but ideas are no longer for Hegel merely "subjective maxims" but take on the character of "objective propositions" (*objektive Sätze*), in the older Platonic sense, existing independently of the mind that thinks them.[63] To discover this idea, he insists, it is not necessary to be in control of any special methodology but only to "abandon" oneself to the "content" one is studying. To return to the Introduction to the *Phenomenology,* Hegel says: "True scientific knowledge . . . demands abandonment to the very life of the object, or, which means the same thing, claims to have before it the inner necessity controlling the object, and to express this only."[64]

On the basis of this passage, some interpreters have suggested that Hegel's famed dialectical method is not really a method at all but a call to abandon all methodology. Alexandre Kojève, for one, has suggested that "when all is said and done, the 'method' of the Hegelian scientist consists in having no method or way of thinking peculiar to this science," and that qua scientist, "his role is that of a perfectly flat and indefinitely extended mirror."[65] From this he goes on to aver that the Hegelian method is purely "empirical" or "positivist," concluding that "Hegel looks at the Real and describes what he sees, everything that he sees, and nothing but what he sees."[66] Likewise, Martin Heidegger, in *Hegel's Concept of Experience,* argues for a reading of this passage in keeping with Heidegger's own fundamental ontology. For him, "our contribution" consists precisely in the omission of all contributions. The Hegelian philosopher, the "we" of the introduction, is distinguished because he knows how to let being be by keeping his own standards out of the investigation. By adopting a purely receptive posture, the philosopher is said somehow to be more in tune with the flow of being.[67]

Hegel's seemingly innocent description of his dialectic as purely descriptive, or "phenomenological," raises once again the issue of whether he does

62. *SL,* p. 590; *Werke* 6 : 261–62.
63. *SL,* p. 738; *Werke* 6 : 442.
64. *PhM,* p. 112; *Werke* 3 : 52.
65. Alexandre Kojève, *Introduction to the Reading of Hegel,* trans. James H. Nichols (New York: Basic Books, 1969), p. 176.
66. Kojève, *Introduction to the Reading of Hegel,* p. 176.
67. Martin Heidegger, *Hegel's Concept of Experience,* trans. Kenley Dove (New York: Harper & Row, 1970), p. 128.

not presuppose more than he wants to admit. The suggestion that dialectical analysis need only "look on" falls afoul of Hegel's avowed intention of having discovered a hidden rationality working its way out in history. Despite interpretations like those of Kojève and Heidegger, the contemporary positivist's distinction between description and prescription, facts and values, is foreign to Hegel's way of thought. The description of this method as purely empirical misses the point that for Hegel empiricism fails to distinguish what is rational and necessary from what is arbitrary and contingent. The task for the Hegelian philosopher is not simply to describe "everything that he sees, and nothing but what he sees," but to show how what he sees contributes to the development of progressively more rational systems of thought and forms of life. Since both the *Phenomenology* and the *Philosophy of History* display not simply a linear succession of forms of consciousness but some progressive development toward higher levels of adequacy, this arrangement is at least in part made by the observer himself or by the observer in conversation with the forms of consciousness themselves. It is this conversational or dialogical relation between thought and the world that captures better Hegel's meaning of dialectic.

ABSOLUTE KNOWLEDGE AND THE END OF HISTORY

Hegel describes his philosophy in the *Phenomenology* as the attainment of absolute knowledge. The very end of the Introduction reads:

> In pressing forward to its true form of existence, consciousness will come to a point at which it lays aside its semblance of being hampered with what is foreign to it, with what is only for it and exists as an other; it will reach a position where appearance becomes identified with essence, where, in consequence, its exposition coincides with just this very point, this very stage of the science proper of mind. And, finally, when it grasps this its own essence, it will connote the nature of absolute knowledge itself.[68]

In describing his philosophy as knowledge of the absolute, Hegel is not making the preposterous claim that he possesses knowledge of everything that is. Such a claim would be demonstrably false. While his grasp of empirical materials was impressive, there were whole areas of historical research, not to mention scientific inquiry, that escaped his attention. Rather, what Hegel claims to possess can be understood in a relatively weaker sense as entailing the following claims: (*a*) that history is a "rational process"; (*b*) that this process has a distinct telos, or purpose; and (*c*) that this telos is

68. *PhM*, p. 145; *Werke*, 3:80–81.

freedom. What Hegel claims to possess is, then, a knowledge of the general structuring principles or patterns that make history into an intelligible whole rather than a haphazard series of events. It is not the totality of all properties or aspects of history, but only those properties or aspects that make it an organized structure.[69]

Even this weaker sense of the term "absolute" will appear too strong to many. As indicated earlier, this claim assumes that history is an intelligible whole and is moving in a progressive direction toward greater degrees of freedom for ever larger numbers of people. Yet one need only think of the experience of two global wars, the rise of totalitarian states and ideologies, and the existence of evil on a previously unimaginable scale to believe that Hegel's faith in the rationality of the historical process has been massively contradicted by the facts. Furthermore, Hegel's claim to absolute knowledge assumes that we are now in possession not only of an intellectually satisfying form of knowledge but a morally satisfying form of life. Absolute knowledge can only be achieved when the philosophic demand for harmony and coherence coincides with its realization in the institutions of a community and its form of ethical life. For Hegel, it was the modern constitutional state produced out of the French Revolution and its Napoleonic aftermath that alone could provide for this rational harmony. Only in such a community, where all the contradictory facets of life and thought have been "sublated," will the need for speculation cease. However, it need hardly be pointed out that in the 150 years since Hegel's death, the institutions of the liberal state have undergone intensive scrutiny and criticism from a variety of perspectives. Hegel's suggestion that he lived to see the "end of history" hardly seems credible to the modern reader.

Before we turn to these problems, there are a number of formal features implied in Hegel's account of absolute knowledge that we must examine. First, Hegel did not regard absolute knowledge as some qualitatively new mode of thought or system in opposition to those that preceded it. It is rather a compendium or completion of all previous knowledge: a synoptic survey of the whole. One could almost say that absolute knowledge is to all previous knowledge as Aristotle said the virtue of magnanimity was to all the virtues: a kind of crown that puts the others in their final form and therefore adds its luster to the whole. Absolute knowledge is, then, a retrospective reconstruction of all previous forms of consciousness. It is not simply an intellectual history, but is a rational reordering of those forms of

69. Burleigh T. Wilkins, *Hegel's Philosophy of History* (Ithaca: Cornell University Press, 1974), pp. 174–75.

thought that have most decisively contributed to the formation of Hegel's own standpoint.

Second, Hegel's emphasis on the emergent character of absolute knowledge brings out another implication. Unlike philosophers such as Kant, who sought to delimit what was to count as knowledge and then specified some particular branch of knowledge, such as mathematics or physics, as satisfying those criteria, Hegel tried to abjure any prejudgment about what should count as knowledge. Accordingly, he tells us that the truth of any set of categories cannot be taken out of context and studied in isolation "as if shot out of a pistol" but must be seen as the result of a formative process out of which truth progressively emerges.[70] Thus, Hegel opposes his view to that of the "ordinary mind," which "takes the opposition between true and false to be fixed." "The diversity of philosophical systems" should be seen as depicting "the progressive evolution of truth."[71]

Hegel's point here about the emergent character of knowledge bears sharply on the way he recommends we study the history of ideas. Knowledge cannot be considered apart from its genesis—how it came into being. Thus, he describes as "dogmatism" the view that truth and falsity have a completely fixed nature and maintains that "truth is not liked stamped coin that is used ready from the mint and so can be taken up and used."[72] One ought not to discard as merely false or illusory the thought of the past but should regard it as contributing to the gradual emergence of higher and truer forms of consciousness. A case in point here is Hegel's treatment of Spinoza's philosophy, which he argues must be understood in terms of its own internal logic and assumptions:

> [O]ne must get rid of the erroneous idea of regarding the system as out and out *false*, as if the *true* system by contrast were only *opposed* to the false . . . the refutation must not come from outside, that is, it must not proceed from assumptions lying outside the system in question and inconsistent with it. The system need only refuse to recognize those assumptions; the *defect* is a defect only for him who starts from the requirements and demands based on those assumptions.[73]

Previous systems of thought should not be regarded as simply true or simply false. Rather they are rational enterprises and need to be criticized mainly for their premature attempts to claim finality for themselves.

70. *PhM*, p. 89; *Werke* 3:31.
71. *PhM*, p. 68; *Werke* 3:12.
72. *PhM*, p. 98; *Werke* 3:40.
73. *SL*, pp. 580–81; *Werke* 6:249–50.

What Hegel is warning against is the tendency to draw sharp meta-physical distinctions dividing truth from falsity, good from evil. As we have already seen, good and evil are intimately bound up with one another in Hegel's conception of rational necessity, so that it is not possible to regard them as categorically distinct. We must see all previous philosophical systems and forms of life as part of an ongoing dialectic, the purpose of which is the disclosure of the rationality contained therein. Truth, then, becomes a functional property of each system. Forms of thought may be regarded as more or less true to the extent that they allow individuals and societies to function within them. When they cease to do this, or when the contradictions they embody become intolerable, they cease to be true. So long as they are capable of reconciling or mediating contradictions, philosophies retain validity. When things fall apart, the owl of Minerva must take flight.

Third, this conception of absolute knowledge is tied to Hegel's conviction that all knowledge must take the form of a system. By this is meant that every form of knowledge must exhibit some degree of rational harmony and coherence. Only what is expressed in the form of a system can be true. "The truth," he says in the Preface to the *Phenomenology,* "is only realized in the form of a system. . . . Knowledge is only real and can only be set forth fully in the form of science, in the form of a system."[74] All knowledge, then, from the lowliest forms of sense experience to the most abstract branches of science, takes the form of an interconnected set of categories and propositions, any one of which is only fully intelligible when considered in the light of all the others. For Hegel, to describe a statement as true does not mean that it adequately pictures or represents a reality independent of itself. Rather, truth lies in the relation between one statement and some internally related set of statements that it presupposes. Thus, the circular or systematic character of knowledge does not imply, as has sometimes been alleged, an abdication of the search for critical standards of truth and rationality.

We discover, then, that all philosophy takes the form of a circle, or a "circle of circles," which reaches completion only when there is nowhere further for it to expand. In a passage from the *Lesser Logic,* we read:

> Each of the parts of philosophy is a philosophical whole, a circle rounded and complete in itself. In each of these parts, however, the philosophical Idea is found in a particular specificity or medium. The single circle, because it is a real totality, bursts through the limits imposed by its special medium, and gives

74. *PhM,* p. 85; *Werke* 3:27–28.

rise to a wider circle. The whole of philosophy in this way resembles a circle of circles [*ein Kreis von Kreisen*].[75]

Fourth, Hegel's conception of absolute knowledge points toward a new form of justification and truth. Henceforth, our knowledge will not be regarded as true because it satisfies some criteria of rationality or objectivity laid down in advance. Truth is not, to use Schelling's phrase, the "point of indifference" where the mind and the external world come into contact. Hegel persistently attacks the main tenets underlying the correspondence theory of truth and its assumption that there is some reality which exists prior to and independent of our knowledge about it. He wants instead to interject a social component in the justification of belief; epistemology becomes a part of social theory. He refers to the knowledge that he has produced as "absolute" not because it is in touch with ultimate reality but because it is at least potentially a source of intersubjective agreement among social agents who have become aware of their interests in freedom. Truth is, then, less a matter of objectivity than of agreement; less a matter of correspondence than of consensus. Like Wittgenstein, Hegel believes that judgments of true and false are matters not only of human agreement but also of forms of life.[76]

When Hegel says that the goal of philosophy is truth and that the truth is something "noble" (*höhes*) he does not mean this in the sense accorded to it by traditional philosophy. Truth, as we have seen, is not confined to the narrow areas of epistemology and logic but exercises a practical function in everyday life. What he is seeking to do is to replace the older conception of truth as agreement with reality with one based on agreement in language, judgment, and culture. As my brief analysis of the dialectic of self-certainty indicated, there is no reality outside of the linguistic categories that we use to describe, explain, and evaluate it. Truth is therefore always realized in some form of community. The virtue of this expressivist theory of truth is that it shifts the burden of proof away from the individual language user to the community. The community becomes the standard for all values, including truth.

Now what is crucial to a community is some standard of mutuality, respect, and esteem. Agreement in judgments cannot be legitimately produced

---

75. *LL*, par. 15, p. 20; *Werke* 8:60.

76. See Wittgenstein, *Philosophical Investigations*, par. 241, p. 88: "So you are saying that human agreement decides what is true and false?—It is what human beings *say* that is true and false; and they agree in the *language* they use. That is not agreement in opinions but in forms of life."

by force or fraud but must be the outcome of discussion, persuasion, and dialogue. This is not unlike the idea of unconstrained dialogue and communication as the only means of arriving at the truth that is spoken of by contemporary social theorists like Jürgen Habermas and H. G. Gadamer.[77] Only when all conditions of domination, coercion, and asymmetrical power relations have been suspended can the participants in such a dialogue be said to be members of a community of speakers. As for the concrete features of such a community, there would no doubt be great disagreement between Hegel, Gadamer, and Habermas, but all would be certain that an inquiry into the conditions of truth must prepare the way for a deliberation over the justice of particular social arrangements.

Fifth, a final implication of Hegel's claim to absolute knowledge is its claim to stand at the "end of history."[78] Whatever his critics (and apologists) have maintained, Hegel believed himself to have lived at that absolute moment in time when the meaning of history would at last be made clear. History, for Hegel, represented the struggle of human beings to achieve complete satisfaction. This satisfaction will be attained only when we have acquired both intellectual and moral mastery over ourselves and the world. The *Phenomenology,* combined with the *Science of Logic,* represents Hegel's path to epistemic sovereignty; the *Philosophy of Right,* along with the *Philosophy of History,* represents the road to moral mastery. Hegelian philosophy, this "circle of circles," claims to have considered all logical and practical possibilities and thus to have put philosophy, and therefore history, in its final form.

For Hegel, his own system completes the closing of the circle of knowledge that had begun over two millennia before in ancient Greece, because it could claim to successfully bring out the rationality of what is. In words that have become firmly etched into the philosophical consciousness of our age, he writes:

> One word about giving instruction as to what the world ought to be. Philosophy in any case always comes on the scene too late to give it. As the thought of the world, it appears only when actuality is already there cut and dried after its process of formation has been completed. The teaching of the concept, which is also

77. Jürgen Habermas, "Towards a Theory of Communicative Competence," *Inquiry* 13 (1970): 360–76; Hans-Georg Gadamer, *Truth and Method* (New York: Seabury Press, 1975), pp. 330–33, 345–51.

78. See R. K. Maurer, *Hegel und das Ende der Geschichte* (Stuttgart: Kohlhammer, 1965); Stanley Rosen, *G. W. F. Hegel: An Introduction to the Science of Wisdom* (New Haven: Yale University Press, 1974), pp. 43–46, 280–83; M. J. Inwood, *Hegel* (London: Routledge & Kegan Paul, 1983), pp. 514–19.

history's inescapable lesson, is that it is only when actuality is mature that the ideal first appears over and against the real and that the ideal apprehends this same real world in its substance and builds it up for itself into the shape of an intellectual realm. When philosophy paints its grey in grey, then has a shape of life grown old. By philosophy's grey in grey it cannot be rejuvenated but only understood. The owl of Minerva spreads its wings only with the falling of the dusk.[79]

Once this insight was achieved, Hegel hoped, philosophy could at last refrain from teaching the world what it ought to be and restrict itself to showing how what is is rational, or "how the state, the ethical universe, is to be understood." Only when we recognize this rationality of the real can we be said to have attained the end of history.

The immanentization of reason has profound political implications. The omnipresence of rationality is the basis of Hegel's much-maligned statement in the Preface to the *Philosophy of Right* that "what is rational is actual and what is actual is rational" (Was vernünftig ist, das ist wirklich; und was wirklich ist, das ist vernünftig).[80] This statement is often taken as evidence of Hegel's virulent conservatism—as evidence that he sought to exclude social criticism of any sort by arbitrarily applying the category of rationality to everything that was. By seeking immanent standards of rationality, it has been argued, Hegel loses whatever critical purchase he might have desired. Thus, as early as the mid-nineteenth century, German liberals like Rudolph Haym could accuse Hegel of attempting to justify reality "as it stood in Prussia in 1821." According to Haym, Hegel was guilty of applying metaphysical categories to contemporary society, thus providing "the absolute formula" for "political conservatism, quietism, and optimism."[81] Haym's charge stuck. Thus we find the same criticism of Hegel being applied by present-day liberal philosophers like Karl Popper, for whom Hegel's identification of the rational with the actual results in a doctrine of pure power politics where "might is right." Furthermore, Popper sees in this dictum an apology not just for Prussianism but for modern totalitarianism with its irrational forms of "state worship" and its "renaissance of tribalism."[82]

Since no present-day reading of Hegel can avoid coming to terms with these criticisms, it is best to do so here. In the first place, when Hegel says

---

79. *PR*, pp. 12–13; *Werke* 7:27–28.
80. *PR*, p. 10; *Werke* 7:24.
81. Rudolph Haym, *Hegel und seine Zeit* (Hildesheim: Olms, 1962), pp. 365, 366, 367–68.
82. Karl Popper, *The Open Society and its Enemies: The High Tide of Prophecy* (Princeton: Princeton University Press, 1963), pp. 30–31.

that the rational is actual, he does not mean to advance the evidently fallacious claim that everything that is is rational. Actuality (*Wirklichkeit*) is a technical term in Hegel's vocabulary which has to be distinguished from mere existence (*Existenz*). In a lengthy footnote to the 1830 edition of the *Encyclopedia,* he explains that actuality consists only of those aspects of reality that are in full agreement with reason. Referring to the famous (or infamous) passage in the preface cited above, Hegel writes:

> In common life, any freak of fancy, any error, evil and everything of the nature of evil, as well as every degenerate and transitory existence whatever, gets in a casual way the name of actuality. But even our ordinary feelings are enough to forbid a casual (fortuitous) existence getting the emphatic name of an actual. . . . In a detailed Logic I had treated among other things of actuality, and accurately distinguished it not only from the fortuitous, which, after all, has existence, but even from the cognate categories of existence and other modifications of being.[83]

And later in the *Encyclopedia* under the heading "Actuality," Hegel further clarifies his point as follows: "So far is actuality . . . from being in contrariety with reason, that it is rather thoroughly reasonable, and everything which is not reasonable must on that very ground cease to be held actual. The same view may be traced in the usages of educated speech, which declines to give the name of a real poet or real statesman to a poet or statesman who can do nothing really meritorious or reasonable."[84]

Two points can now be made about Hegel's maxim. First, when Hegel attributes rationality to the actual, he does not mean to encompass by that term everything that is. He is as aware as anyone of the role played by chance, contingency, and caprice in human affairs. "Actuality" in Hegel's technical sense may be understood as the conceptual opposite of what is arbitrary or contingent. Perhaps a better word for actuality would be "necessity," since for Hegel what is actual must be permanent and therefore not subject to whim or essential alteration. Whatever is not simply arbitrary is in Hegelian terms necessary.

Of course, what is regarded as necessary and beyond the power of human willfulness may itself be a contingent matter. Advances in genetic engineering, for instance, and the breaking of the DNA code, once thought to be impossible, have proven amenable to change. Indeed, there is no reason to believe that similar sorts of developments will not occur in the future. The Hegelian riposte would be to say that if the boundaries between necessity and contingency are themselves subject to change, this is itself a matter

83. *LL,* par. 6, p. 9; *Werke* 8:47–48.
84. *LL,* par. 142, p. 201; *Werke* 8:280–81.

of necessity. As Charles Taylor has put it: "Hegel does not hold that the world has no contingency in detail, as it were. On the contrary, there is contingency, and also must be of necessity, according to the structure of things!"[85]

Second, despite Hegel's qualifications, he gives us no clear standard for distinguishing the actual from the existent, the real from the apparent. At times he appears to go out of his way to emphasize how no clear-cut standard is possible. Thus, in the *Philosophy of Right* he says that "the state is no ideal work of art; it stands on earth and so in the sphere of caprice, chance, and error, and bad behaviour may disfigure it in many respects."[86] Since he can tolerate no external guarantee for rationality, such as natural law, presumably the only way we have of knowing whether a social institution or belief is fully in accord with reason is its ability to adapt and survive over time. If it proves to be unable to adapt to changing circumstances, then it cannot be fully rational, in the way that the Greek polis, being unable to survive the period of Hellenistic expansion, was not a real state. This is not merely to substitute a doctrine of *Machtpolitik* for one of philosophical reason, for unlike Mao Zedong, Hegel refuses to believe that power comes out of the barrel of a gun. Rationality is a fully functional concept, so we can attribute necessity or actuality to a social practice or institution if it allows for adaptation to its environment.

However one assesses the status of these arguments, Hegel's claim to be standing at the end of history will no doubt strike the skeptical reader as an unparalleled piece of arrogance, or even chauvinism. In the first place, his claim to have put knowledge in its final form seems to be empirically unsupportable. Historical change is, on Hegel's own account, brought about to a large degree by radical conceptual innovation. But there is no way to predict with certainty when such innovation may cease. As Karl Popper has shown, since history is controlled in part by the direction of knowledge, and since the direction of knowledge cannot be predicted, we cannot predict the future direction of history. Hegel seems to have drastically underestimated the essential openness and unpredictability of experience.[87] Furthermore, as we have seen, Hegel's claims to have achieved absolute knowledge are tied to his views on the attainment of a morally and politically satisfying form of life. A form of life is satisfying if it allows agents to realize their interest in freedom. But it is not yet clear whether the institu-

85. Taylor, *Hegel and Modern Society,* pp. 30–31.
86. *PR*, par. 258A, p. 279; *Werke* 7:404.
87. Karl Popper, *The Poverty of Historicism* (New York: Harper & Row, 1964), pp. vi–vii.

tions of postrevolutionary Europe (and America) allow this freedom. Until consensus can be reached on this issue, which at this point in our history seems an unlikely possibility, the issue of the end of history will remain unresolved.

Finally, even if Hegel were right that his was the last word in the community of free men, the result might not be elevating but debilitating. For Nietzsche, whose essay *The Use and Abuse of History* remains the most trenchant critique of Hegelian historicism, "there has been no dangerous turning point in the progress of German culture in this century that has not been made more dangerous by the enormous and still living influence of the Hegelian philosophy." The danger in question is that contemporary man, "by a neat turn of the wheel," is suddenly elevated by Hegel to "the perfection of the world's history." Such an insight, for Nietzsche, would have the effect of turning modern men into mere epigones, with nothing great or noble left to do. What Hegel ought to have said, then, is "that everything after him was merely to be regarded as the musical coda of the great historical rondo—or rather, as simply superfluous." The end of history, if such a thing were possible, would not mean the complete satisfaction of human desire but would result in a kind of generalized aimlessness and loss of meaning. The land of Minerva's Owl would be for Nietzsche nothing so much as the world of the "last man," the one great herd without a shepherd.[88]

In a similar vein, Alexandre Kojève saw the Hegelian thesis of an end of history as a combination or "synthesis" of the "pagan" or "aristocratic" morality of ancient Greece with the "bourgeois-Christian" morality of the modern world.[89] From antiquity, and in particular from "Socratic-Platonic" philosophy, we have inherited the idea of a "universal state or empire." But ancient universalism was distinguished from modern in one decisive respect. It was predicated upon the idea of human inequality. For the ancients, there could be no "mixture" between masters and slaves, for these were taken to be two distinct classes or natures. The pagan morality was transformed by Christianity, which for the first time in history introduced some conception of the "fundamental equality" of the species. But this equality was as yet only an equality of faith in a single God. It was not yet equality in the human or terrestrial, that is, the political sense of the term. It only remained for these two distinct strands of morality to be synthesized

88. Friedrich Nietzsche, *The Use and Abuse of History,* trans. Adrian Collins (Indianapolis: Bobbs-Merrill, 1979), p. 51.

89. Alexandre Kojève, *Tyrannie et sagesse* (Paris: Gallimard, 1954); reprinted as "Tyranny and Wisdom," in Leo Strauss, *On Tyranny* (Ithaca: Cornell University Press, 1975).

by Hegel into the idea of a "politically universal state" which is also at the same time a "socially homogeneous state or 'classless society.'"[90] Such a state—first enunciated during the French Revolution and brought to further realization by the great political upheavals of the twentieth century—is universal because it will encompass the whole of humanity, allowing for no further planetary expansion. It is homogeneous because it will absorb and unite all previous distinct nations, tribes, and classes into a single "concrete universal."

The end of history, then, is the culmination of a lengthy historical process which originates in the necessity to engage in labor and struggle, what Kojève called "ontological negativity."[91] History, which began with an act of "negation," will end with the "negation of the negation." The end of history will put an end to the need for struggle, labor, and "otherness." This otherness will be overcome when the mind comes to regard reality as its own creation, when it sees itself reflected in nature and the social world. This reconciliation of self and other is, for Kojève, the solution to the problem of alienation within history and also the beginning of wisdom. Unlike the "theological" philosophy of Plato, which posited an end to this problem only in an "ideal" world outside of history, Hegelian "atheism" posits nothing outside of human doing, what man has done for himself. Alienation will be overcome once men have learned to dominate nature, conquer *fortuna,* and in general exert rational mastery over their own affairs. History will be complete, then, when nothing human is alien to us.

It is here that Kojève reminds us that this "Hegelian theme," the end of history, was "taken up by Marx" at the end of *Capital,* volume 3. Here Marx made a distinction between "the realm of necessity" (*Reich der Notwendigkeit*) and "the realm of freedom" (*Reich der Freiheit*).[92] The former consists of "history properly so-called, in which men ('classes') fight among themselves for recognition and fight against Nature by work," while the latter refers to that "beyond" (*jenseits*) in which "men (mutually recognizing one another without reservation) no longer fight, and work as little as possible (Nature having been definitively mastered—that is, harmonized with Man)."[93] The end of history will not only mean the instauration of social harmony and

90. Kojève, "Tyranny and Wisdom," p. 183.
91. Kojève, *Introduction to the Reading of Hegel,* p. 222.
92. For some critical comments casting doubt on Kojève's use of Marx, see Patrick Riley, "Introduction to the Reading of Alexandre Kojève," *Political Theory* 9 (1981): 5–48, esp. 13–18; see also my own *Reading Althusser, An Essay on Structural Marxism* (Ithaca: Cornell University Press, 1984), pp. 46–59.
93. Kojève, *Introduction to the Reading of Hegel,* p. 159n.

the pacification of nature but also the end of historical, negating action of any kind. The transition from the realm of necessity to the realm of freedom will culminate in "the disappearance of Man," not to be sure as a biological phenomenon but "Man properly so-called—that is, Action negating the given . . . or in general, the Subject opposed to the Object." The disappearance of man at the end of history will also mean the end of philosophy, because when "man himself no longer changes essentially, there is no longer any reason to change the (true) principles which are the basis of his understanding of the World and of himself."[94]

Kojève was only the most prominent of those Hegelian philosophers who worried that the end of history would herald, not the triumph, but the "death of man."[95] What Nietzsche, writing from the perspective of 1873, feared would become a reality, Kojève, writing from the experience of the twentieth century, feared had become a reality. In a lengthy footnote appended to the 1958 edition of his *Introduction to the Reading of Hegel*, he came to question whether the complete satisfaction of human desire promised at the end of history would mean, not the fulfillment, but the "reanimalization" of humanity. The elimination of the need for struggle would introduce the reign of frivolity, ennui, and boredom. If labor, struggle, or alienation, have brought men to their present height, there might be reason to think that the complete transcendence of alienation would result in the abolition of man as a term of distinction. "[I]t would have to be admitted," Kojève wrote, "that after the end of History, men would construct their edifices and works of art as birds build their nests and spiders spin their webs, would perform musical concerts after the fashion of frogs and cicadas, would play like young animals and would indulge in love like adult beasts. But one cannot then say that this 'makes Man happy.'"[96]

In the same footnote, Kojève left no doubt that the completion of history which had only been announced by Hegel in 1807 with the battle of Jena had now been accomplished in the "classless" societies of both the contemporary United States and Soviet Russia. If, he says, "the Americans give the appearance of rich Sino-Soviets," this is only because "the Russians and Chinese are only Americans who are still poor but are rapidly proceeding to get richer." In either case, Kojève thought he saw in the triumph of the

---

94. Kojève, *Introduction to the Reading of Hegel*, p. 159n.

95. It is not often noted that Kojève's analysis significantly predated the more fashionable "antihumanisms" of the 1960s identified with Althusser and Foucault; see my *Reading Althusser*, pp. 192–200.

96. Kojève, *Introduction to the Reading of Hegel*, p. 159n.

"American way of life" the actual completion of "post-history" and the return of man to the "eternal present."[97]

The end of history, then, which had originally been greeted as a promise of paradisaic satisfaction on earth, came later to appear as the nightmarish triumph of an utterly rationalized, "disenchanted" world, a world increasingly populated by a race of industrious ants. Kojève himself responded to this prospect with the kind of sage stoicism one would expect from an Hegelian "wise man." Not even the philosopher, however, could hope to project an ideal beyond the existing horizon. All that would be left to do was to describe this inhuman end in the fullness of its self-satisfaction.

These gloomy reflections need not be accorded the last word. Kojève's conception of a fully satisfied (or sated) humanity depends upon the coming-into-being of an economy of abundance, which today seems scarcely likely. Indeed, Hegel would have resisted Kojève's "naturalist" reading, which identifies human happiness with the satisfaction of material needs. Furthermore, Hegel did not share the snobbish European prejudice of seeing the "American way of life" as the final degradation of man. Rather, he describes America as "the land of the future," where we cannot rule out new developments of the human spirit. In the *Philosophy of History* he writes:

> America is therefore the land of the future, where, in the ages that lie before us, the burden of the World's History shall reveal itself—perhaps in a contest between North and South America. It is a land of desire for all those who weary of the historical lumber-room of old Europe. Napoleon is reported to have said: "*Cette vielle Europe m'ennuie.*" It is for America to abandon the ground on which hitherto the History of the World has developed itself."[98]

Hegel's thesis about an end of history cannot be dismissed merely as an antiquated metaphysical prejudice left over from an age of faith, as some have patronizingly claimed.[99] If we understand the phrase "the end of history" to mean a condition characterized by an overall consensus on the ends of life, we can see that it bears an uncanny resemblance to another movement, namely, the "end of ideology" thesis proclaimed by many American intellectuals throughout the 1950s and 1960s.[100] The proclama-

97. Kojève, *Introduction to the Reading of Hegel*, p. 161n.

98. *PH*, pp. 86–87; *Werke* 12:144.

99. This, I take it, is the view of Karl Löwith, in *Meaning in History* (Chicago: University of Chicago Press, 1962).

100. For a sample of this literature, see Daniel Bell, *The End of Ideology: On the Exhaustion of Political Ideas in the Fifties* (New York: Free Press, 1960); S. M. Lipset, *Political Man* (New

tion of an end of ideology rested on the assumption that the passions that had generated the political fanaticisms of the past were now spent and that the imperatives of the postwar industrial society would form the basis for a new consensus. This new consensus would not, so it was claimed, be just another ideology, but would be an anti- or counterideology where men would resolve their differences in a more pragmatic piecemeal fashion. Such political disagreements as continued to exist would be over questions of means, to be settled by experts in public policy and the other social sciences. Henceforth, terms like "right" and "left" would disappear altogether as inappropriate to an age characterized (in the ingenious phrase of Arthur Schlesinger) by "the vital center."

The case against the "end of ideology" thesis has been stated forcefully elsewhere.[101] In any case, I take it to be self-refuting for the same reasons as Hegel's end of history thesis. Far from genuinely marking an end of history, Hegel's thesis was itself a key expression of the history of his time and place. Hegel was not the first, and certainly not the last, philosopher to succumb to the temptation of endowing his thought with a permanence and validity that he denied to others. At the conclusion of the *History of Philosophy,* he presented the entire history of thought as so many progressive approximations of his own standpoint, which would be the attainment of wisdom. In the rational society that Hegel thought he saw coming into being, where all traces of the divided self had been dissipated, there and only there would philosophy in the sense of abstract speculation cease. This is not to make the obvious point that Hegel underestimated the peculiar limitations of the time and circumstances in which he wrote. The point is that if Hegel was correct to say that all philosophy is "its own time apprehended in thoughts," then his own efforts to insulate his philosophy from the historical process that he so brilliantly analyzed and described could not but meet with failure.

Hegel was, I believe, profoundly right to regard history as a logical process where great and liberating ideas become impediments to the development of future thought and thus unwittingly provoke their own demise. When applied to itself, Hegel's thesis about an end of history could not but

---

York: Doubleday, 1959); Raymond Aron, *The Opium of the Intellectuals,* trans. Terence Kilmartin (New York: Doubleday, 1957).

101. See, for example, Charles Taylor, "Neutrality in Political Science," *Philosophy, Politics, and Society,* 3d series, ed. Peter Laslett and W. G. Runciman (Oxford: Blackwell, 1967), pp. 25–57; Alasdair MacIntyre, "The End of Ideology and the End of the End of Ideology," *Against the Self-Images of the Age* (Notre Dame: Notre Dame University Press, 1978), pp. 3–11.

become another stifling orthodoxy that would generate its own antithesis, namely, an end to the end of history. Thus, if we consider some of the more promising candidates to succeed Hegel—existentialism, hermeneutical philosophy, deconstruction—all began with an initial rejection of Hegelian premises. All of the various anti-Hegelianisms of our time are characterized by a dependency on what they claim to reject. One may choose to call this a negative dependency, but it is a dependency nonetheless. If my analysis of Hegel is correct, then the worst thing that can fairly be said is that his philosophy was the first casualty of its own success.

8   HEGEL AND THE LIBERAL LEGACY

Political theory has prospered over the last generation or two, because of a sense of impending crisis. This crisis is often attributed to the liberal tradition of thought and practice. It is now virtually a commonplace that as a theory of politics, not to mention human personality, liberalism is seriously impoverished. Liberalism has emphasized individual rights at the expense of cultivating any conception of the public good and has consequently become anomic, rootless, and uncertain of its purposes. The focus on such private ends as security and property has led to a specifically liberal form of conformism, mediocrity, and philistinism. The decline of any sense of "the political" or the res publica has furthermore left liberal societies defenseless in dealing with other societies equipped with alien political doctrines.[1]

The crisis of liberalism, it is sometimes alleged, is rooted in a larger crisis facing "modernity" or even "the West."[2] Modernity essentially predated liberalism and gave rise to it. For our purposes, the origins of modernity can be traced back to Descartes, who opened up the theoretical possibility of the total "mastery and control" of nature. Modernity was thus presented as driven by man's desire to conquer the world in the service of human power. Whether modernity is to be understood as a "secularization" of earlier Judeo-Christian views or rests upon a rejection of earlier positions will have to remain for now an open question. The fact is that early modernity— especially that identified with the men of the Enlightenment and their hope for universal peace and prosperity—could not be sustained in the face of skeptical doubts. Science, which the enlighteners had hoped to harness for the relief of man's estate, turned out to be a double-edged sword. The rise of global technology, as later critics of modernity have pointed out, has often left men powerless before enormous bureaucratic structures which increas-

1. See Sheldon Wolin, *Politics and Vision: Continuity and Innovation in Western Political Thought* (Boston: Little, Brown, and Co. 1960), chap. 10; William Sullivan, *Reconstructing Public Philosophy* (Berkeley: University of California Press, 1982); Ronald Beiner, *Political Judgment* (Chicago: University of Chicago Press, 1983).

2. Leo Strauss, *The City and Man* (Chicago: University of Chicago Press, 1964), pp. 1–12; Alasdair MacIntrye, *After Virtue* (Notre Dame: University of Notre Dame Press, 1981).

ingly dominate all facets of life. While modernity was originally presented as the triumph of enlightened reason over the forces of darkness and superstition, its critics have seen it as promoting new and more ominous orthodoxies supported by the power of modern science. Indeed, this dialectic of modernity has been the subject of works from Horkheimer and Adorno's *Dialectic of Enlightenment* to Allan Bloom's recent *The Closing of the American Mind*.

It is in this context of impending crisis that the recent Hegel renaissance should be understood. Yet even here, Hegel's relation to this crisis is far from unambiguous. Some see Hegel's form of historicism as destroying the tradition of natural rights that has been the core of the liberal tradition. His views on the historically immanent character of reason has led to a "lowering of the standards" of political life, such that the best regime is simply whatever happens to exist. Others see in Hegel's ontology and metaphysics the chief enemy of liberalism properly understood. Liberalism is said to work best when it operates with a sense of skeptical detachment about itself. Some sense of moral indeterminacy is necessary if liberalism is to retain an open, free, and tolerant politics. Hegel's demand for metaphysical closure thus remains an obstacle to the fuller realization of liberal ends and purposes.

While conceding much to the power of these criticisms, I would like to suggest in conclusion that Hegel's views on the state and political community remain his most enduring influence on the liberal legacy. Typically, liberals in the past have shied away from these concepts, treating them as a sort of monolith inimical to freedom. Hegel's emphasis on authority, order, sovereignty, and law have seemed to many to conceal a conservative, if not a reactionary, intent. If I am right, however, Hegel's chief accomplishment has been to show that the state and community are not just a precondition for, but a dimension of, freedom. The state is not simply an instrument of force and coercion but a locus of shared understandings. A state is more than an instrument for ensuring civil peace; it is a wider network of shared ethical ideas and beliefs. A state is ultimately a meeting of minds, since it depends on a common cultural history and a sense of civic identity.

The state, then, is charged with the business of articulating some notion of the common good, which traditional forms of liberalism seem unable to do. That the state is not just a broker between competing interest groups but has the positive function of promoting a way of life, some substantive conception of human flourishing, is in turn tied to Hegel's ideas about human nature in general. For Hegel, human beings are not just Benthamite utility maximizers but are defined by a range of powers, skills, and capacities that can only be developed in association with others. Rather than serving as an obstacle to the realization of the human good, politics satisfies the noninstrumental human need to belong to a community of rational citizens.

To be sure, the idea of a community of rational citizens is not self-evident. The use of the term "rationality" has become widely associated in our culture with the language of economics and the psychology of self-interest. Rationality has become a more or less descriptive term for how people behave under market conditions. However, on Hegel's account, rationality is not simply a given of human behavior but a goal to be achieved. To be rational is not just to be an effective calculator of means to already-posited goals, but requires the ability to articulate and defend some idea about what goals are worthy for a human being to pursue. Rationality is not just a descriptive, but an evaluative, concept, since some people will be able to define more articulately and persuasively the goals they seek and how these fit into a coherent plan of life. The idea of rational citizenship, then, is tied to some idea of human flourishing or, to use Hegelian language, "personality." The benefits of citizenship, we can now begin to see, are not just instrumental to the attainment of nonpolitical goals but are valuable because they allow us to clarify, defend, and if necessary revise our ideas about what contributes to our sense of well-being. "Political activity," as Stephen Salkever has written, "can thus provide the forum for the development of a self-critical capacity which is indispensable to the rational person."[3]

Underlying Hegel's argument, then, is a claim not just about the state but about the kinds of persons that inhabit the state. One aspect of liberalism, especially in its Kantian forms, has been a tendency to attach priority to the self over all communal ends and purposes. The detached, free-floating, or "unencumbered" self of liberal theory achieves completion in a political setup that is purportedly neutral to questions of the human good and recognizes only the right of people to pursue their own conceptions of the good within that framework. The implication of a deontologically liberated self, inhabiting a world void of meaning and empty of telos, free to choose its own ends and order its own priorities, has been marvelously captured by Iris Murdoch in her book *The Sovereignty of Good:*

> Kant believed in Reason and Hegel believed in History, and for both this was a form of a belief in an external reality. Modern thinkers who believe in neither, but who remain within the tradition, are left with a denuded self whose only virtues are freedom, or at best sincerity, or, in the case of the British philoso-

3. Stephen Salkever, "Is it Rational to Vote?" *Ethics* 90 (1980): 213–14.

phers, an everyday reasonableness. Philosophy, on its other fronts, has been busy dismantling the old substantial picture of the "self," and ethics has not proved able to rethink this concept for moral purposes. The moral agent then is pictured as an isolated principle of will, or burrowing pinpoint of consciousness, inside, or beside, a lump of being which has been handed over to other disciplines, such as psychology or sociology.[4]

Hegel's response to this morally deracinated sense of the self, which Murdoch identifies with the works of Stuart Hampshire and Jean-Paul Sartre, is to remind us of the formative role of history or, to use another term for it, "narrative" in the construction of the self. Politics and ethical life are, for Hegel, deeply embedded in the stories, myths, and "forms of consciousness" which tell us about ourselves. We are, to use the phrase of Alasdair MacIntyre, "story-telling animals," that is, our identities are crucially bound up with our individual life histories and the histories of the peoples and cultures to which we are attached.[5] One way in which narrative functions is by configuring those virtues or publicly recognized qualities that together constitute an ideal of human character. Human character, as both Hegel and Aristotle understood, is not simply a product of our own making but is in large part the result of the upbringing and cultural context to which we have been habituated. This, I take it, is Hegel's point in saying that while a morality may require choice, it is not itself the product of choice. A choice can only be made within the context of a meaningful way of life, and a moral choice can only be made within the context of morality. This is the rationale behind Hegel's distinction between *Moralität* and *Sittlichkeit*. His apparent depreciation of the sphere of autonomy and free action is not to deny the fact of choice but only to bring out the contextual features within which choices are made.

Hegel's views gain credibility, in my opinion, when we consider the dominant alternatives to them. One such alternative is libertarianism, the present-day heir of the seventeenth- and eighteenth-century natural rights theorists. Like their early modern forebears, libertarians are concerned to limit state action, to liberate society, especially the marketplace, from the dead hand of government. The state is regarded here as nothing more than an umpire for the oversight of efficient market transactions that can be modeled along game-theoretic lines. On this market theory of politics, human beings engage in political activity, not to develop certain traits of char-

---

4. Iris Murdoch, *The Sovereignty of Good* (Boston: Ark, 1985), pp. 47–48.
5. MacIntyre, *After Virtue*, p. 201; the literature on the political use of narratives has become immense, but for a brilliant exposition, see Paul Ricoeur, *Time and Narrative*, 3 vols. (Chicago: University of Chicago Press, 1984–88).

acter deemed to be desirable, but as a cost to be incurred in order to enjoy certain private, nonpolitical goods. The type of research agenda typically generated by this kind of approach is the "paradox" of why voters who are taken to be rational decision makers continue to vote at all, given that their individual contributions will have at best a marginal effect on the political outcome. It is no surprise, then, to see economic theorists of democracy depict the political system as a marketplace where voters are likened to buyers and politicians to sellers of vendible commodities. The aim of the political process is thus to guarantee an equilibrium between individuals or groups of individuals competing for scarce resources under competitive market conditions.[6]

Like the libertarians of our own day, Hegel also celebrated the separation of civil society from the state and welcomed the separation as one of the great accomplishments of modernity. Civil society brought with it an unprecedented growth in freedom, understood here as sheer indeterminacy. But even as he delights in the liberation of individual self-interest from an oppressive politics of the common good, Hegel is also highly critical of those commercial societies, notably England, where everything is judged in terms of exchange value alone. Market liberalism characteristically sees human beings as egoistic calculators of pleasures and pains who regard political activity as a necessary evil to be endured for the ultimate ends of safety, peace, and comfort.

It is precisely because Hegel does not wholeheartedly applaud the emancipatory interests at work within civil society that many have complained of his reactionary politics. But this is to misunderstand. Hegel was a liberal, but a pre- (and perhaps even a post-) market liberal, or what I called earlier a corporate liberal. By a corporate liberal, I mean one who regards the existing corporations, voluntary associations, and other institutions of civil life as a means of checking the power of a centralizing, rationalizing bureaucratic state, on the one hand, and the development of rootless, deracinated, anomic populaces (*Pöbel*), on the other. These intermediary associations, we must recall, are forms of ethical life and therefore play an important tutelary function in shaping the individual's capacities for shared moral experience and civic involvement. Only by membership in one of the publicly authorized corporations can a person avoid the corrosive effects of

6. Anthony Downs, *An Economic Theory of Democracy* (New York: Harper & Row, 1957); J. M. Buchanan and G. Tullock, *The Calculus of Consent* (Ann Arbor: University of Michigan Press, 1962); Mancur Olson, *The Logic of Collective Action* (Cambridge, Mass.: Harvard University Press, 1965).

the kind of apolitical individualism unleashed by a commodity-producing society. These lesser groups are important, because they help to prepare men and women for active citizenship. They appear here, as in the work of later pluralist writers, as a training ground for virtue, where various modes of cooperation and competition are inculcated.

The second alternative is utopianism, especially of the Marxist variety, which can trace its lineage back to Rousseau and the French Revolution. According to this perspective, the separation of the state from civil society and the corresponding distinction between public and private carries out a deep diremption in the modern world that Marx, following Hegel and Rousseau, traces back to the decline of the ancient polis. In modern times, civil or private life has become wholly emancipated from political limitations; it has become completely independent of any considerations relevant to the commonwealth or public good. Consequently, modern man is divided into two distinct beings, the "citizen" who is expected to participate in cooperative association with others and the "bourgeois" who is liberated to pursue his own egotistical needs and interests. Marx's suggestion is that while civil man has been emancipated from the previous ethico-political restraints upon acquisitive activity, this liberation has been incomplete, since it left man dependent upon the vagaries of the market. Personal arbitrariness of the kind that obtained between lord and vassal was replaced by the impersonal arbitrariness of the system of needs. The "withering away of the state" and the *Aufgehoben* of the whole civil-political, private-public, split would occur only when the increase in human productive powers could make possible an economy of abundance. Only then would it be possible to dispense with the institutions of law, the state, and the rules of justice and for men to live in peaceful, spontaneous harmony with one another.[7]

Except in his very early writings, Hegel's superior realism never permitted infatuation with this intoxicating vision. In his own time, this vision turned on Rousseau's attempt to revive the cult of ancient citizenship, with its demand for radical freedom and autonomy. The kind of freedom taught by Rousseau and his revolutionary disciples was not merely the freedom of the bourgeois who wants nothing more than to pursue his own interests in the marketplace. Freedom means rather the freedom of the citizen, the ra-

---

7. The classic statement of this position is Karl Marx, "On the Jewish Question," *The Marx-Engels Reader,* ed. Robert Tucker (New York: W. W. Norton, 1978), pp. 26–52; for the best account of the Rousseauist origins of Marx's critique, see Galvano della Volpe, *Rousseau and Marx,* trans. John Fraser (London: NLB, 1978).

tional will, who desires liberation from private interests altogether so as to dedicate himself more fully to the pursuit of universal goals. The culture of democracy assumes, then, that no one is free until all participate in the collective decision making of the community. For reasons that should by now be clear, Hegel rejects the radical democratic alternative for presupposing what no longer exists. What is presupposed is a kind of harmony in opinions, customs, and traditions, which in the modern world has not survived. The attempt to create such a community by force can only result in terror, as in the French Revolution, or in tyranny, as in present-day totalitarian regimes. If current talk of "repoliticizing" the public sphere is to be taken seriously at all, it will have to confront seriously Hegel's objections to direct democracy.[8]

Was Hegel successful in mediating between the two extremes just discussed? What would success look like?

In the American context, it would seem as if some of Hegel's worst fears have been realized. According to perhaps the most influential interpretation, America is a nation of Lockean individualists. Indeed, Locke has often been referred to as America's philosopher-king. So great has been the dominance of Lockean individualism that it has rarely been challenged, making it one of the few self-evident truths shared by most Americans. "[T]he reality of atomistic social freedom," Louis Hartz wrote with Locke in mind, "is [as] instinctive to the American mind . . . as in a sense the concept of the polis was instinctive to Platonic Athens or the concept of the church to the mind of the middle ages."[9]

To be sure, the dominance of Lockeanism has recently been challenged by a number of scholars proclaiming the virtues of alternative political and intellectual traditions. These revisionist interpretations open up the exciting prospect of a more communitarian source of American political culture. The republican tradition, for example, which is said to have originated in Greece and Rome, been reborn in sixteenth-century Florence and reached America by way of the radical Whig opposition in England, was essentially anticapitalist and antibourgeois. It evinced an unstinting devotion to the public good at the expense of one's own private interests. American politics has, accordingly, more to do with the preservation of virtue, understood as requiring the people's direct involvement in civic affairs, than the protec-

8. For the "repoliticization" thesis see Jurgen Habermas, *Legitimation Crisis,* trans. T. M. McCarthy (Boston: Beacon Press, 1973); *Strukturwandel der Öffentlichkeit* (Berlin: Luchterhand, 1962).

9. Louis Hartz, *The Liberal Tradition in America* (New York: Harcourt, Brace & World, 1955), p. 62.

tion of interests. The defense of an ideal of active citizenship against all manner of political corruption is the central motif of this revisionist camp.[10]

The attempt to revive an older preliberal tradition as an antidote to Locke's alleged materialism and hedonism is based in part on a distortion of Locke. As a number of dissenting neo-Lockean scholars have argued, this critique is based more on a caricature of Locke as a "possessive individualist" than on his real views. Far from being bereft of virtues, Lockean liberalism can be seen as a vigorous canon of human excellences, including justice, courage, self-denial, civility, humanity, industry, and truthfulness. Liberalism, which forms the moral and intellectual core of the American political tradition, if anything does, has never been without its internal theory of the human good.[11] Thus, Locke supplemented the strict juridical doctrine of the *Second Treatise* with a book entitled *Some Thoughts Concerning Education,* where he develops a model of human character appropriate for the new liberal order. As Nathan Tarcov has argued in his recent study of Locke's educational writings, Locke "constructs modern moral virtues, including civility, liberality, justice, and humanity, on the basis of his egoistic and hedonistic psychology. . . . To understand this view of human life as an entirely degraded one, bereft of any dignity, is to do an injustice not only to Locke but to liberalism and ourselves."[12]

Even accepting this revisionist, or "non-Lockean," Locke, it is arguable that there has been another, more "Hegelian," conception of statehood and political development at work in our tradition. According to Samuel Beer, America is more than a collection of semisovereign states united for the purposes of security and prosperity. It is, to use the language of Daniel Webster, a genuinely "national community," one where "liberty and union" are "one and indivisible." By a community, Beer means first of all "an emotional fact: a massive background feeling of 'belongingness' and identifica-

10. For some of the more important works arguing this thesis, see Bernard Bailyn, *The Ideological Origins of the American Revolution* (Cambridge, Mass.: Harvard University Press, 1967); Gordon Wood, *The Creation of the American Republic, 1776–1787* (New York: W. W. Norton, 1972); J. G. A. Pocock, *The Machiavellian Moment: Florentine Political Thought and the Atlantic Republican Tradition* (Princeton: Princeton University Press, 1975), chap. 15; for a relentless critique of the civic republican influences on the framers, see John P. Diggins, *The Lost Soul of American Politics: Virtue, Self-Interest, and the Foundations of Liberalism* (Chicago: University of Chicago Press, 1984).

11. William A. Galston, "Defending Liberalism," *American Political Science Review* 76 (1982): 621–29; Rogers Smith, *Liberalism and American Constitutional Law* (Cambridge, Mass.: Harvard University Press, 1985), chap. 8.

12. Nathan Tarcov, *Locke's Education for Liberty* (Chicago: University of Chicago Press, 1984), p. 210.

tion." On such a view "we are joined with a vast national community by a distinctive kind of emotional tie: by *public* joy, grief, pride, anger, envy, fear, hope, and so on."[13] The idea of a national community, then, means something more than the sheer centralization of power. A national community consists of people who share a life in common, presenting a range of resemblances and differences linked in a diverse and sometimes confusing pattern. Those invoking the national idea have been variously the Federalists, the Whigs, the Republicans, and after 1930, the Democrats. In a subsequent article, Beer seeks to defend this tradition against its "Jeffersonian" rival with its call for a "new federalism." "Today," Beer warns, ". . . [a] destructive pluralism—sectional, economic, and ethnic—disrupts our common life." The task remains "to keep alive in our speech and our intentions the move toward the consolidation of the union."[14]

A skeptical critic of Beer's position might well say that while there are important consolidating or "Hegelianizing" tendencies in our tradition, it does not follow that the national idea represents some kind of historical absolute in the way Hegel thought it did—the final reconciliation of reason and reality. It is just this metaphysical interpretation of the state, so this argument runs, that condemns whatever apparent merits Hegel's criticism of liberalism may have to irrelevancy. One could argue, as we have seen some of Hegel's defenders do, that Hegel's political insights can still be saved by disentangling them from the skeins of his speculative metaphysics and philosophy of history. But to be consistent, one would have to admit that Hegel's depiction of the modern state as the apex of world history is simply wrong.

This kind of skepticism about the validity of the Hegelian project actually takes two forms. The first argues that Hegel's idea of a national community is just inadequate for dealing with the problems of the modern world, which is dominated by global technology and multinational corporations that transcend the control of any state. The Hegelian state is today nothing more than an anachronism, or is rapidly on its way to becoming one. The increasing economic and technological interdependence of states has just about doomed the nation-state to extinction as an autonomous political unit. World government, as a leading liberal economist has asserted, seems "the only rational method for coping with the world's economic prob-

---

13. Samuel Beer, "Liberalism and the National Idea," *Left, Right, and Center,* ed. Robert Goldwin (Chicago: Rand McNally, 1967), p. 165.

14. Samuel Beer, "The Idea of the Nation," *The New Republic,* 19 and 26 July 1982, pp. 23–29.

lems."[15] Furthermore, those seeking to rehabilitate the state today are putative reactionaries seeking a return to such traditional values as order, authority, sovereignty, and the rule of law.

The second form of skepticism stems from Hegel's own interpretation of the modern state as the culmination of history, where reason and reality, theory and practice, are finally made one. The overcoming of alienation, even if desirable, cannot be accomplished in the state. This criticism is often premised on an alleged inconsistency in Hegel's thought. His attempt to portray history as a completed (or completable) process moving toward a final telos is said to betray the dialectical element in his thought, with its endless negativity and rebellion against all fixity. The true Hegel is not the conservative idealist, but the revolutionary dialectician, for whom "overcoming" and "self-transcendence" are all that matter. Consider, for example, the following passages from writers of quite different perspectives:

> The speculative, systematic, abstract aspects of [Hegel's] philosophy are rejected. But philosophy does not just vanish as if it had never been. It leaves behind it the spirit of radical criticism, dialectical thought which grasps the ephemeral side of existence, dissolves and destroys it—the power of the negative.[16]

> Hegel has emasculated his own dialectic with its never-ending power of criticism and negation by virtue of his arrogant system which halts at the Rubicon of ideology and partial truth.[17]

> [W]e can now begin to say, what irremediably disfigures the Hegelian conception of History as a dialectical process is its *teleological* concept of the dialectic, inscribed in the very *structures* of the Hegelian dialectic at an extremely precise point: the *Aufhebung* . . . directly expressed in the Hegelian category of the *negation of the negation* (or negativity).[18]

I regard these objections ot Hegel's theory as flawed. The first claim, regarding the obsolescence of the state, is either premature, mistaken, or

15. Harry Johnson, cited by Thomas J. Biersteker, "The Limits of State Power in the Contemporary World Economy," *Boundaries: National Autonomy and its Limits*, ed. Peter G. Brown and Henry Shue (Totowa, N.J.: Rowman & Littlefield, 1981), p. 148.

16. Henri Lefebvre, *The Sociology of Marx*, trans. Norbert Guterman (New York: Vintage Books, 1968), p. 6.

17. George A. Kelly, "Mediation versus Compromise in Hegel," *Compromise in Ethics, Law, and Politics*, ed. J. R. Pennock and J. H. Chapman (New York: New York University Press, 1979), p. 88.

18. Louis Althusser, *Politics and History: Montesquieu, Rousseau, Hegel, and Marx*, trans. Ben Brewster (London: NLB, 1972), p. 181.

both. Such claims usually rely on the assumption that politics and the state can be reduced to more fundamental subpolitical social, cultural, economic, or psychological realities. Typically, they affirm some kind of "scientism," whereby the world of politics is seen as so many variables to be seized and manipulated by policy experts. Technology is really the master concept of the policy scientist, with its claim to provide mastery and control over all the diverse and chaotic aspects of political life. At the core of this attitude, then, is the belief that political problems are no different in kind, only in degree of complexity, from problems facing a doctor or an engineer. Political decisions are thought here to be formulated in accordance with technical rules where the choice between alternative strategies is constrained once certain "givens" have been postulated. Arguments in these fields do not concern the ends to be pursued but the most efficient means to arrive at ends already laid down in advance. It should not be surprising that it is precisely from the partisans of this fundamentally technocratic approach to politics that the recent Hegelian call to "bring the state back in" has met with the greatest resistance.[19]

The second charge—that Hegel arbitrarily arrests the dialectic of history, forcing it to culminate in the present—is a more serious objection. As we have already seen, though, the distinction between dialectic and system, between methodology and metaphysics, is entirely foreign to Hegel's thought. This distinction has been foisted onto his thought by those latter-day disciples seeking to put his dialectic into the service of the revolution. Hegel's dialectic is, however, more concerned with the "mediation and overcoming" (*Vermittlung und Aufhebung*) of conflicts than their intensification. The crucial role assigned by Hegel to these concepts is lost if we persist in regarding the dialectic simply as the power of the negative and see all societal forms as so many varieties of unfreedom. The Hegelian dialectic is concerned with the resolution of contradictions by means of speculative reason. This involves, as we have seen, the conceptual grasp of opposites by means of some new concept which shows us that things we thought to be incompatible are in fact mutually dependent.

The chief conflict that Hegel set himself to resolve was that between the

19. For the resurgence of this state-centered approach, see Stephen Skowronek, *Building a New American State* (Cambridge: Cambridge University Press, 1982); Peter B. Evans, Dietrich Rueschmeyer, and Theda Skocpol, *Bringing the State Back In* (Cambridge: Cambridge University Press, 1985); for two fiercely hostile attacks upon the new state theorists, see David Easton, "The Political System Besieged by the State," *Political Theory* 9 (1981):303–25; Leonard Binder, "The Natural History of Development Theory," *Comparative Studies in Society and History: The International Quarterly* 28 (1986):3–33.

"substantial" culture of the Greek world and the principle of subjective freedom developed initially by Socrates and reaching its culmination in the liberal commercial order of modernity. The Greek polis, Hegel tells us, was *unmittelbar;* it was a "lived" rather than a reflective culture. The "beautiful" harmony of Greek antiquity had to collapse to make room for the higher levels of moral and intellectual achievement attained by postclassical civilization. The mediation of these two principles forms the basis of Hegel's idea of the modern state. It is my contention that far from being at odds with his politics, Hegel's dialectical logic is profoundly consistent with the ethical community sketched out in the *Philosophy of Right.*

Nevertheless, the contemporary outlook is virtually defined by its skepticism about Hegelian "metanarratives" and their progressivist philosophies of history. Postmodern critics like Jacques Derrida and Jean-François Lyotard have seen in Hegel's monumental "system"—with its periodization of history into distinct phases of spirit—nothing but a thinly veiled attempt to gain control over the past; furthermore, the Hegelian belief in the end of history instantiated in a rationally ordered state appears as a form of domination over the future. In place of Hegel's attempted synthesis of reason and history, postmodernism claims to offer no new philosophical system or "grand theory" but rather a "hermeneutics of suspicion," a perpetual watchfulness over the purveyors of schemes proclaiming universal emancipation and enlightenment.[20]

The question that must be faced, then, by the student of Hegel today is this: What can be retained of his progressivist philosophy of history once it has been submitted to the skeptical attacks of the masters of suspicion? One answer could be a more supple or provisional notion of an end of history. While our criteria of rationality and standards of epistemic validity may not be timeless, they are still all that we have to go by. Take them away and we simply don't know how to think. Unless we are prepared to give up the idea of a critical perspective altogether, every historian must find himself in the role of the last historian, at least until something better comes along. Such a standpoint need not be metaphysically grounded but can perhaps be discovered immanently or pragmatically in the forms of human discourse, by what seems rational to us. As a number of recent works have tried to show, it is not inconceivable that the analysis of discourse can pro-

20. For a good overview of some of these views, see Quentin Skinner, ed., *The Return of Grand Theory in the Human Sciences* (Cambridge: Cambridge University Press, 1985); for a devastating critique, see Frederick Crews, "The Grand Academy of Theory," *Skeptical Engagements* (New York: Oxford University Press, 1986), pp. 159–78.

vide the telos of agreement that Hegel sought in his phenomenology of the "forms of consciousness."

The most ambitious attempt to date to discover an absolute standpoint through an analysis of language use has been Jürgen Habermas's theory of communicative rationality. Drawing on the work of Wittgenstein, Austin, and others, Habermas wants to show that language is a social institution and as such is oriented towards a telos of mutual understanding. Not conflict but consensus is the implicit end of all speech acts. For Habermas, the very fact that we are language-using creatures presupposes the possibility of truth—of reaching agreement or consensus. In the appendix to his work *Knowledge and Human Interests,* Habermas writes: "The human interest in autonomy and responsibility is not mere fancy, for it can be apprehended a priori. What raises us out of nature is the only thing whose nature we can know: *language.* Through its structure, autonomy and responsibility are posited for us. Our first sentence expresses unequivocally the intention of universal and unconstrained consensus."[21]

The idea that speech aims at the attainment of consensus rests on a number of premises. It assumes (1) that the ability to communicate in language implies the possibility of understanding by others; (2) that the possibility of mutual understanding suggests criteria for distinguishing between real and only apparent agreement; (3) that a real consensus cannot be based on force and fraud but only on the force of the better argument; (4) that the force of the better argument can prevail only where the participants in the dialogue share equally in the process, that is, where there are no gross asymmetries of power that can distort the outcome. The condition that obtains where the disparities of power have been removed is called the "ideal speech situation."

Habermas's notion of an ideal speech situation has been the subject of scathing criticism.[22] It is often alleged that Habermas moves too quickly in affirming that to understand a statement is to agree with it. This assumes that for every situation, and given enough time, competent reasoners will in principle come up with the one correct answer for dealing with whatever is the problem at hand. But this conception of rationality is too strong to be realistic. It does not take note of the "essentially contestable" character of our most basic political concepts. To grasp this point it is only necessary to

21. Jürgen Habermas, *Knowledge and Human Interests,* trans. Jeremy Shapiro (Boston: Beacon Press, 1971), p. 314.
22. See John B. Thompson and David Held, eds., *Habermas: Critical Debates* (London: Macmillan, 1982).

ask ourselves questions like, How much is the right amount of equality? Or, to what extent ought the state to be responsible for alleviating poverty? To ask these questions is already to acknowledge the limits of reason in dealing with important normative issues. This is not to say that reason is useless in dealing with these problems, but only that reasonable persons may disagree on what an answer should be, and that we should therefore not expect more from rationality than it can deliver.

Habermas's ideal speech situation might seem to be a transcendent utopian ideal but for the fact that it has one compelling historical analogue, namely, the Greek polis. Indeed, the condition of "unconstrained discourse" represents Habermas's attempt to give a linguistic basis to the demand for greater participation in politics. But language, as the Greeks, and especially Aristotle, well understood, produces not just consensus but conflict. Aristotle's famous statement that man is by nature the being endowed with speech, or logos, means that man alone among the animals has the capacity, not just to agree, but to disagree over the meaning of basic moral terms and concepts. Such disagreement cannot be regarded as the result of "systematically distorted communication," as Habermas believes, but rather expresses the multifaceted and ambivalent character of language as such. Aristotle knew that political speech contains grave risks and the possibility of much abuse, but on the whole he believed it to be a risk worth taking.

The Habermasian ideal speech situation is today the equivalent of the left Hegelian demand to bring about the "realization" of philosophy. Indeed, the problem of realizing philosophy has become virtually *the* problem of the Hegelian left ever since the 1840s. The proposition that philosophy should be realized has been interpreted to mean that philosophy should foresake its transcendent pretentions and become more worldly or practical; likewise, reality should, through the spread of ideas and general enlightenment, become more amenable to theory, more "modern." Only when philosophy lowers its sights and sets itself more practical goals, and only when the mundane world is purged of all that is merely customary or traditional, will the "realization" of philosophy occur. This fusion of the rational and the real is, then, the final goal of philosophy.

It is often alleged, correctly in my view, that modern critical theory which envisages an emancipated society based on our interest in autonomy vastly overestimates the role of reason in human affairs. It avers that through the power of their own self-critical rationality people can come to an understanding of themselves and their affairs and thus reorder their collective lives to express better their desire for freedom. But what this demand conceals is the problem of exactly how the insights of universal reason are to be applied to particular situations. What is absent from the modern critical project is a theory of political judgment, or *phronesis,* a form of reason or ethical know-how which involves complex judgments specific to the particular practices or situations at hand.[23] *Phronesis* is the Aristotelian virtue especially required in political decision making and is akin to the quality of moral reasonableness, which consists of knowing the myriad details relevant to a case and what the parties to it would be likely to accept as a solution. Without some notion of political judgment, the Habermasian ideal speech situation, like the Hegelian end of history, remains an empty possibility. To the extent that modern critical theory remains wedded to a belief in the self-realization of reason, its problems remain the problems of Hegel.

23. For the importance of this concept, see Hans-Georg Gadamer, *Truth and Method* (New York: Seabury, 1975), pp. 278ff.; see also Richard J. Bernstein, *Beyond Objectivism and Relativism: Science, Hermeneutics, and Praxis* (Philadelphia: University of Pennsylvania Press, 1983), pp. 156ff.

INDEX

Abrams, M. H., 176
Absolute knowledge, 170, 177, 211, 217–22. *See also* Truth
Actuality, 223–25
Adorno, Theodor, 233
Alexander the Great, 209
Alienation, 17, 86. *See also* Divided self
Althusser, Louis, 134 n, 153 n, 208 n, 241 n
America, 229, 238–41
Antigone, 112
Apel Karl-Otto, 1
Appearance and Reality, 203–4, 213
Aquinas, Saint Thomas, 62, 65
Archimedean point, 10, 126, 167
Arendt, Hannah, 35 n, 77, 92
Aristotle, 13, 166; compared to Hegel, 104, 107, 124, 130, 141, 161, 208, 218; compared to Kant, 76; Hegel's critique of, 113; and logical theory, 195; *Nicomachean Ethics,* 19, 63, 136, 138, 139, 161; *Politics,* 37, 104, 113, 137, 139; on practical reason, 245–46; and practical philosophy, 136–39; and slavery, 118–19; on theory and practice, 18–19; and typology of regimes, 37; on volition, 62–63
Atomism, 7, 84, 140, 238
Aufhebung, 53, 190–93, 237, 242
Augustine, Saint, 20, 37: *De libero arbitrio,* 20
Austin, J. L., 1, 244
Avineri, Shlomo, 10

Bacon, Francis, 23, 25, 59
Bad infinity, 55, 83–84
Bayle, Pierre, 26, 30
Beautiful soul, 54, 76–80; and Kant, 79–80; Nietzsche's view of, 80
Beer, Samuel, 239–40
Begriffsgeschichte, 203
Bell, Daniel, 202, 229 n
Bentham, Jeremy, 101, 140, 233

Berkeley, George, 58
Bildung, 42–43, 120, 143, 175–80
Bismarck, Otto von, 132, 135, 139–40, 152. *See also* Prussia
Bloch, Ernst, 209
Bloom, Allan, 93, 233
Blumenberg, Hans, 21
Bonaparte, Napoleon, 49, 85, 96–97, 160, 164, 209, 212
Bureaucracy, 140, 149–52; impartiality of, 149–50; Marx's critique of, 150–51; Weber's critique of, 151–52
Bürger, 123
Burke, Edmund, 37, 86, 103, 130, 168

Caesar, Julius, 209, 212
Carlsbad Decrees, 139–40
Cicero, 141
Civility, 112, 140, 141
Civil Society (*Bürgerliche Gesellschaft*), 104–5, 132, 140–45, 157–58, 236
Cole, G. D. H., 142
Collingwood, R. G., 35 n, 168 n, 178, 206 n
Common sense, 68–69, 182–83
Communism, 103. *See also* Marx, Karl
Constant, Benjamin, 46
Constitutionalism, 149–50, 152–53, 155; ancient versus modern views, 149–50; and separation of powers, 153
Contingency, 9, 224–25. *See also* Necessity
Contradiction: logical character of, 198–200; moral/psychological character of, 191–92, 199; social/structural character of, 198–99, 202
Corporation, 13, 140–45; and *Bildung,* 143, 237; and corporatism, 142–43, 144–45; and representation, 144; welfare functions of, 143–44, 236
Cropsey, Joseph, 24
Cunning of Reason (*List der Vernunft*), 95, 210–12

Deconstruction, 231
De Gaulle, Charles, 155
Deontology, 4, 125, 234
Derrida, Jacques, 243
Descartes, René, 10, 59, 137; alleged conservatism of, 23; and epistemology, 21–22, 169–70, 182; and *générosité,* 24–25; and mastery of nature, 24–25, 81, 232; provisional morality of, 23–25; reductionism of, 58, 165–66
Desire, 115–17
Determinate negation, 13, 187–93
Dialectics, 51–53, 165–69; dialogical character of, 167–68; historical character of, 168–69; and immanent critique, 167; misinterpretations of, 202–4
Diderot, Denis, 58, 87; *Le neveu de Rameau,* 87
Divided self, 7, 11, 17–31, 177, 191–92
Durkheim, Emile, 33
Dworkin, Ronald, 98n, 122, 125, 128

"Earliest System-Programme of German Idealism," 39; disputed authorship of, 40
Elster, Jon, 204n, 209, 210
Empiricism, 65–70, 70–71, 184
End of history, 13, 164, 169, 222–31, 243–46
End of ideology, 229–30
Enlightenment, the: dialectic of, 61, 232–33; and liberalism, 7–8; and naturalism, 26–28; and natural law, 25–26; and revolution, 35–38, 85; and science, 59–61, 212; and skepticism, 181; and tradition, 57–59
Equality, 62, 128, 201
Existentialism, 152, 163, 231

Fackenheim, Emil, 213n
Fascism, 142, 144, 152, 212
Ferguson, Adam, 32
Feuerbach, Ludwig, 207
Fichte, Johann Gottleib, 10, 12, 80–85, 106, 169; and action, 81; and a priorism, 213n; and conservatism, 132; and labor, 82, 120; and moral aspiration, 83–84; and the police state, 80–81, 84; and transcendental argument, 70
Findlay, J. N., 198, 204, 205
Forbes, Duncan, 156
Forster, E. M., 167
Frankfurt, Harry, 117
Frankfurt School, 1, 180

Free speech, 123–24
French Revolution, 7, 12, 32, 164, 191, 218; and "absolute freedom," 79, 87–88, 108; German response to, 34–36; Hegel's critique of, 85–97, 237–38; Hegel's disillusionment with, 49, 55; philosophical character of, 85–86; and republic of virtue, 93–94; Rousseau's influence on, 88–91; tragic character of, 86–87
Freud, Sigmund, 129
Fries, Jacob, 79, 129

Gadamer, H. G., 58n, 136n, 137n, 178, 188n, 208, 222, 246n
Galbraith, J. K., 143
Galileo, 59, 141
Galston, William A., 4n, 36n, 128, 239n
Geist (Mind/Spirit), 45, 49, 50, 55, 56, 176, 177
Gellner, Ernest, 5
Gemeinschaft/Gesellschaft, 6, 33, 123
Gibbon, Edward, 46
Goethe, Johann Wolfgang von, 17, 175, 196; *Werther,* 175
Greece: decline of, 45–48, the Enlightenment and, 181; idealization of, 31–34; and *paideia,* 43, 175; philosophy and, 18–20; and civil religion, 41–45
Grice, H. P., 116

Habermas, Jürgen, 1, 222, 244–45
Haller, L. von, 148
Hampshire, Stuart, 235
Hare, R. M., 78
Hartmann, Klaus, 130n, 131n, 198
Hartz, Louis, 238
Haym, Rudolph, 132, 223
Hegel, Georg Wilhelm Friedrich: and Aristotle, 119, 147; "Bonapartism" of, 49, 96–97; alleged conservatism of, 132, 135, 139–40, 223, 233, 241; as critic of Christianity, 43–49; and dialectics, 51–53, 165–69, 203; and empiricism, 67–70, 170–71; and the French Revolution, 49, 55, 85–97; and functionalism, 209–10; and Hölderlin, 34–35; and immanent critique, 10, 13, 167, 169–75; and Judaism, 51; and Kant, 51–52, 70–80, 162–63, 171–73, 213–16; and love, 50–54, and need for philosophy, 17; and Plato, 113–14; postmodern criticism of, 243–46; realism of, 55, 237–38; alleged relativism of, 130–31, 168–69, 178–79;

renaissance of interest in, 1–6; and Schelling, 39–40, 221; Schiller's influence
on, 31–34; technocratic criticism of,
240–42; and tyranny, 48–49, 94–97,
160
Works: *Early Theological Writings*, disputed character of, 40–41; *The German
Constitution*, 49, 94; *Jena Philosophy of
Mind*, 49, 95, 96; *Lectures on the History of
Philosophy*, 185, 187, 230; *Lesser Logic*,
68, 154, 173, 190, 220; *Natural Law*, 65,
70, 72, 75, 159; *Phenomenology of Mind*,
and "beautiful soul," 79; and *Bildungsideal*,
43, 175–77; and cultural disintegration,
87; and epistemology, 169, 170; mastery
and slavery in, 115, 162; and "negative
dialectics," 179, 189, 201, 216, 217; war
in, 159, 161; *Philosophy of History*, and
America, 229; French Revolution in, 85,
91; and teleology, 207, 217; *Philosophy of
Right*, ambiguities of, 103, 105; democracy
criticized in, 129; interpretations of, 132,
135, 150; mastery and slavery in, 121;
practical intention of, 136, 139; state depicted in, 113, 114, 225; war in, 159, 160,
163; *Science of Logic*, and "bad infinity,"
84; and contradiction, 200–201; cunning
of reason in, 210; and negativity, 189
Heidegger, Martin, 1, 152, 163, 216, 217
Heine, Heinrich, 61
Henrich, Dieter, 27 n, 190 n, 198
Herder, Johann Gottfried von, 42, 50, 103
Hermeneutics, 231
Hitler, Adolph, 135
Hobbes, Thomas, 7, 12, 59, 70, 90, 106,
115, 155, 157; compared to Hegel, 104,
134; and desire, 116–18; egalitarianism
of, 62; and law, 147; naturalism of,
26–27; and rationality, 62, 116–17, 208;
reductionism of, 64; and rights, 65–66;
and volition, 63, 107, 109, 113
Hölderlin, Friedrich, 12, 50; and divided
self, 17; on "eccentric circle," 34; *Hyperion*, 34
Hook, Sidney, 156
Horkheimer, Max, 233
Hume David: empiricism of, 170; on facts
and values, 102; on history, 26; and naturalism, 30; and the nightwatchman state,
7; on reason, 8, 208; and skepticism, 183
Hypocrisy, 79, 92–93

Ilting, Karl-Heinz, 139, 140, 156

Immanent critique, 10, 13, 169–75

Kant, Immanuel, 7, 12–13, 44, 70–80, 85,
88, 102, 106, 125, 132, 157, 168, 181,
187, 200; and autonomy, 2–3, 59, 71,
79, 109; and Categorical Imperative,
73–74, 108–11, 139; and critical philosophy, 28, 164–66; dualism of, 29–30;
Eichmann's use of, 77–78; and epistemology, 171–73, 194–95, 219; formalism of,
73–75; on French Revolution, 36; and
"perpetual peace," 75, 162; and Pietism,
79–80; and Rawls, 2–3, 28–29, 76; and
republicanism, 29, 145; and Schiller, 31;
teleology of, 110–11, 213–16
Kelly, George A., 8, 121, 140, 175, 241 n
Kepler, Johannes, 141, 211
Knox, T. M., 49
Kojève, Alexandre, 96, 97, 116, 121, 216,
217, 226–29
Koselleck, Reinhart, 35 n, 37 n, 60, 203 n,
207
Kristol, Irving, 4 n
Kroner, Richard, 35

Labor (*Arbeit*), 81–82, 119–21
Laski, Harold, 142
Law (*Gesetz*), 104, 132, 145–48; command
theory of, 147; public character of, 148
Lenin, V. I., 36
Liberalism: alleged crisis of, 232–33; at-
tacks on, 100–103; Hegel's contribution
to, 6–9, 236–38; and libertarianism,
235–36; republicanism and, 238–39; re-
vival of, 2–3; and rights, 61–65, 98–100
Locke, John, 7, 12, 13, 157; and empiricism,
170–71, 184; *Essay Concerning Human
Understanding*, 66, 71; and liberalism, 99,
132, 135, 141, 238–39; and natural
rights, 65–67, 70; and revolution, 37
Louis XVI, 36
Lowi, Theodore, 143
Lukàcs, Georg, 40, 49 n, 75 n, 81, 145 n,
175 n, 180
Lycurgus, 48
Lyotard, Jean-François, 243

Machiavelli, Niccolò, 64; compared to Descartes, 23, 24; on Christianity, 42; on
political foundings, 48, 94–95
MacIntyre, Alasdair, 4 n, 71, 230 n, 232 n,
235
Macpherson, C. B., 4, 82

Maine, Henry, 123
Maistre, Joseph de, 132
Mandeville, Bernard de, 209–12
Mao Zedong, 225
Marx, Karl, 33, 36; compared to Hegel, 53, 86, 120–21, 237; criticism of bureaucracy, 150–51; criticism of dialectic, 9, 134–35, 192–93, 207–8, 242; criticism of monarchy, 155–56; criticism of natural rights, 100–101; and end of history, 164, 169, 227
Mastery and slavery, 8, 12, 52, 118–22, 162
Mazzini, Giuseppe, 161
Melanchthon, Philipp, 139
Mercier, Louis Sebastian, 35
Mill, J. S., 102, 127
Monarchy, 13, 152–56; and presidency, 154; necessity for, 155
Montesquieu: compared to Hegel, 41, 42, 50, 72, 73, 87, 132, 143; *De l'esprit des lois,* 47, 73; on ancient versus modern liberty, 46–47; and republicanism, 12; on separation of powers, 153
Moses, 20, 48, 94
Murdoch, Iris, 17, 76, 234–35
Mussolini, Benito, 142

Naturalism, 12, 26–27, 65–70. *See also* Empiricism
Naturalistic fallacy, 65–66
Natural Law, 26–27
Nazism, 77–78, 103, 212–13
Necessity, 9, 13, 56, 203–17; contextual character of, 203; and contingency, 224–25; logographic character of, 205–6; practical character of, 206; rational (teleological) character of, 206–17
Neo-Conservatism, 4
New Institutionalism, 13, 242
Nietzsche, Friedrich, 68, 80; as critic of Hegel, 226, 228; *The Use and Abuse of History,* 80, 226
Nihilism, 55, 103, 107–8, 186
Nohl, Hermann, 40
Novalis, 152

Oakeshott, Michael, 72, 97, 103, 104 n, 132 n, 153
Ockham, William of, 20, 21
Organicism, 1, 133, 153–54, 207

Paine, Thomas, 35, 135
Pascal, Blaise, 93
Pelczynski, Z. A., 10, 133–34

Personality, 109; as basis of rights, 111–14; and citizenship, 234; legal conception of, 122–23, 146; and moral self-realization, 129–30; Plato's denial of, 113–14
Pietism, 79–80
Plant, Raymond, 40
Plato: compared to Aristotle, 137; compared to Hegel, 104, 107, 130, 175–76, 187; conception of reason, 18–19, 208; Hegel's critique of, 113–14; and regime transformation, 37; *Republic,* 18, 37, 104, 113, 114
Polybius, 37
Popper, Karl, 103, 132, 133, 202, 223, 225
Positivism, 184
Practical philosophy, 13, 132–40. *See also* Aristotle
Prejudice, 58–59
Progress, 37–38, 54–55, 59–61, 169
Property, 123, 146
Proust, Marcel, 200
Prussianism, 223. *See also* Bismarck, Otto von
Pyrrho of Elis, 180, 183

Rawls, John, 98 n, 124, 125; Kantianism of, 2–3, 28–29, 76
Reason: actuality of, 223–25; autonomy of, 27, 29–30, 71, 79; dialectical conception of, 4–5, 9–10, 17, 56, 152–53, 156, 197, 223–25, 234; erotic power of, 51–53, 208; instrumental conception of, 3, 145; Judeo-Christian conception of, 20–21; Platonic-Aristotelian conception of, 18–19
Rechtsstaat, 13, 112, 123, 140; differences with polis, 149, 155; and rule of law, 145 ff.
Recognition (*Annerkenung*), 12, 114, 124–31
Reductionism, 64, 165–66
Reformation, 86, 114
Relativism, 102–3, 130; and Hegel, 168–69, 178–79
Ricardo, David, 141
Rights: an ambiguity of, 125; of association, 143; contextual character of, 71–73, 114, 125–26, 162–63 (*see also* Sittlichkeit); criticisms of, 100–103; development of, 115–22; and free expression, 123–24; general features of, 61–65; and Hobbes, 65–66; and international law, 162–64; neo-Kantian theory of, 2–3, 125–26; and Locke, 66–67; and needs, 99; of property, 123, 146; to recognition, 122–31; of representation, 144; and the will, 107–14
Riley, Patrick, 74

Ritter, Joachim, 10, 139n
Robespierre, Maximilien, 12, 35, 55, 93, 95
Romulus, 94
Rorty, Richard, 1
Rosen, Michael, 204, 205
Rosen, Stanley, 11
Rousseau, Jean-Jacques, 7, 12, 105, 106, 115, 116, 118, 148, 185; and autonomy, 108–9; and Christianity, 42; *Discourse on the Origins and Foundations of Inequality Among Men,* 27, 92, 116, 185; *Emile,* 175; compared to Hegel, 104, 114, 175; compared to Kant, 29; and naturalism, 27–28; on public/private split, 43, 47, 92–93, 237; *Social Contract,* 42, 88, 104; and general will, 47, 64, 88–91
Ryan, Alan, 120

Saint-Just, Louis Antoine de, 93
Salkever, Stephen, 107n, 234
Sandel, Michael, 4n, 5n
Sartre, Jean-Paul, 81, 235
Say, Jean-Baptiste, 141
Schaar, John, 125
Schelling, F. W. J. von, 12, 50, 56; and divided self, 18; and French Revolution, 34–35, 38–39; differences with Hegel, 39–40, 221
Schiller, Friedrich, 50, 163; and aesthetic state, 33–34; and divided self, 17; and freedom, 31; and specialization, 32–33
Schlesinger, Arthur, Jr., 230
Schliermacher, Friedrich, D. E., 178
Schulze, Johannes, 181
Secularization, 229, 232
Sextus Empiricus, 180, 186
Shell, Susan, 82
Shklar, Judith, 76, 92
Sincerity, 92–93
Sittlichkeit (social ethics), 8, 12, 71–72, 121–22, 130–31, 158, 166, 235
Skepticism, 20, 170, 180–87; and *ataraxia,* 180–81; contrasted with common sense, 182–83; and Hume, 183; political implications of, 187
Skinner, Quentin, 15
Smith, Adam, 141, 209, 212
Socrates, 106, 113, 191, 199
Solon, 48

Spinoza, Baruch de, 27, 30, 170, 189, 207, 219
Strauss, Leo, 103n, 145n, 205n, 232n
Struggle for recognition, 115–22

Tacitus, 46
Tarcov, Nathan, 239
Tawney, R. H., 142
Taylor, Charles, 1, 166, 200, 225
Teleology: criticism of, 212–13, 241; and Hegel, 206–11; and Kant, 110–11, 213–15
Theory and practice, 19, 137, 167
Theseus, 48, 94, 96, 97, 160
Tocqueville, Alexis de, 142, 143
Tönnies, Ferdinand, 33, 123
Towes, John, 35
Trotsky Leon, 36, 161
Truth: as correspondence, 13, 174; evolutionary character of, 219; as recollection, 176; systematic character of, 220–21; verification of, 221–22. *See also* Absolute knowledge

Utilitarianism, 30, 101–2, 117, 135, 140
Utopianism, 237

Verstand (understanding), 43, 51, 184, 188, 194–97, 205; and formal logic, 195–96; and principle of non-contradiction, 199
Vico, Giovanni Battista, 171
Volksgeist, 40–43, 47, 49; and *Bildung,* 42–43; and Montesquieu's *esprit general,* 41; and social solidarity, 41–42, 47
Voltaire, François-Marie Arouet de, 181
Voting paradox, 236

Walzer, Michael, 4n, 122n, 128, 157
War, 156–64; and courage, 160–62; and peace, 162–63
Weber, Max, 83, 126, 160; critic of bureaucracy, 151–52
Webster, Daniel, 239
Williams, Bernard, 1
Wilson, Woodrow, 162
Wittgenstein, Ludwig, 1, 183, 185, 201–2, 221, 244

Yack, Bernard, 79